CASS SERIES ON THE SOVIET (RUSSIAN) STUDY OF WAR

The Bear Went Over the Mountain

GW00568940

CASS SERIES ON THE SOVIET (RUSSIAN) STUDY OF WAR
Series Editor: David M. Glantz
ISSN 1462-0960

This series examines what Soviet military theorists and commanders have learned from the study of their own military operations.

1. Harold S. Orenstein, translator and editor, *Soviet Documents on the Use of War Experience*, Volume I, *The Initial Period of War 1941*, with an Introduction by David M. Glantz. (ISBN 0 7146 3392 5 cloth)

2. Harold S. Orenstein, translator and editor, *Soviet Documents on the Use of War Experience*, Volume II, *The Winter Campaign 1941–1942*, with an Introduction by David M. Glantz. (ISBN 0 7146 3393 3 cloth)

3. Joseph G. Welsh, translator, *Red Armor Combat Orders: Combat Regulations for Tank and Mechanized Forces 1944*, edited and with an Introduction by Richard N. Armstrong. (ISBN 0 7146 3401 8 cloth)

4. Harold S. Orenstein, translator and editor, *Soviet Documents on the Use of War Experience*, Volume III, *Military Operations 1941 and 1942*, with an Introduction by David M. Glantz. (ISBN 0 7146 3402 6 cloth)

5. William A. Burhans, translator, *The Nature of the Operations of Modern Armies* by V.K. Triandafillov, edited by Jacob W. Kipp, with an Introduction by James J. Schneider. (ISBN 0 7146 4501 X cloth, 0 7146 4118 9 paper)

6. Harold S. Orenstein, translator, *The Evolution of Soviet Operational Art, 1927–1991: The Documentary Basis*, Volume I, *Operational Art, 1927–1964*, with an Introduction by David M. Glantz. (ISBN 0 7146 4547 8 cloth, 0 7146 4228 2 paper)

7. Harold S. Orenstein, translator, *The Evolution of Soviet Operational Art, 1927–1991: The Documentary Basis*, Volume II, *Operational Art, 1965–1991*, with an Introduction by David M. Glantz. (ISBN 0 7146 4548 6 cloth, 0 7146 4229 0 paper)

8. Richard N. Armstrong and Joseph G. Welsh, *Winter Warfare: Red Army Orders and Experiences*. (ISBN 0 7146 4699 7 cloth, 0 7146 4237 1 paper)

9. Lester W. Grau, *The Bear Went Over the Mountain: Soviet Combat Tactics in Afghanistan*. (ISBN 0 7146 4857 4 cloth, 0 7146 4413 7 paper)

The Bear Went Over the Mountain

Soviet Combat Tactics in Afghanistan

Edited by

LESTER W. GRAU

Foreign Military Studies Office
Fort Leavenworth, Kansas

FRANK CASS
LONDON • PORTLAND, OR

First published in Russian in 1991 by the Frunze Academic Press
First published in English in 1996 by the
National Defence University Press, Washington, DC
This edition first published in 1998 by
FRANK CASS PUBLISHERS
Newbury House, 900 Eastern Avenue
London IG2 7HH

and in the United States of America by
FRANK CASS PUBLISHERS
c/o ISBS, 5804 N.E. Hassalo Street
Portland, Oregon, 97213-3644

Reprinted in 2001

Website: http://www.frankcass.com

British Library Cataloguing in Publication Data

The bear went over the mountain : Soviet combat tactics in
  Afghanistan. – (Cass series on the Soviet (Russian) study of war)
  1. Guerrilla warfare – Afghanistan. 2. Afghanistan – History –
  Soviet occupation, 1979–1989. 3. Afghanistan – History –
  Soviet occupation, 1979–1989 – Personal narratives
  I. Grau, Lester W.
  958.1'045

ISBN 0-7146-4857-4 (cloth)
ISBN 0-7146-4413-7 (paper)

Library of Congress Cataloging-in-Publication Data

The Bear went over the mountain : Soviet combat tactics in Afghanistan
/ edited by Lester Grau.
     p.   cm. – (Cass series on the Soviet (Russian) study of war)
  Translated from Russian.
  Originally published: Washington, D.C. : National Defense
University Press, 1996.
  Includes bibliographical references (p.   ) and index.
  ISBN 0-7146-4857-4. – ISBN 0-7146-4413-7 (pbk.)
  1. Afghanistan–History–Soviet occupation, 1979–1989. 2. Soviet
Union–Military policy. 3. Soviet Union–History, Military.
I. Grau, Lester W. II. Series.
DS371.2.B4   1998
958.104'5–dc21

98-6417
CIP

Printed in Great Britain by
Bookcraft (Bath) Ltd., Midsomer Norton, Somerset.

CONTENTS

FOREWORD

When the Soviet Union decided to invade Afghanistan, they evaluated their chances for success upon their experiences in East Germany, Hungary and Czechoslovakia. Unfortunately for their soldiers, as well as the people of Afghanistan, they ignored not only the experiences of the British in the same region, but also their own experience with the Basmachi resistance fighters in Central Asia from 1918-1933. Consequently, in Afghanistan the Soviet army found its tactics inadequate to meet the challenges posed by the difficult terrain and the highly motivated *mujahideen* freedom fighters.

To capture the lessons their tactical leaders learned in Afghanistan and to explain the change in tactics that followed, the Frunze Military Academy compiled this book for their command and general staff combat arms officers. The lessons are valuable not just for Russian officers, but for the tactical training of platoon, company and battalion leaders of any nation likely to engage in conflicts involving civil war, guerrilla forces and rough terrain. This is a book dealing with the starkest features of the unforgiving landscape of tactical combat: casualties and death, adaptation, and survival.

Battalion and company commanders, platoon leaders and sergeants will find realistic issues within these vignettes to discuss with squad and team leaders, and with vehicle commanders and drivers. Basic and Advanced Infantry Officer and NCO courses will find useful applications for both classroom and field instructions. Senior leaders may find invaluable insights into the dangers and opportunities tactical units under their command may face in limited wars. Above all, the lessons in this book should help small unit leaders understand the need for security, deception, patrols, light and litter discipline, caution, vigilance, and the ability to seize the initiative in responding to unpredictable enemy actions and ambushes.

Hans Binnendijk
Director, Institute for National Strategic Studies

ACKNOWLEDGEMENTS

Many people contributed to this book. Colonel General Fedor M. Kuzmin, the Commandant of the Frunze Academy, made this book possible. Other Frunze Academy officers who helped me immensely were General Major Ivan N. Vorob'ev and Colonel Analtoli Malin. Mary Fitzgerald of the Hudson Institute suggested the present book layout. Michael Orr of the United Kingdom's Combat Studies Research Centre in Sandhurst and Allen Curtis of the National Training Center, Fort Irwin, California read and commented on the manuscript. Colonel (Ret) Dave Glantz, the former director of the Foreign Military Studies Office (FMSO), read and commented on the manuscript and wrote the introduction. My directors, Colonel Tod Milton and Colonel Charles Johnston, and my co-workers at FMSO, Dr. Graham Turbiville, Colonel (Ret) Bill Mendel, Dr. Jacob Kipp, LTC (Ret) Tim Thomas, LTC (Ret) Bill Connor, LTC John Sray, LTC Geoff Demerest, Major Brian Dando, Major Ray Finch and Major Steve Button read and commented on the manuscript. Randy Love of FMSO and my good friend Michael Gress painstakingly checked my translation. Stephen Stewman of FMSO did a fantastic job on the maps. General Yahya M. Nawroz, former Chief of Operations of the Afghanistan Ministry of Defense, *mujahideen* strategist, and interim Minister of Defense, read and corrected my manuscript and identified and corrected place names. Colonel Ali Ahmad Jalali, former Afghan Army and *mujahideen* commander and noted author, also read and corrected my manuscript and identified and corrected place names. SPC Marcin Wiesiolek cleaned up and scrubbed the graphics. Peter D. Neufville provided good counsel and direction based on his experience in Afghanistan and research on the Panjsher operations. James H. Brusstar and Fred Kiley guided the manuscript through the acceptance process at National Defense University. Richard Stewart of the Special Operations Command at Ft. Bragg found additional publication funds, and Jonathan Pierce of NDU Press did the final edit and design. Finally, Gina Grau, my bride of 29 wonderful years, helped with encouragement and understanding. Thank you all for your help. The mistakes are mine, the product is ours.

INTRODUCTION

Sixteen years after its commencement and six years after its cessation, the Soviet-Afghan War remains an enigma for Westerners. Set against the backdrop of earlier successful Soviet military interventions in East Germany (1953), Hungary (1956), and Czechoslovakia (1968), and occasional Soviet military pressure on Poland, the stark military power of the Soviet state seemed to be an irresistible tool of indefatigable Soviet political power. Ever concerned about the specter of a Soviet theater strategic offensive across the plains of Europe, the West was thankful that nuclear deterrence maintained the Cold War balance, and was conditioned to accept, albeit reluctantly, the results of Soviet intervention within its Socialist commonwealth or in Soviet border regions. Having suffered through the trauma of Vietnam, Americans, in particular, watched curiously to see how the vaunted Soviet military machine would deal with the ill-equipped tribesmen of this inhospitable region. A few recollected the Afghan experiences of the British in the late Nineteenth Century, when British imperial power was humbled by the ancestors of these very same tribesmen. Few Westerners, however, doubted that the Soviets would ultimately prevail. Some even projected their European fears to Asia, and pondered the applicability of the Soviet theater-strategic offensive to southern Asia. More than a few strategic pundits and military planners envisioned a bold Soviet strategic thrust from southern Afghanistan to the shores of the Persian Gulf, to challenge Western strategic interests and disrupt Western access to critical Middle Eastern oil.

Despite these fears and dire warnings, the Soviet Afghan military effort soon languished as the British experience began to repeat itself. Although appearing to have entered Afghanistan in seemingly surgical fashion and with overwhelming force, the Soviet military commitment was, in reality, quite limited, and the immense and stark territory of Afghanistan swallowed the invaders up. Across the largely barren landscape, guerrilla fighters multiplied, and, within months, the hitherto curious word *mujahideen* took on new meaning. The anticipated short sharp struggle became prolonged as the West watched transfixed, wondering when the Soviet military machine would prevail. In time, the question of prevalence imperceptibly faded, and was replaced by doubts over whether the Soviets would prevail at all. In the end, ironically, even the Soviets could not cope, and the disease of the Afghan adventure infected Soviet society and the Soviet body politic itself. What began as yet another step in the expansion of Soviet power ended in a welter of systemic institutional self doubt that exposed the corruption within the Soviet system and ultimately brought that system and its parent state to ruin.

To this day the Western view of the Afghan War has been clouded in mystery and shadows. Soviet writers have presented Westerners with a mixture of political diatribe, military fable, allegory, and analogy, set against the backdrop of few facts. Westerners have recounted the war based on this Soviet material, sketchy *mujahideen* accounts, the reports of the occasional Western war correspondents in Afghanistan, and pure supposition. This volume, the first factual material to shed real light on the conflict, represents a unique first step in setting the Afghan record straight.

Several stark realities immediately emerge which place the Afghan War in proper perspective and permit its proper assessment in the context of Soviet military, political, and social development. First, although violent and destructive, the war was a limited one, in particular, in comparison with other notable recent local wars. Its ferocity and decisiveness did not match that of the series of short Arab-Israeli wars which scarred the Cold War years. It lacked the well-defined, large-scale military operations of the Korean War and the well-defined political arrangements that terminated that war. It also differed significantly from the oft-compared U.S. war in Vietnam. In Vietnam, American military strength rose to over 500,000 troops and the Americans resorted to many divisional and multi-divisional operations. By comparison, in Afghanistan, a region five times the size of Vietnam, Soviet strength varied from 90-104,000 troops. The Soviet's five divisions, four separate brigades and four separate regiments, and smaller support units of the 40th Army strained to provide security for the 21 provincial centers and few industrial and economic installations and were hard-pressed to extend this security to the thousands of villages, hundred of miles of communications routes, and key terrain features that punctuated and spanned that vast region.

Second, faced with this imposing security challenge, and burdened with a military doctrine, strategy, and operational and tactical techniques suited to theater war, the Soviet Army was hard pressed to devise military methodologies suited to deal with the Afghan challenges. Afghanistan aside, the 1980's were a challenging period militarily for the Soviet Union as it struggled to come to grips with changing political-military and military technical realities. The burgeoning arms race and increasing military strength of western democracies placed undue and unprecedented strains on the already weakening Soviet economy and forced the Soviets to face increased military expenditures at at time when the older policy of "Detente" had increased popular contacts with and knowledge of things Western and raised expectations of Soviet consumers. Soviet military authorities were increasingly unable to cope with military-technical realities in the form of a technological revolution in weaponry, which produced the looming specter of a proliferation of costly high-tech precision weaponry. In the short term, while an economic and technological solution was being sought, the military was forced to adjust its operational and tactical concepts and its military force structure to meet the new realities. Coincidentally, this was done while the military searched for appropriate ways to fight the Afghan War.

As a result of these twin military challenges, the Soviets formulated new concepts for waging war in non-linear fashion, suited to operating on battlefields dominated by more lethal high-precision weapons. This new non-linear battlefield required the abandonment of traditional operational and tactical formations, a redefinition of traditional echelonment concepts, and a wholesale reorganization of formations and units to emphasize combat flexibility and, hence, survivability. During the early and mid 1980s, the Soviet military altered its concept of the theater strategic offensive, developed new concepts for shallower echelonment at all levels, developed the concept of the air echelon, experimented with new force structures such as the corps, brigade, and combined arms battalion, tested new, more-flexible, logistical support concepts (for material support), and adopted such innovative tactical techniques as the use of the *brone-*

gruppa [armored group]. Afghanistan not only provided a test bed for many of these lower-level concepts, but it also demanded the employment of imaginative new techniques in its own right. Hence, the brigade, the material support battalion, and the *bronegruppa* emerged on the Afghan field of battle, reconnaissance-diversionary [SPETSNAZ] units sharpened their skills, and air assault techniques were widely employed.

Third, the inability of the Soviet military to win the war decisively condemned it to suffer a slow bloodletting, in a process that exposed the very weaknesses of the military as well as the Soviet political structure and society itself. The employment of a draft army with full periodic rotation of troops back to the Soviet Union permitted the travails and frustrations of war and the self doubts of the common soldier to be shared by the Soviet population as a whole. The problems so apparent in the wartime army soon became a microcosm for the latent problems afflicting Soviet society in general. The messages of doubt were military, political, ethnic, and social. In the end they were corrosive and destructive. As evidence, one needs only review the recently released casualty figures to underscore the pervasiveness of the problem. Soviet dead and missing in Afghanistan amounted to almost 15,000 troops, a modest percent of the 642,000 Soviets who served during the ten-year war. And the dead tell no tales at home. Far more telling were the 469,685 casualties, fully 73 percent of the overall force, who ultimately returned home to the Soviet Union. Even more appalling were the numbers of troops who fell victim to disease (415,932), of which 115,308 suffered from infectious hepatitis and 31,080 from typhoid fever. Beyond the sheer magnitude of these numbers is what these figures say about Soviet military hygiene and the conditions surrounding troop life. These numbers are unheard of in modern armies and modern medicine and their social impact among the returnees and the Soviet population, in general, had to be immense.

This volume puts a human face on the Soviet Afghan experience and begins to add flesh and blood to our previously skeletal appreciation of the war. In time-honored fashion, this volume also continues the Soviet General Staff's penchant for conducting detailed analysis of combat based on concrete combat experiences during the course of war. All the warts and blemishes are present, as they must be if an army is to change. The book provides a revealing portrait of war in general, tactics in particular, and, coincidentally, the soldiers' human condition. It also reveals that Western intelligence's picture of how the Soviets operated tactically lagged about 10 years behind reality. It captures the pain and frustration suffered by the Soviet military and, most important, provides acute insights into why and how these military experiences ultimately ignited political and social turmoil in the Soviet Union.

This is the first of the Soviet Afghan revelations. Let us hope that it will not be the last.

David M. Glantz
Colonel, US Army (Retired)
Carlisle, Pennsylvania

Colonel Glantz is the West's leading expert on the Soviet Army in World War II and a leading figure in current Russian/American military cooperation initiatives. He is the author of *When Titans Clashed: How the Red Army Stopped Hitler, Soviet Military Deception in the Second World War, Soviet Military Operational Art in Pursuit of Deep Battle, Soviet Military Intelligence in War, The Military Strategy of the Soviet Union: A History, The Soviet Conduct of Tactical Maneuver: Spearhead of the Offensive, The History of Soviet Airborne Forces, From the Don to the Dniepr: Soviet Offensive Operations December 1942 August 1943,* and *The Initial Period of War on the Eastern Front: 22 June-August 1941.* He is series editor of *The Soviet Study of War* series and editor of *The Journal of Slavic Military Studies.* His last military position was the director of the Foreign Military Studies Office, Fort Leavenworth, Kansas.

PREFACE

The Armed Forces of the Soviet Union structured, equipped and trained their forces for nuclear and high-intensity war on the great northern European plain and the plains of northern China. However, their political leadership thrust them into the middle of the Afghanistan civil war to reconstitute and to support a nominally Marxist-Leninist government. The terrain, the climate and the enemy were entirely different from what they had prepared for. In this locale, their equipment functioned less than optimally, their force structure was clearly inappropriate and their tactics were obviously wrong. The citizens of the Soviet Union did not understand why their sons were being conscripted for battle in a strange land and failed to see how their sacrifices contributed to the security of the fatherland. Those with connections sought to avoid the draft. Unlike their fathers who fought the Nazi invaders, the returning soldiers were not welcomed as heroes or treated with respect. They were shunned and often scorned by their fellow citizens. A gap opened between the Armed Forces and the citizenry and many veterans found they could not fit back into the lifestyle of the complacent and self-centered citizenry. The effects of the Afghanistan war reverberate throughout Russia today.

The Communists took power in Afghanistan on 27 April 1978 with a bloody military coup. President Nur M. Taraki, the new president, announced sweeping programs of land distribution, changed status for women and the destruction of the old Afghanistan social structure. The new government enjoyed little popular support. The wobbly new government was almost immediately met by armed resistance fighters who contested this new order. The combat readiness of the Army of the Democratic Republic of Afghanistan plummeted as bloody government purges swept the officer ranks. In March 1979, the city of Herat revolted. Most of the Afghan 17th Infantry Division mutinied and joined the rebellion. Forces loyal to Taraki advanced and occupied the city while the Afghan Air Force bombed the city and the 17th Division. Thousands of people reportedly died in the fighting, including some Soviet citizens.

Soldiers, units and entire brigades deserted to the resistance and by the end of 1979, the actual strength of the Afghan Army was less than half of its authorized 90,000. The government purges and executions of serving officers, coupled with officer desrtions to the resistance, halved the size of the officer corps. In September 1979, Taraki's Prime Minister, Hafizullah Amin, seized power and executed Taraki. Amin's rule was no better and the Soviet Union watched this new communist state spin out of control and out of Moscow's orbit. The Soviet Politburo moved to stabilize the situation.

On 27 December 1979, Moscow struck with a Coup de Main. Using the same techniques as they employed during the invasion of Czechoslovakia, the Soviets rapidly seized the major cities, radio stations and centers of power. They executed Amin and put an Afghan communist exile, Babrak Karmal, in power. They crushed the resistance by the Afghan Army and began consolidating their power.

The Soviets soon discovered that Afghanistan was not going to be a repeat of their Czechoslovakian experience. Their force commitment, initially assessed as requiring several months, was to last over nine years and require increasing numbers of Soviet forces. It proved a bloody experience in which the Soviet Union reportedly killed 1.3 million people and forced five and a half million Afghans (a third of the prewar population) to leave the country as refugees. Another two million Afghans were forced to migrate within the country. The countryside is ravaged and littered with mines. Clearly, on a percentage basis, the Soviet Union inflicted more suffering on Afghanistan than Hitlerite Germany inflicted on the Soviet Union during World War II.

The Soviet concept for military occupation of Afghanistan was based on the following:

- stabilizing the country by garrisoning the main routes, major cities, airbases and logistics sites;
- relieving the Afghan government forces of garrison duties and pushing them into the countryside to battle the resistance;
- providing logistic, air, artillery and intelligence support to the Afghan forces;

- providing minimum interface between the Soviet occupation forces and the local populace;
- accepting minimal Soviet casualties; and,
- strengthening the Afghan forces, so once the resistance was defeated, the Soviet Army could be withdrawn.[1]

In the end, the Soviet Union withdrew from Afghanistan and the communist government was defeated. Approximately 620,000 Soviets served in Afghanistan. Of these, 525,000 were in the Soviet Armed Forces while another 90,000 were in the KGB and 5,000 were in the MVD. The Soviets invested much national treasure and lost 13,833 killed. Of their 469,685 sick and wounded, 10,751 became invalids. The Soviets lost 118 jets, 333 helicopters, 147 tanks, 1314 armored personnel carriers, 433 artillery pieces and mortars, 1138 radio sets and CP vehicles, 510 engineering vehicles and 11,369 trucks.[2]

There are some striking parallels between the Soviet role in Afghanistan and the United States' role in Vietnam. Like the United States, the Soviets had to restructure and retrain their force while in the combat zone. Eventually, military schools and training areas began to incorporate Afghanistan combat experience and to train personnel for Afghanistan duty. Mountain warfare training centers sprang up in many districts. However, unlike in the United States Army, the Afghanistan war was not an all encompassing experience for the officer corps. Barely 10 percent of the Soviet motorized rifle, armor, aviation and artillery officers served in Afghanistan. However, a majority of airborne, air assault and Spetsnaz[3] officers served in Afghanistan.

---

[1] Scott R. McMichael, *Stumbling Bear: Soviet Military Performance in Afghanistan,* London: Brassey's 1991, p. 10; and Boris Gromov, *Ogranichennyy kontingent* [Limited contingent], Moscow: Progress, 1994, p. 172.

[2] Manuscript of Aleksandr Lyakhovskiy, *Tragediya I doblest' Afghan* [The Tragedy and Valor of the Afghan Veterans], Moscow: Iskona, 1995

[3] Spetsnaz are "forces of special designation" or special troops and can include a variety of branches and jobs. The highly-trained, hardened

As in Vietnam, tactics needed a major overhaul to meet the changed circumstances. Units which adapted enjoyed relative success while units which did not paid a price in blood. During the Vietnam war, the changes in U.S. tactics were disseminated through the branch schools, special courses at Fort Bragg, branch journals, special training publications and a series of books published by *Infantry* magazine entitled *The Distant Challenge*. These last books were a compilation of successful U.S. actions in Vietnam with commentary on what was done correctly and what needed work. The Soviets also (though belatedly) discussed tactical changes in their tactical journal *Voyenney vestnik* [Military herald] and taught mountain warfare in their training center in Ushgorod in the Turkestan Military District as well as the other new mountain training centers.

With the breakup of the Soviet Union, U.S. relations with the Russian military have slowly changed. Tentative military-to-military contact programs are developing and attempts are being made to bridge the vast differences between our two forces with the possibility of future joint operations and peacekeeping. A considerable amount of formerly classified or hidden material is now being offered to the West. Recently I received a 1991 book entitled *Combat Actions of Soviet Forces in the Republic of Afghanistan*. This book was compiled by the History of Military Art department at the Frunze Combined Arms Academy in Moscow. The Frunze Academy is a three-year command and staff college for Russian combat arms officers. The Academy is named for M. V. Frunze, a famous Soviet military theoretician, Minister of Defense and the architect of Soviet victory in the mountain-desert region of Soviet Central Asia in the 1920s. The history faculty of the Frunze Academy interviewed Afghanistan veterans, analyzed their actions and then recorded the incidents and their commentary as lessons learned for future combat in mountain-desert terrain.

The book was intended for internal use only and, as such, shows both the good and the bad. Mistakes and successes both illustrate the

---

Spetsnaz who performed long-range reconnaissance, commando and special forces functions are the ones referred to throughout this book. Figures of percentages of officers of various branches serving in Afghanistan are the author's estimate based on a variety of conversations and sources.

hard lessons-learned in fighting a guerrilla in rough terrain. These lessons learned are not peculiarly Russian. Many of the mistakes and successes fit equally well with the experiences of an American army in the jungles and mountains of Vietnam and should apply equally well in future conflicts involving civil war, guerrilla forces and rough terrain. Indeed, Afghanistan is not all mountains and desert. It has forests and tangled "green zones"--irrigated areas thick with trees, crops, irrigation ditches and tangled vegetation. This then is not a history of the Afghanistan war. Rather it is a series of snapshots of combat as witnessed by young platoon leaders, company commanders, battalion commanders, tactical staff officers and advisers to the Afghan government forces. It is not a book about right or wrong. Rather, it is a book about survival and adaptation as young men come to terms with a harsh, boring and brutal existence punctuated by times of heady excitement and terror. I have translated and commented on these vignettes in the hope that the tactical ground commander of the future can use them to meet the challenges of the future and to help keep his soldiers alive.

There are 47 Frunze Academy vignettes in this book, each with its own map. I have translated the text, but put the combat narrative in the first person instead of the third person. The commentary provided by the Frunze Academy follows. To this I have added my own commentary. In addition, I have interjected my own comments as footnotes and marked them as "(ed.)". I have added two more vignettes from *Voyenney vestnik*, since I felt that they would add significantly to the defensive chapter. Finally, I have added my own concluding chapter to the book. I derived much of the concluding chapter from the dozens of conversations that I have had with Afghanistan veterans--Soviet generals, officers and soldiers as well as resistance fighters. The map of Afghanistan is indexed to each action in the book. Some of the translation is rather free in order to clarify certain points for the reader. I have tried to put as much of the experience into American military English as possible. So, for example, in an air assault I talk about "first lifts" instead of "forward groups" and "ground-support aircraft" instead of "sturmoviks". The Russian term is referenced in the glossary.

Stephan Stewman has done a yeoman's job in redrawing all the Russian maps in the book. We have translated them into English, but retained Russian map graphics. I have worked with Soviet graphics for over 13 years of my 26 year military career. Quite frankly, I find their graphics more "user friendly" than Western graphics, flexible and illustrative. The Russians can show the sequential development of an action by adding times or identifying lines to their graphics. These lines are explained in the legend. What follows is a table of Russian map graphics. Since this is not printed in color, enemy forces are shown by double lines on the map.

There are several problems with the book. First, the place names are often pure transliterations from the Russian. Western maps of Afghanistan are often pure transliterations from the Pushtu or Dari original. Often, it is difficult to tell what the name of the actual place is--especially when dealing with small towns which may have two or three names, depending on who surveyed the map. So, it is often difficult to pinpoint the exact site of the vignette. I have used the *Gazetteer of Afghanistan* Second Edition published by the Defense Mapping Agency in June 1983 where possible. General Yahya M. Nawroz, formerly Chief of Operations of the pre-communist Afghanistan Ministry of Defense and strategist of the *Mujahideen* Military Committee, has graciously assisted me in pinpointing many other locales. Colonel Ali Ahmad Jalali, a reknown commander in both the Afghanistan Army and the resistance and a noted author in his own right, has also reviewed the book and helped clear up many of the mystery locales. But others remain mysteries to both of them.

Further, many of the maps that accompany the vignettes are problematic. Apparently, most of the maps were drawn from memory, although some of them show evidence of access to the original mapsheet. Over time, details fade and many of the sketch maps are rough approximations. Distances, directions, place names and geographic features may differ from the actual ground. Distances are transcriptions from the original except where clearly in error. Still, the maps must be used as an approximation and not as an accurate depiction of the ground.

Finally, some of the original editing of the Russian text was slipshod. Typing errors, differences in place name spellings between the map and the text, and transcription errors are evident in the Russian texts. I have done my best to correct these where possible.

Still, these vignettes are an absolute gold mine for any tactician.

They are an intimate look at a battlefield where a modern, mechanized army tried to defeat a guerrilla force on rugged terrain in the middle of a civil war. Despite their best efforts, they were unable to achieve decisive military victory and their politicians finally ordered them home. Other armies would do well to study their efforts.

Lester W. Grau
Lieutenant Colonel, U.S. Army (Ret.)
Leavenworth, Kansas

A BRIEF CHRONOLOGY OF THE SOVIET–AFGHAN WAR, 1979–1989

Afghanistan has always been a loose collection of tribes and nationalities over which central governments had moderate influence and control. There are three dominant languages and numerous minority languages. Although overwhelmingly Islamic, the Islamic community is split among Hanafi Sunnis, Inmami Shia, Ismailis Shia and Sufis. The land is dominated by high mountain and desert and modern travel is primarily restricted to a highway ring connecting the various cities. There is no railroad network. The country and economy are primarily rural and there is a long, unbroken tradition of tribal, religious and ethnic blood feuds that continues to the present. The Afghans have a history of uniting against foreigners and then reverting to intertribal conflict.

The Great Game[1]
Russian expansionism and empire building in Central Asia began in 1734 and Moscow's interest in Afghanistan was apparent by the late 1830s. As a result of the Russo-Persian War of 1826–28, the Persian court was under some Russian influence and Russian advisers and mercenaries were part of a Persian force which attempted to seize the city of Herat in 1837. British diplomatic and military pressure, reacting to this incursion as a Russian threat against the Afghan city-state of Kandahar and India (then controlled by the British East India Company) intervened to turn back the Persian incursion. This was probably the opening round in what became known as "The Great Game". The Great Game described the British and Russian struggle

---

1. Section derived from Richard F. Nyrop and Donald M. Seekins (eds), *Afghanistan: A Country Study*, fifth edition, Washington: US Government Printing Office, 1986, 22–73.

for influence along the unsettled northern frontier of British India and
in the entire region between Russia and India. Afghanistan lay
directly in this contested area between two empires. Russia described
her motives in the Great Game as simply to abolish the slave trade
and to establish order and control along her southern border. The
British, however, viewing Russian absorption of the lands of the
Caucasus, Georgia, Khirgiz, Turkmens, Khiva and Bukhara, felt
threatened by the presence of a large, expanding empire near India
and ascribed different Russian motives. The British believed that
Russian motives were to weaken British power and to gain access to
a warm-water port. British motives were to protect the frontiers of
British India and Britain felt that gains or losses of power and
influence in the region were reflected as gains or losses of power and
influence in Europe proper.

The Great Game spilled into Afghanistan when British forces
invaded during the First Anglo-Afghan War (1839–42). Britain
claimed that the invasion was supposed to counter Russian influence.
After hard fighting, the British withdrew. By 1869, the Russian empire
reached the banks of the Amu Darya (Oxus) river – the northern
border of Afghanistan. This caused additional British concern. In
1878, the arrival of a special Russian diplomatic mission to Kabul led
to another British invasion and the Second Anglo-Afghan War. The
British Army again withdrew. In the Anglo-Russian Treaty of 1907, the
Russians agreed that Afghanistan lay outside its sphere of interest and
agreed to confer with Britain on all matters relating to Russian–
Afghan relations. In return, Britain agreed not to occupy or annex any
part of Afghanistan nor interfere in the internal affairs of that country.
Although the Amir of Afghanistan refused to recognize the treaty,
Russia and Britain agreed to its terms and honored them until 1919
when Afghan troops crossed into British India, seized a village and
attempted to raise a popular revolt in the area. The British responded
with yet another invasion and the Third Anglo-Afghan War.

During this short war, the Afghanistan government quickly
recognized the new Bolshevik government in Russia and asked for
military aid against the British. The war ended without this aid, but
the new relationship between Afghanistan and the Soviet Union
continued. In 1920, the Soviet Union sponsored the Congress of
Peoples of the East in Baku. This congress called for a holy war
against British Imperialism. In 1921, the Afghan–Soviet Treaty was
the first international agreement that the Soviets entered after taking
power. Soviet economic and military aid to Afghanistan followed.

Still, there were disagreements between the neighboring states. Soviet expeditionary forces entered Afghanistan in 1925 to seize a small disputed island in the Amu Darya river.   When Amin Amanullah, the head of Afghanistan, was overthrown in 1929, the Soviet government sent a 1,000 man expeditionary force, disguised as Afghans, to try to restore him to power. International condemnation eventually caused the Soviets to withdraw. Again in 1930, Soviet forces entered 13 miles into Afghanistan as they followed a Moslem rebel who had taken refuge in the south.

In the 1920s and 1930s, the Soviets were more concerned with fighting a determined guerrilla resistance and re-establishing control throughout Central Asia. However, Britain and the Soviet Union continued to vie for advantage and influence in this buffer state between India and the Soviet Union. In 1947, the British withdrew from the newly independent states of India and Pakistan, leaving a political power vacuum in Afghanistan which the Indian Communist Party sought to fill. Following the death of Stalin, the Soviets again showed interest in the area and, in the 1950s, the Soviets became the single source of armaments for Afghanistan. The Soviets also increased trade and economic aid. Aid projects included hospitals, airfields, hydroelectric dams, and the Salang Pass highway tunnel. By 1963, Soviet military advisers were assigned throughout the Afghan Army's school and units. Some 4,000 Afghan officers were sent to the USSR for training. Soviet presence and influence were pervasive. In 1978, a small leftist group of Soviet-trained Afghan officers seized control of the government and founded the Democratic Republic of Afghanistan, a client state of the Soviet Union. Civil war broke out in Afghanistan.

Soviet Intervention

The Soviet–Afghan War began over the issue of control. The Democratic Republic of Afghanistan was nominally a socialist state governed by a communist party. However, the state only controlled some of the cities, while tribal elders and clan chiefs controlled the countryside. Furthermore, the communist party of Afghanistan was split into two hostile factions. The factions spent more time fighting each other than trying to establish socialism in Afghanistan. Government proclamations of land distribution, emancipation of women and the destruction of traditional society in order to construct a new "egalitarian" society found little support among the traditional, Islamic peoples. While the communists did little to implement these modernization programs effectively, their attempts galvanized the opposition against these radical ideas. Communist infighting increased as the President of Afghanistan was overthrown and executed by his prime minister (from the opposing faction). The prime minister became the new president and proved even more unpopular and less effective than his predecessor. Meanwhile, units of the army mutinied, civil war broke out, cities and villages rose in revolt and Afghanistan began to slip away from Moscow's control and influence. Leonid Brezhnev, the aged Soviet General Secretary, saw that direct military intervention was the only way to prevent his client state from disintegrating into complete chaos. He decided to intervene.

The obvious models for intervention were Hungary in 1956 and Czechoslovakia in 1968. The Soviet General Staff planned the Afghanistan invasion based on these models. However, there was a significant difference that the Soviet planners missed. Afghanistan was embroiled in a civil war and a *coup de main* would only gain control of the central government, not the countryside. Although participating military units were briefed at the last minute, the Soviet Christmas Eve invasion of 1979 was masterfully planned and well executed. The Soviets seized the government, killed the president and put their own man in his place. They planned to stabilize the situation, strengthen the army and then withdraw Soviet forces within three years. The Soviet General Staff planned to leave all fighting in the hands of the army of the Democratic Republic. But Afghanistan was in full revolt, the dispirited Afghan army was unable to cope, and the specter of defeat following a Soviet withdrawal haunted the Politburo. Invasion and overthrow of the government proved much easier than fighting the hundreds of ubiquitous guerrilla groups. The Soviet Army was trained for large-scale, rapid-tempo operations. They were not trained for the platoon leaders' war of finding and closing with small, indigenous forces which would only stand and fight when the terrain and circumstances were to their advantage.

Back in the Soviet Union, there was no one in charge and all decisions were committee decisions made by the collective leadership. General Secretary Brezhnev became incapacitated in 1980 but did not die until November 1982. He was succeeded by the ailing Yuri Andropov. General Secretary Andropov lasted less than two years and was succeeded by the faltering Konstantin Chernenko in February 1984. General Secretary Chernenko died in March 1985. Although the military leadership kept recommending withdrawal, during this "twilight of the general secretaries" no one was making any major decisions as to the conduct and outcome of the war in Afghanistan. The war bumped on at its own pace. Finally, Mikhail Gorbachev came to power. His first instinct was to order military victory in Afghanistan within a year. Following this bloodiest year of the war, Gorbachev realized that the Soviets could not win in Afghanistan without unacceptable international and internal repercussions and began to cast about for a way to withdraw with dignity. United Nations' negotiators provided that avenue and by 15 October 1988, the first half of the Soviet withdrawal was complete. On 15 February 1989, the last Soviet forces withdrew from Afghanistan.

Soviet Operations in Afghanistan[2]
Modern armies think in terms of tactics supporting operations and operations building campaigns. This theoretical framework failed in the Soviet Army in Afghanistan as large-scale operations proved ineffective and were practically a hindrance. Still, the Soviets continued to mount operations. The Soviet Army was probably the world's most operationally competent army in terms of theory, planning and execution. Historic Soviet victories were operational and Soviet war-fighting was operationally oriented (compared to Western armies which had more of a tactical orientation). Afghanistan, however, was a tactical war and Soviet tactics were initially inadequate for fighting guerrillas. This book is a record of their tactical evolution. There were three phases to the war. The first was the invasion and consolidation phase from 1979 to 1981. Phase two sought military victory and lasted from 1982 to 1986. Phase Three was the withdrawal phase which lasted from 1986 to 1989. What remains then is to provide a chronological list of the war's major events and operations from the Soviet perspective. Tactical events recorded in this book are tied to the chronology where appropriate, but there are few matches, since most instructive tactical events occurred away from the clumsy large-scale operations.

1979
15–21 March. Anti-Communist demonstrators seize Herat and the

---

2. Chronology of operations derived from David C. Isby, *War in a Distant Country: Invasion and Resistance*, London: Arms and Armour Press, 1989, and Mark Urban, *War in Afghanistan*, New York: St Martin's Press, 1988.

Afghan 15th Division, ordered to restore the situation, joins the opposition. Between 28 and 200 Soviet civilians and advisers butchered in Herat. Herat is bombed by Afghan and Soviet aircrews leaving an estimated 5,000 Afghan dead.

April. Soviet-piloted Mi-24 HIND helicopters support a DRA offensive in the Kunar valley which kills an estimated 1,000 when the village of Kerala is razed.

17 May. Afghan mechanized brigade from the 7th Division defects to the resistance.

July. Battalion of Soviet paratroopers lands in Bagram airbase to protect Soviet helicopter force.

August. 5th Brigade of the 9th Afghan Division mutinies and joins resistance in the Kunar valley.

August–October. General Pavlovskiy, Chief of Ground Forces (and Soviet commander of the invasion of Czechoslovakia), leads a group of 50 Soviet officers on a planning reconnaissance throughout Afghanistan.

14 September. Prime Minister Amin's faction kills President Taraki in a gun battle. Amin becomes president.

October. Insurrection in the 7th Division.

24 December. Soviet airborne division begins air landing in Kabul.

27 December. Soviet divisions cross border and begin advance south along the eastern and western highways. Soviet airborne and Spetsnaz forces overthrow government and kill the president.

28 December. Barbak Karmal declared new president of the Democratic Republic of Afghanistan.

1980
1 January. Kandahar revolts and Soviet citizens and troops are hacked to pieces.

21 February. Kabul protests the Soviet occupation and hundreds are killed and thousands are arrested (and later executed). Anti-Soviet riot in Shindand put down by Soviet forces.

February. Soviet sweep of Kunar valley.

March. Soviet push into Paktia results in the loss of a Soviet battalion. Soviet sweep of Kunar valley.

April. Soviet offensive in Pandshir valley.

May. Soviet sweep of Ghazni. Soviet sweep of Kunar valley.

June. Soviet sweep of Ghazni.

September. Soviet sweep of Kunar valley. Pandshir I.

October. Pandshir II.

November. Soviet sweep of Kunar valley. Soviet sweep of Wardak province. Lowgar valley offensive until mid-December.

1981
February–May. Fighting in Kandahar.

April. Pandshir III.

June–July. Nangahar offensive.

4 July. 108th MRD offensive in Sarobi valley. Heavy fighting in Herat.

August. Pandshir IV.

5 September. 5th MRD offensive in Farah province.

October. 5th MRD sweeps around Herat. Unsuccessful DRA operation at Marmoul Gorge, Balkh province. Soviet offensive in Kandahar.

December. Combined sweeps with DRA and 66th MRB in Nangahar. Fighting in Herat.

1982
January. Fighting in Herat.

February. City fighting in Kandahar.

May. Pandshir V, largest operation yet launched in retaliation for attack on Bagram air base. 108th MRD governing headquarters for composite force drawn from three divisions (108th MRD, 201st MRD and 103rd ABD) (aftermath vignette 29).

July. Sweep against Paghman hills near Kabul.

August–September. Pandshir VI.

November. Laghman valley offensive.

1983
January. Lowgar valley offensive. Soviets negotiate cease-fire in Pandshir valley.

April. Sweeps around Herat.

June. Ghazni offensive.

August. Paktia province offensive.

November. Shomali offensive.

1984
April. Gora tepa offensive. End of cease-fire in Pandshir valley. Pandshir VII, largest offensive yet, launched under control of 108th MRD. Operation also includes push up Andarab valley and Alishang valley. Soviets garrison lower valley and fighting continues throughout summer.

June. Lowgar valley offensive. Herat and Kandahar offensives (vignette 42).

July–August. Lowgar and Shomali valley offensive.

August–October. Relief of Ali Khel garrison in Paktia by 70th MRB and 345th ABR.

September. Pandshir VIII (aftermath in vignette 8).

October. Fighting in Herat (vignette 14).

November. Paktia operation.

December. Kunar valley offensive with 66th MRB, 345th ABR. Lasts until February.

1985
April. Maidan valley offensive.

May–June. Kunar offensive and relief of Barikot garrison.

June. Pandshir IX launched in retaliation for fall of Pechgur.

July. Heavy fighting in Herat and Kandahar.

August–September. Paktia offensive. Largest offensive since Pandshir VII. Relieved Khost, but failed to take Zhawar (vignette 23).

1986
March. Offensive around Andkhoy (vignette 11 and 16).

April. Paktia offensive takes Zhawar.

May. President Karmal replaced by Najibullah. Offensive in the Arghandab near Kandahar.

June. Khejob valley offensive.

August. Lowgar valley offensive.
October. Six Soviet regiments withdrawn.

November. 66th MRB offensive in Naizan valley.

1987
January–February. Temporary cease-fire for national reconciliation.

May–June. Arghandab offensive. Paktia offensive near Jadji.

14 July. Loss of Kalafghan garrison in Takhar province.
November–January. Operation Magistral to relieve Khost (vignette 17).

1988
March. Offensive to relieve Urgun in Paktia province.

April. Kandahar to Ghazni offensive.

14 April. Geneva Accords signed (talks in process since 1982).

April. Soviet withdrawal from Barikot, upper Kunar valley and Ali Khel, Chowni and Chamkani in Paktia, Qalat in Zabul.

May. 66th MRB withdrawal from Jalalabad.

15 October. Half of Soviet force withdrawn.

1989
15 February. Last Soviet combat units withdrawn.

ВОЕННАЯ ОРДЕНОВ ЛЕНИНА И ОКТЯбРЬСКОЙ РЕВОЛЮЦИИ КРАСНОЗНАМЕННАЯ ОРДЕНА СУВОРОВА АКАДЕМИЯ имени М. В. ФРУНЗЕ

Order of Lenin and the October Revolution, Red Banner and Order of Suvorov Military Academy named in honor of M. V. Frunze

Кафедра истории военного искусства

by the Department of the History of the Military Art

бОЕВЫЕ ДЕЙСТВИЯ СОВЕТСКИХ ВОЙСК В РЕСПУБЛИКЕ АФГАНИСТАН

COMBAT ACTIONS OF SOVIET FORCES
IN THE REPUBLIC OF AFGHANISTAN

Тематический сборник тактических примеров

(A thematic collection of tactical examples)

Москва

Moscow

Издание академии

The Frunze Academy Press

1991

Frunze Title Page

FRUNZE COMMENTS ABOUT THE
PREPARATION OF THIS COLLECTION

This collection of tactical experiences is based on the personal experience of student-officers at the academy who, during various years, served in combat as part of the Limited Contingent of Soviet Forces in Afghanistan . The following group of military historians assisted them in the preparation of this book: Chapter One-LTC S. A. Shumaev, LTC A. M. Korelov, Major V. V. Titov and Major S. N. Zagorul'kin; Chapter Two-Major I. I. Latynin and Major Yu. B. Sinel'shchikov; Chapter Three-Major Yu. G. Legtyarev; Chapter Four-Major Yu. B. Sinel'shchkov. Chapter Five-Major S. V. Ionov; and, Chapter Six-LTC S. A. Morozov and Major A. V. Reznichenko.

The teaching faculty of the Academy's History of Military Art Department provided assistance in the collection and editing of materials.

Candidate of Historical Science Colonel Yu. N. Yarovenko headed the team of authors and served as editor-in-chief.

FRUNZE FOREWORD

The Limited Contingent of Soviet Forces in the Republic of Afghanistan garnered valuable combat experience and significantly expanded the theory and practice of combat in mountainous-desert terrain. Battalion and regimental-level[1] combat was fought primarily in the mountains against separate detachments of *mujahideen* [insurgents]. The war was fought under conditions where the enemy lacked any aviation capabilities, but had modern air defense systems and modern mines. A lack of front lines and advances along varied axes (which were not mutually supporting) characterized the decisive actions of the opposing sides as they attempted to seize the initiative and gain control over certain territories.

The Soviet forces encountered several unique combat characteristics which necessitated that they adopt more effective methods for combating guerrilla forces of *mujahideen.*

Combat experience disclosed that the principal types of combat included: company, battalion and regimental raids; blocking off areas where the enemy was located prior to searching out and destroying guerrilla forces; and the simultaneous attack on several groups of the enemy located at various depths and locations. The specific combat conditions influenced the way in which the advance through mountains and inhabited areas was conducted; led to a change in air assault tactics; changed the methods of conducting marches and providing convoy security; and caused a change in the tactics of organizing and conducting ambushes.

At the present time, a number of studies have been published based on the combat lessons of Afghanistan. These analyze the conditions in this Theater of Military Operations, focusing especially on the tactics of the *mujahideen* guerrilla forces, and the

[1]Here the Russian text employs the generic terms subunits (podrazdelenie) and units (chasti). I put them into Western equivalent (ed.).

changed nature of the combat missions of Soviet battalions and regiments. This material serves as the basis for further improvement of the education of the officer corps and should be used in commanders' preparations for combat and in training exercises in higher command-staff colleges.

At the same time, far from all is done to synthesize and analyze Afghanistan combat experience. Thus, insufficient attention is devoted to specific combat episodes and to the analysis of good and bad points in the combat situations. Further, coordination between military history and operational-tactical training of the command cadre needs improvement.

In this respect, the team of authors has made an attempt to draw general conclusions about the little-investigated experiences in the training and the conduct of combat which were influenced by Afghanistan experience. These include specific mission decisions involving blocking and destroying guerrilla forces, the offense in mountains and through populated areas, the use of air assault tactics, the conduct of the defense in a security detachment, the conduct of a march and convoy security, and the conduct of ambushes.

This is not an exhaustive study of the training and conduct of battle by the Soviet battalions and regiments in Afghanistan. Rather, it is a collection of material which describes and analyzes individual combat episodes.

The Bear Went Over the Mountain:

Soviet Combat Tactics in Afghanistan

CHAPTER 1:
BLOCKING AND DESTROYING GUERRILLA FORCES

Research on the combat experience acquired by the Soviet forces in Afghanistan showed that one of the fundamental methods for fulfilling combat missions was to block off a region in which guerrilla forces were located and then to thoroughly comb the region to find and destroy the *mujahideen.*

Successful accomplishment of this task required thorough preparation of personnel and weapons for combat; skillful coordination between the blocking and combing forces, their *bronegruppa*, artillery and aviation; the application of military cunning and the application of reasoned initiatives; and the brave and decisive actions of the commander and personnel. Excellent results were achieved by suddenly blocking-off those regions which had been the site of military activity several days prior.

---

[1]The *bronegruppa* (armored group) is a temporary grouping of 4-5 tanks, BMPS or BTRs, or any combination of such vehicles. The BMPs (tracked combat vehicles) or BTRs (wheeled combat vehicles) are deployed without their normally assigned infantry squad and fight away from their dismounted troops. The grouping has a significant direct-fire capabilitiy and serves as a maneuver reserve (ed.)

An airborne battalion searches
Sherkhankhel village
by Major S. N. Petrov[2]

In the spring of 1982, guerrilla forces began combat activities in Parvan Province. Guerrillas hit our convoys, outposts and separate groups of soldiers. They regularly shelled the Bagram airport and the base camp of our airborne regiment. Intelligence reports indicated that a well-armed group of approximately 40 *mujahideen* were operating out of Sherkhankhel village.

The airborne regiment commander received orders to destroy this guerrilla force. Preparations for combat were rapidly completed. Sufficient ammunition for three days combat was issued to every paratrooper and two combat loads of ammunition were loaded onto the combat vehicles. The regimental commander personally inspected the battalion's readiness.

The 3rd Airborne Battalion commander planned to move his battalion secretly to the Sherkhankhel region and to seal it off with two companies of paratroopers while a third company would search the village. One airborne company would remain in reserve. An artillery battalion and four Mi-24 helicopter gunships would provide support with the initiation of combat.

In the predawn hours of 20 March, the battalion moved out from Bagram to Sherkhankhel. A reconnaissance patrol moved 300 meters in front of the column. The approach march moved on a wide, straight road. Along the left side of the road stretched a thick, high, long adobe wall while on the right side lay a concrete lined canal which was five meters wide and two-and-a-half meters deep. Suddenly, through an embrasure cut in the adobe wall, and practically at point-blank range, the enemy opened fire on the reconnaissance patrol. The survivors scrambled for safety into the canal. A machine gun opened fire from a house 150 meters further north from the ambush site. The battalion column halted and the battalion commander called in artillery and helicopter support.

The battalion finally began to maneuver its reserve company in an effort to encircle the enemy, but only after the *mujahideen* ceased

[2]S.N. Petrov served in the OKSVA from 1981 to 1983 as the commander of an airborne company.

fire. But even this attempt was stopped by a veritable hurricane of enemy fire. The *mujahideen* used the system of *karez*[3] to successfully break contact and withdraw. There was no thought of conducting a pursuit or continuing the action. The 3rd Airborne Battalion lost eight men killed and six wounded. Two of the dead were officers. The battalion did not search the village since the *mujahideen* were already gone. Instead, the battalion returned to its base camp.

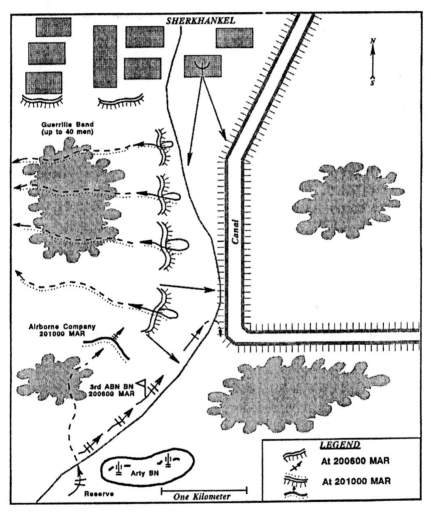

Map 1: The sweep of Sherkhankhel village on 20 March 1980.

[3]A system of underground tunnels used for the collection of ground water and for carrying water for surface irrigation.

FRUNZE COMMENTARY: In spite of our measures to prepare for combat secretly, the enemy was able to determine the intention of Soviet tactical elements. Exploiting the arrogance of the battalion commander, the enemy hit him with an ambush. The battalion's subunits, which were prepared to conduct a sweep, conducted an approach march along a single march route which was so constricted as to prevent maneuver by the subunits. The battalion commander merely put a reconnaissance patrol to his front and did not consider using flanking patrols.

EDITOR'S COMMENTARY: Operations security is difficult, particularly when fighting on someone else's turf and working with an indigenous force which may not be 100% on your side. Yet operations security is absolutely imperative for preserving your force and winning battles. In this vignette, the regimental commander thoroughly inspected his force prior to its moving out. This sounds like a good idea, however, this was the dread *stroevoy smotr* [ceremonial inspection] which was an unwelcome part of peace-time, garrison soldiering in the Soviet Army. The entire regiment would lay out all its equipment on the parade ground. All equipment would be laid out on tarps in front of the vehicles. Every piece of equipment would be formally checked and accounted for, the correct spacing on uniform items would be checked with a template, and displays would be aligned with pieces of string. The process could take three days. Although inspections are good ideas, these massive formal inspections were almost always conducted before a planned action. Any *mujahideen* in the vicinity were tipped off that an action was pending and could sound the warning. This Soviet pattern often compromised operational security. In this vignette, the *mujahideen* definitely were warned and punished the careless Soviet force. The *stroevoy smotr* may have been part of the Soviet problem.

Searching a populated area in the Charikar Valley
by LTC A. L Makkoveev[4]

Throughout the winter of 1980, Kabul and the surrounding provinces were quiet and there was no combat in this region. However, with the arrival of spring, organized guerrilla groups initiated an active campaign.

I commanded the 7th Motorized Rifle Company[5] which was mounted on BMPs. On the morning of 21 July, I was given the mission to conduct a road march from Kabul to Charikar and then reinforce one of the mountain rifle battalions which would conduct a deep raid and search.

Preparations for combat began in garrison. The company had 100% fill in personnel, weapons and equipment. We carried three days worth of dry rations[6] and the vehicles were topped-off with POL. After a thorough inspection, I reported to my battalion commander that we were ready for combat.

We completed our road march to the AO (area of operations) of the 3rd Mountain Rifle Battalion. That evening, the battalion commander, Captain Yu. P. Levintas, explained the 3rd Battalion mission and instructed me to prepare my company to move in the main body of the battalion along a designated route and search all the nearby villages.

At 0500 hours on 22 July, the 3rd Mountain Rifle Battalion, reinforced by my 7th Motorized Rifle Company, moved out. Riding on

---

[4]A.L. Makkoveev commanded a motorized rifle company in the Limited Contingent of Soviet Forces in Afghanistan from December 1979 to November 1981. He was decorated with the Military Order "For Service to the Fatherland in the Armed Forces of the USSR" Third Class.

[5]Evidently a part of the 108th Motorized Rifle Division (ed.).

[6]Dry rations are similar to the old U.S. Army C-ration. There were three types of dry rations. The first contained a can of meat, some crackers or toast, some jam and a tea bag. The second contained two cans of meat mixed with oatmeal. The third contained a can of meat and a can of vegetables or fruit (ed.).

our combat vehicles allowed us to overcome many natural obstacles. At one stage of our advance, I dismounted my company. While we were dismounted, I received the order to search a nearby village and, following the search, to take the road [which ran through the village] to rejoin the battalion main body. I dispatched a squad-sized patrol to establish a defensive position at the entrance to the village. I wanted the squad to cover the company as it deployed. On the outskirts of the village, I established firing positions for the machine gun-

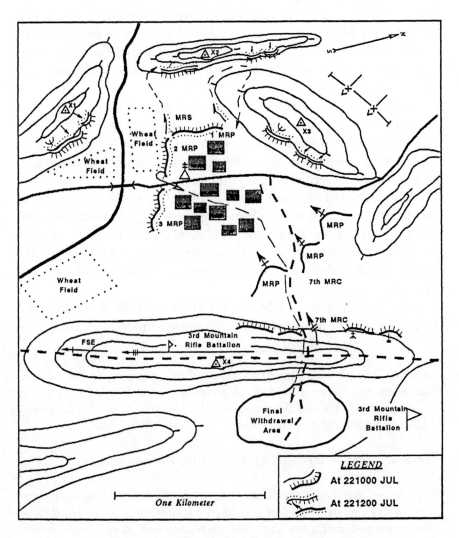

Map 2: Motorized rifle company searching a village while separated from the main force on 22 July 1980.

grenade launcher platoon.[7] The company then descended from the heights, formed into a line and combed the village, searching the houses and basements. After two hours, we finished the search and the company assembled on the road to exit the village.

At that moment, the enemy suddenly opened up on us with heavy fire from hill #2. The company went to the defense and took up positions behind the adobe walls on the south and southwest edges of the village. I decided to send two squads from the first platoon to envelop hill #2 and then destroy the enemy by an attack from the front and rear. I also decided to dispatch a patrol squad to the top of hill #1. However, just as the platoon started to move to carry out its tasks, the *mujahideen* opened fire [from hills # 1, 2 & 3]. My forces had to stay in place and return fire. After 30 minutes, I received orders to withdraw my company to the hill from which we started [#4]. During the withdrawal from the village, my company was pinned down by fire from hill #3. After we destroyed the enemy on hills #2 and #3 with small arms fire and helicopter gunship strikes, I moved my company to the designated area.

FRUNZE COMMENTARY: The positive aspect of this skirmish was that the personnel displayed high morale and rapidly reacted to all orders even though this was their first time under fire. Further, the helicopter gunships displayed great skill as they made gun runs on the enemy. However, the skirmish also showed that the company had insufficient experience in conducting combat in mountainous regions and neither the officers, sergeants, nor soldiers knew the enemy's tactics. If the enemy had held his fire until the entire company was moving on the path between hill # 1 and # 2 (where there was nothing but open wheat fields to the right and left), the company would have been in a very serious predicament. Instead, the enemy opened fire immediately when the company reached the southern outskirts of the village. The Soviet force did a weak job of reconnaissance. Their failure to seize the dominant terrain allowed the enemy to suppress practically the entire company area with fire. Another shortcoming was that the company had never rehearsed

---

[7]The machine gun/grenade-launcher platoon was the fourth platoon of a motorized rifle company and provided suppressive fire from PKS or *Utes* machine guns and AGS-17 automatic grenade launchers. This platoon disappeared during force reorganization in the mid-1980s.

breaking contact and withdrawal during training.

Data from this skirmish further shows that it is necessary to devote greater attention to commanders' training, especially tactical training. This should be done separately from platoon, company, battalion and field training. This includes training junior commanders. Courage and bravery are excellent characteristics, however the skillful handling of squads and, consequently, of platoons in battle is what is necessary and training did not achieve this.

EDITOR'S COMMENTARY: The commander learned that he must control dominant terrain and position over-watch forces before beginning the sweep. Failure to properly employ reconnaissance forces and failure to control high ground are constant problems throughout this book.

This 1980 example gives a partial look at one of the innovations in force structure which the Soviet Army made in an attempt to deal with the guerrilla forces–the mountain rifle battalion. Apparently, most of these came from the mountain training center in the Turkestan Military District.

Blocking and destroying a guerrilla force in Kunar Province
by Major V. A. Gukalov

In December 1980 in Kunar Province, a 50-man guerrilla force slipped across the border from Pakistan and crossed the Kunar river at night. Then it stopped to rest in a canyon. We decided to destroy the *mujahideen* within the confines of the canyon which was located to the southwest of Chaghasarai. The commander planned to conduct the battle as follows: Insert an airborne company (minus one platoon) by 0400 hours, 15 December to block the southern lip of the canyon and simultaneously insert an airborne platoon and the regimental airborne reconnaissance platoon to block enemy exits to the north and west. At 0500 hours, move the rest of the battalion (minus the blocking company) into the canyon to search for and destroy the enemy which was resting in the village located in the canyon.

At 2200 hours 14 December, the blocking group moved out on GAZ 66 trucks. The trucks headlights were off. They drove from the battalion lager, which was located along the highway, north toward Chaghasarai. In order to deceive *mujahideen* reconnaissance, several GAZ 66 trucks also drove south from the lager. The trucks dropped the first group two kilometers south of the canyon and then continued north. The first group walked to their blocking positions. The second part of the blocking force was dropped north of the canyon and walked to their positions. By 0400, 15 December the exits from the canyon were sealed.

At 0500 hours, the battalion (minus the blocking company) began its sweep into the canyon. The *mujahideen* security discovered this force at 0600. Adhering to their tactics, part of the enemy initiated combat with our main force while the rest began a withdrawal. The withdrawing forces were caught in our ambushes.

The enemy lost 24 killed and 4 captured. We had one wounded.

FRUNZE COMMENTARY: This example contains typical elements used to deceive the enemy (complete light discipline; insertion by trucks; running trucks in opposite directions; final movement into

---

[8]V.A. Gukalov served in the OKSVA in 1979-1981 as the senior assistant to the Chief of the Operations Section on the staff of an airborne division.

position on foot). The action succeeded despite our inability to conduct prior reconnaissance in the battle area due to time constraints and the lack of reinforcements and supporting elements.

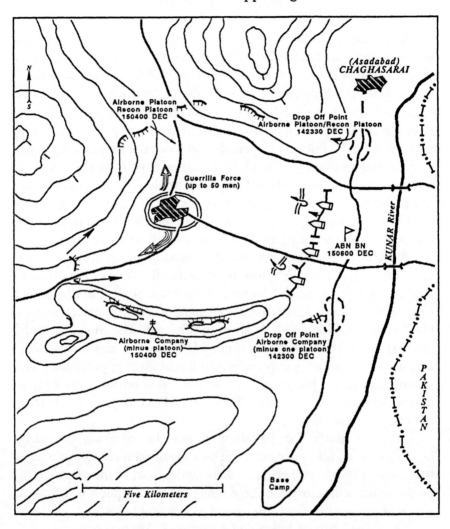

**Map 3: Blocking and destroying a guerilla force
in Kunar Province on 15 December 1980.**

Combing the city of Bamian and its outlying towns during the course of a raid
by Major A. P. Pivovarenko

During the winter of 1980, the situation along the roads between Termez and Kabul worsened. Enemy activity was particularly heavy in the area of the Salang pass leading to the critical Salang tunnel. Guerrilla forces struck convoys of military vehicles and trucks. Our motorized rifle regiment, composed of three reinforced motorized rifle battalions, was tasked to secure this sector from February until May of 1980. By May, the situation along this section of road had become even more acute. Consequently one of our battalions was structured as a raiding detachment. The battalion was reinforced with a tank company, a self-propelled artillery battery from division artillery, the regiment's reconnaissance company, a platoon of ZSU-23-4s[11] and a squad of sappers.

The reconnaissance company carried out its first raid in the area of Ghorband during the pre-dawn hours of 20-21 May and arrived at the village at daybreak. The detachment quickly broke into Ghorband and killed up to 10 *mujahideen*. After this, we began a thorough search of all the houses of the village. During the search, we only found some *mujahideen* small arms, for the bulk of the guerrilla force had secretly withdrawn to the north. On the following day, the entire raiding detachment finally began to move onto the city of Bamian. The detachment moved by road and fell into a *mujahideen* ambush, losing one BMP and one ZSU-23-4. The detachment seized the city. Our companies assaulted and searched the city's blocks. Our search showed that the *mujahideen* had abandoned the city. Our detachment stayed in the city for several days. During that time we searched the nearby villages but found no *mujahideen*. The enemy had temporarily abandoned the populated areas. My reconnaissance company

---

[9]A.P. Pivovarenko served as a reconnaissance platoon leader in the OKSVA from January 1980 to December 1980.

[10]Most likely, the regiment was a part of the 108th Motorized Rifle Division (ed.).

[11]The ZSU-23-4 is a self-propelled air defense weapon which fires four 23mm machine guns simultaneously. This weapon proved extremely effective in counter-ambushes and in the destruction of ground targets (ed.).

received information from our Afghan agent network which was
located in that city and, from that information, we were able to seize
63 weapons. The rest of the battalion was only able to capture two
weapons—both of them antiques.

The detachment conducted further raids which combed outlying
villages and canyons. But, again the *mujahideen* had successfully
withdrawn and the battalion swept empty blocks and areas.

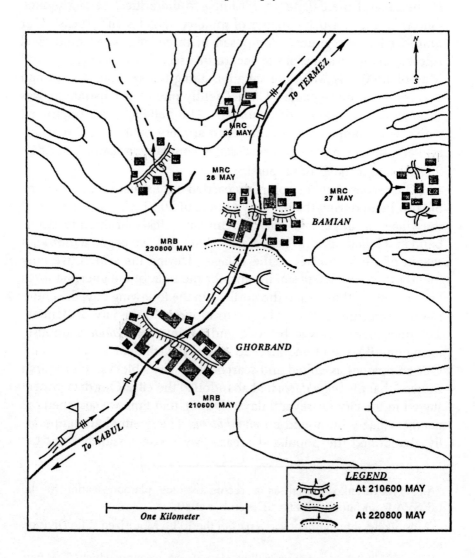

**Map 4: Sweeping Bamian and the surrounding villages in the
course of a raid by a motorized rifle battalion.**

FRUNZE COMMENTARY: Military experience shows that three basic tasks must be fulfilled to conduct a successful block and sweep. First, preliminary reconnaissance must disclose the location of the guerrilla forces as well as their composition and probable course of action. Second, the maneuverability of the guerrilla force must be constrained–tactical air assault landings and raiding groups must deny all paths and routes of withdrawal to the enemy and prevent his disengagement from the strike of the blocking groups. Third, the enemy must be destroyed by the main sweeping force or by a frontal attack. The unsuccessful accomplishment of any one of these tasks resulted in a failed mission. Combat experience demonstrated that it is necessary to establish close contact with the enemy, pin him down by battle while simultaneously maneuvering blocking forces into position, and then surrounding and destroying his guerrilla force. It is absolutely essential to search for the enemy, and this requires the effective utilization of reconnaissance forces. In order to successfully accomplish their combat mission, subunits need to be expeditiously divided into search, support, and fire support groups and the main body.

EDITOR'S COMMENTARY: The commander fought the *mujahideen* rear guard and made no efforts to pin the main body of the guerrilla force in place, cut off its escape route and aggressively outmaneuver it. The commander did not use his reconnaissance, fought his way through in a by-the-numbers manner, and did nothing to accomplish the mission rapidly. Sweeping an area without first posting blocking forces is, at best, a waste of time and a good way to get one's nose repeatedly bloodied. The commander showed little initiative and less field sense. Originally, this was the lead-off example to the book, but it was so weak that I moved it. I left it in as a prime example of the problems of the Soviet Army in 1980 in Afghanistan. Their army was trained for the European battlefield and was unable initially to cope with this new environment. Tactical commanders lacked initiative and the *mujahideen* took advantage of this.

Soviet commanders used their reconnaissance forces for combat and did not restrict them to reconnaissance missions. Reconnaissance forces were better trained and motivated than motorized rifle forces, but their casualty rate must have been much higher. The misuse of reconnaissance forces may have also been dictated by the fact that there were not enough Soviet forces in-country to do the job. Soviet field units were often chronically under strength.

Finally, the Bamian in this example is not the province capital of Bamian province, which was controlled by government forces throughout the war and which is not on the road to Termez, but approximately 150 kilometers to the east of it.

Blocking and searching the green zone
of the Arghandab River
by LTC S. V. Zelenskiy[12]

In October 1982, our reconnaissance learned that 10 guerrilla forces with a total strength of approximately 350 men were operating north of Kandahar city in the "green zone" bordering the Arghandab River. This fertile "green zone" stretches for 15-20 kilometers along the northern bank of the river and is up to seven kilometers wide. It is an agricultural region of gardens and vineyards bisected by a network of irrigation ditches. It is practically impassible for vehicles.

The brigade received an order to destroy these *mujahideen.*[13] The commander's concept was to seal off the north with the *bronegruppa* of three battalions. Helicopter gunship patrols would fly patrol patterns to seal off the south and the east.

Two motorized rifle battalions and an air assault battalion would search the area from the west to detect and destroy the enemy. An artillery battalion would support the action.

The force moved to its assembly areas and designated positions at night. By 0500 hours 6 October, the battalions' *bronegruppa* had all occupied their designated positions, the dismounted troops had closed in their assembly areas, the artillery battalion had occupied their firing positions and were prepared to conduct firing missions, and the helicopters were on station and flying their standing patrols.

At 0530 hours, the brigade commander gave the signal and the force began their sweep on a wide front. The 3rd Motorized Rifle Battalion was on the left, the 1st Motorized Rifle Battalion was in the center and the air assault battalion was on the right flank. Almost immediately, an irregular group of five-to-seven men began long-range small-arms fire on our forces and then withdrew to the northeast. Our subunits went in pursuit of them.

At 1600 hours, the 2nd Air Assault Company, commanded by

---

[12]S. V. Zelenskiy served in the OKSVA from 1981 to 1983 as the commander of an air assault company and as the senior assistant to the Chief of a brigade operations section. He was decorated with the "Order of the Red Star."

[13]The 70th Separate Motorized Rifle Brigade (ed.).

Senior Lieutenant Dyuby, made contact with approximately 40 *mujahideen*. The enemy was deployed in a well-organized defense occupying about a kilometer of frontage. The battalion commander ordered the right-flank 1st Air Assault Company to "envelop from the right the enemy force which is defending in front of the 2nd Company. Block the enemy route of withdrawal to the northeast. Prepare to destroy the enemy in concert with the 2nd Company."

I was a senior lieutenant at the time and commanded the 1st Air Assault Company. It took me a half hour to form up my platoons and begin the maneuver. During this time, the 2nd Company sus-

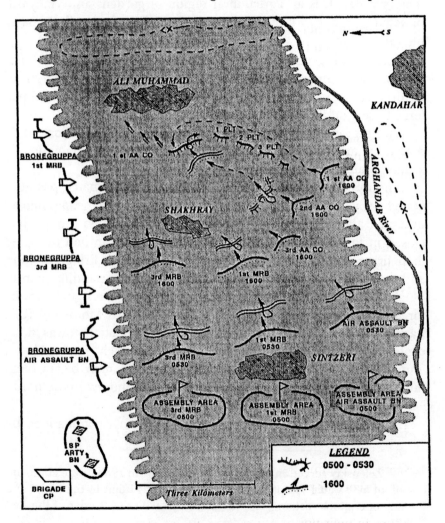

Map 5: Block and search of a green zone along the Argandab River.

tained casualties, but the enemy began to withdraw. By 1700 hours, I had maneuvered my platoons into blocking positions covering a *mujahideen* breakout to the northeast. I personally positioned each platoon behind adobe walls working consecutively from the southeast to the north. When I finished positioning my forces, my command post element and I were at the extreme right flank of my position. I had seven soldiers, including myself, in the command group.

Before I could reposition, approximately 70 enemy soldiers approached my command post. My six soldiers and I took the enemy under fire. At that point, I lost radio communications with both battalion headquarters and my subordinate platoons. However, I still had radio contact with brigade headquarters. The brigade commander demanded the exact coordinates of my position in order to call in artillery fire. However, I was unable to determine my precise location. I could only give an approximate location which I felt would be accurate to within 50 meters. The artillery refused to shoot the mission without more precise data.

The enemy force attacked three times. During the third assault, the command post was running out of ammunition. Each member of the command group, at my direction, simultaneously threw a grenade and broke contact with the enemy and withdrew to the first platoon position. Even when we had joined forces with the first platoon, we did not pursue the enemy because of his clear numerical superiority.

Enemy losses were 20 killed. My company had no casualties.

FRUNZE COMMENTARY: From this local episode, one can evaluate the following characteristic features associated with a larger brigade-size block and search action:

- using helicopters to seal off areas;
- tight coordination between subunits;
- skillful leadership and the ability to make the right decisions on the battlefield;
- initiative and steadfastness by our conscript soldiers at the command post of the air assault company;
- failure of communications;
- the absence of platoon leaders' initiative (a significant battle was taking place to their right, yet the platoon leaders kept their platoons in their positions awaiting orders from the company commander); and,

- deception by the enemy (instead of withdrawing straight back from his forward positions, he withdrew parallel to his forward positions toward the north).

EDITOR'S COMMENTARY: This encirclement differs from Soviet European tactics, since Soviet forces usually physically block all sides of an encircled area. In Afghanistan, they only used physical blocking forces when dominant terrain or a village marked a side. This was probably done to avoid fratricide between closing elements and the blocking forces. Frequently in Afghanistan, the Soviets used helicopter patrols, *bronegruppa* and RDM as an economy of force measure to block a side. In this vignette, the Soviets used *bronegruppa* and helicopter patrols. One wonders how effective the eastern helicopter patrol was overflying a forested area.

The vignette points out that small unit leaders need to be trained and given the freedom to react to combat in their area when radio contact is lost. The question is whether the platoon leaders knew that they had lost radio contact with their commander and if they took any steps to determine whether they still had contact or not.

The vignette also points out that the artillery would not fire unless the ground force commander knew his exact location. The ground commander could determine his location within 50 meters, yet the brigade commander would not fire artillery beyond that point and allow the commander to adjust that fire onto the enemy force. The company did not have a FO with it and the air assault company commander either could not adjust artillery fire or he was not trusted enough to do so. Soviet artillery was normally fired according to a preplanned schedule with all fire concentrations plotted from surveyed firing points. Normative fire destruction was used instead of more-accurate, adjusted artillery fires. Soviet artillery was hard pressed to "hip shoot" without their own FO on the ground. Soviet normative firing methodology was unsuited for combating mobile guerrilla forces who refused to stay put for massed artillery fires. One wonders whether the brigade commander refused the artillery fire, since he might personally suffer more from an investigation for deaths from "friendly" fire than for enemy-inflicted deaths.

Blocking, searching for and destroying a guerrilla force in Ishkamesh region
by Major A. M. Kovyrshin[14]

The enemy established a base and training center near the village of Ishkamesh, 60 kilometers southeast of the city of Kunduz. Guerrilla forces trained at this center engaged in firing at aircraft landing at Kunduz Airport and attacked supply convoys along the Kunduz–Puli-Khumri road. This made it difficult to supply and sustain the garrisons and forces located in the province.

LTC V. M. Akimov commanded the motorized rifle regiment which was ordered to prepare for combat to destroy the guerrilla forces operating in this region.[15] For this mission, the regiment was reinforced with a separate reconnaissance battalion, a separate helicopter squadron, and two artillery battalions. In addition, an Afghan infantry division supported the regiment.[16]

On 19 January 1984, the regiment and its subunits received their combat orders:

The reconnaissance battalion, reinforced with an 82mm mortar platoon and a flamethrower squad, air assaults into the Fuloli, Marzek, and Kokabulak region to cut off the enemy in Ishkamesh and Fuloli by 0900 hours 20 January. Be prepared to cooperate with the 2nd Battalion in blocking and destroying the enemy in Fuloli.

The 2nd Motorized Rifle Battalion, reinforced with a flamethrower squad, air assaults into the Kuchi, Badguzar and Apikutan region and destroys the enemy located there. Link up with your *bronegruppa* no later that 0700 hours and conduct a raid in the direction of Kuchi, Badguzar and Pil'kha to destroy the enemy located between Pil'kha and Ilig and to seize the ammunition stores located there. Subsequently, be prepared to link up with the reconnaissance battalion on the axis Kokabulak-Fuloli to block and destroy the enemy in the village of Fuloli.

---

[14]A. M. Kovyrshin served in the OKSVA from September 1982 through November 1984 as a platoon leader in a motorized rifle company. He was decorated with the Order of the Red Star.

[15]Most likely the 149th Motorized Rifle Regiment of the 201st Motorized Rifle Division (ed.).

[16]The 20th Infantry Division (ed.).

The 1st Motorized Rifle Battalion, reinforced with a artillery battalion and a flamethrower squad, conducts a road march to arrive at Marzek by 0800 hours, 20 January and destroy the enemy located in the Marzek-Ishkamesh region. Be prepared to advance on the axis Ishkamesh-Darayi-Pashay.

Regimental subunits and the reconnaissance battalion were at 70% personnel strength and 90% equipment fill. Enemy personnel in the area numbered 1,100-1,300 men armed with approximately 70 grenade launchers, 25 DShK 12.7 mm heavy machine guns, 40 mor-

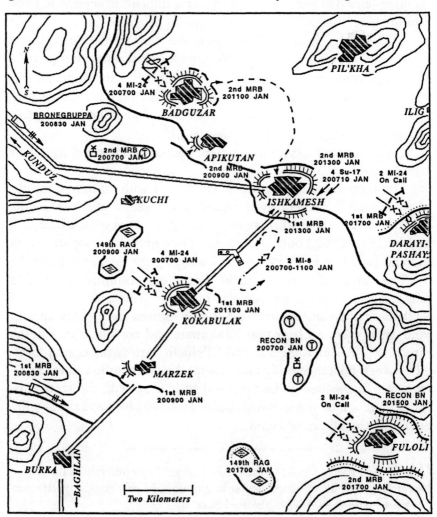

**Map 6: Destruction of the enemy in his training center in the
vicinity of Ishkamesh**

tars, and 10 artillery pieces. Intelligence revealed approximately seven caches in the area containing weapons, ammunition and supplies.

At first light on 20 January, after we conducted an airstrike on the area between Kokabulak and Marzek, the reconnaissance battalion made an air assault landing east of Marzek while the 2nd Motorized Rifle Battalion made an air assault landing two kilometers north of Kuchi. The *mujahideen* did not react to the helicopter flight since we used Mi-6 helicopters–a cargo helicopter not usually used for air assaults. This deception effort against the enemy paid off.

The reconnaissance battalion, commanded by LTC Tikhonov, cut the guerrillas southern route of withdrawal and blocked them in the strongpoints of Kokabulak and Marzek.

The 1st Battalion, commanded by Major A. V. Vlasov, exploiting the success of the reconnaissance battalion, arrived at the villages of Marzek and Kokabulak by 0830 hours and joined forces with the reconnaissance forces. Over the course of the next two and one-half hours, they destroyed the enemy in these strong points.

The 2nd Battalion, commanded by LTC V. Krokhin, landed and destroyed the enemy in the strong point of Kuchi. By 0830 hours, they had linked up with the approaching *bronegruppa*, which had driven there under the command of the 6th Company's commander, Senior Lieutenant R. S. Zarifov. The 2nd Battalion mounted its vehicles and conducted a raid on the axis Apikutan-Badguzar with the missions of searching and destroying weapons and ammunition caches.

The enemy, while conducting delaying actions withdrew part of their force into the mountains, while the other part withdrew into Ishkamesh-the main strong point in this *mujahideen* training center.

The 1st Motorized Rifle Battalion, having destroyed the enemy in Marzek and Kokabulak, moved on Ishkamesh from the south and arrived there at 1300 hours. Meanwhile, the 2nd Battalion, having destroyed the enemy in Badguzar and Apikutan, moved on Ishkamesh from the north. The *mujahideen* in Ishkamesh were blocked from two sides.

After a ten-minute artillery barrage by three artillery battalions, both motorized rifle battalions, supported by a flight of helicopter gunships, attacked Ishkamesh. By 1500 hours, Ishkamesh had fallen. The 1st Battalion pursued a group of *mujahideen* who managed to break out and flee toward Darayi-Pashay. The 2nd Battalion moved to the area south of Fuloli to link up with the reconnaissance battalion and join forces to seal off and destroy the enemy in Fuloli.

By 1600 hours, the enemy had broken off his main attacks and concentrated his main forces to defend the villages of Fuloli and Darayi-Pashay.

The 1st Battalion having reached the village of Darayi-Pashay at 1700, was unable to take the village from the march mounted on BMPs. They dismounted and tried to encircle the village by climbing the mountain and coming over the southern flank. However, they were unable to do this since the encircling force came under interlocking enemy fire. The battalion fought for possession of the village for the next 24 hours, but was unable to take it.

The 2d Battalion attacked Fuloli from the march mounted on BMPs. They were also unsuccessful, so they dismounted and blocked Fuloli from the south. The 2d Battalion and the reconnaissance battalion fought for possession of Fuloli for the next 24 hours. They were finally able to take it, but discovered that most of the enemy had slipped out under the cover of fog and darkness and escaped into the mountains to the southeast.

During 20 and 21 January, we destroyed the organized, main guerrilla force in the Ishkamesh region. The enemy lost up to 150 men killed and captured. Further, we captured a large amount of weapons and ammunition.

FRUNZE COMMENTARY: The following points are particularly noteworthy:

- deception against the enemy (using the Mi-6 helicopter instead of the normal Mi-8);
- misleading the enemy as to the actual region in which the combat actions were planned (through information supplied to the Afghan division);
- wide spread use of maneuver, combining frontal strikes with flanking attacks, encirclements, vertical envelopment, and on foot as well as mounted on various carriers;
- tight coordination between the combined arms subunits and the aviation and artillery support (an artillery FO accompanied every company and TO&E FACs accompanied every battalion, while additional FACs accompanied every company. They all had adequate communications);

- inadequate quantity of forces for a 20x10 kilometer area denied us the opportunity to seal off and destroy all the guerrilla forces;
- use of reconnaissance forces as combat forces; and
- paying closer attention to the increasing scale of activities which lead toward sealing and destroying the enemy.

EDITOR'S COMMENTARY: Tactical surprise gained from air landings and air assaults dissipates rapidly. Once the enemy has dug into a mountainside, green zone or village, heavy forces with superior numbers and superior fire power are necessary to blast them out. Once the surprise had worn off on this raid, the Soviets were fighting two separated actions and lacked the combat power to win either of them.

The use of the Mi-6 transport helicopters for the air assault fits the motto "never set a pattern but do the unexpected." One has to ask, however, was it deliberate deception or were they just lucky that these were the aircraft available?

Sweeping a green zone in Helmand Province
by Major V. I. Kurochkin[17]

In May 1984 we conducted an army operation to clear guerrilla forces from Helmand Province. The *mujahideen* in this region were very well trained and bore an undying hatred toward the government of Afghanistan. By this time, Soviet forces had accumulated a great deal of experience in conducting sweeps of separate regions and inhabited areas. Usually, motorized rifle soldiers dismounted from their carriers and conducted the sweeps on foot without their carriers. Practically speaking, this meant that they conducted these sweeps without the immediate fire support of tanks, artillery and BMPs (or BTRs). The *mujahideen* had also amassed experience in countering subunits conducting these sweeps in various regions and developed tactics and techniques to deal with the sweep. As a rule, they would lure us into predetermined areas and then open fire on us at a distance of no more than 50 to 100 meters. They would only fight in close contact to us since we could not use our artillery or aviation support within 100 meters of friendly forces. The *mujahideen* knew the local area and local terrain features quite well and were thus able to outmaneuver the Soviet forces.

Planning for this operation began long before its start and was very thorough. After being briefed on the concept of the operation, LTC Romanov, the commander of an airborne battalion, decided to push his attached tanks and his personnel carriers into the green zone ahead of his dismounted paratroopers. The tanks would provide armored cover for the paratroopers while cutting firing lanes in front of them. This was a very bold and original idea since the enemy usually mined those areas where tanks could maneuver and the terrain was laced with irrigation canals and potential ambush sites. The battalion commander planned that the combat formation would consist of two *bronegruppa* in column, each one led by tanks followed by personnel carriers which would push through the green zone. An airborne company would move on each flank of the *bronegruppa*.

The sweep began at 0800 on the morning of 11 May and by the day's end of 13 May, we had completely cleared the *mujahideen* out

---

[17]V. I. Kurochkin served in the OKSVA from February 1984 until April 1986.

of the oasis. We captured a large amount of weapons and ammunition. Despite the fact that one of the companies came under fire more than 10 times and that over 40 RPG rounds were fired at our tanks, our battalion did not have a single casualty.

FRUNZE COMMENTARY: The battalion's success was mainly due to the skillful use of tanks to destroy the enemy by direct fire. Engineer subunits found the enemy obstacles, particularly their mine fields, in timely fashion. The dismounted sappers worked under the

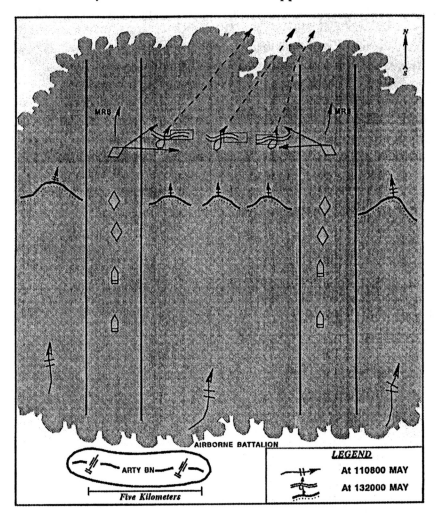

**Map 7: Sweeping the green zone with an airborne battalion
11-13 May 1984**

cover of armored vehicles. The commander skillfully used artillery fire to suppress the enemies' fires. The tanks and dismounted soldiers coordinated their movements as they moved from line to line. They would not move forward until the enemy was suppressed by artillery fire from the supporting artillery battalion. An artillery officer from the supporting battery accompanied the company it supported and adjusted artillery fire for that company. Thus, as soon as the enemy was spotted, firing data was transmitted to the supporting battery. The enemy was unable to conduct accurate, aimed fire, since such fire instantly resulted in an answering artillery barrage. Consequently, not one of the antitank RPG rounds hit a tank. Thus, thanks to well organized fire control and engineer support, the battalion was able to use tanks successfully in the green zone and successfully fulfill its mission in a short time with no casualties.

EDITOR'S COMMENTARY: This vignette could be subtitled "if it's dumb and it works, it's not dumb". On the other hand, this is a slow and expensive way to clear a zone. No *mujahideen* casualties are mentioned, so at the end of three days, the force blasted it's way through 14 kilometers of vegetation and owned it until they left. Then the *mujahideen* came back.

Sweeping villages with Afghani
and Soviet subunits
by Major S. G. Davydenko[18]

Throughout the time that Soviet forces operated in Afghanistan, the Panjsher Valley was the site of the sharpest ideological and military struggles between the government of Afghanistan and the armed opposition led by Ahmed Shah Massoud.[19] Operations which had been conducted in this valley earlier had resulted in heavy casualties. The mountain massif (located high above sea level)and the severe climate limited the capabilities of machines and men.

I was an adviser to a battalion of the Afghan Army's "Commando" Brigade garrisoned in the Barak fortress.[20] We received an order to sweep the villages of Tal'khana, Dashtak, Turkha, Kalatak and Chislak to capture or destroy *mujahideen* operating in the area. In addition, we were to find and destroy prepared firing positions and supply caches of ammunition, equipment and food.

Preparations for the operation began upon receipt of the mission. However, due to the massive disaffection and desertions of Afghan brigade officers and men to the *mujahideen*, the Afghan concept of the operation was almost immediately known to the enemy. On the morning of 28 October 1984, I received the order to start the mission. The concept of action for the battalion was as follows: Move out of the fortress and precede on foot to conduct a sweep of the designated villages. In the event that the enemy offered any resistance, call in artillery fire on them from the artillery battalion that belonged

---

[18]S. G. Davydenko served with the OKSVA from September 1984 to September 1986 as the adviser to an Afghan battalion commander.

[19]Ahmed Shah Massoud is one of the best-known guerrilla leaders in the West. He is a minority Tadjik who assembled the largest single guerrilla army in Afghanistan. This army, put at 11,000 regulars by the Soviets, may have numbered 50,000 when part-time partisans are added. Massoud was born around 1950, studied engineering in Kabul and is fluent in French. His control of the 70-mile-long Panjsher Valley was frequently challenged by the Soviets, yet in the end Massoud dominated the valley. Massoud became the West's favorite Afghan when Ken Follett based his best seller, *Lie Down with Lions* on this tough guerrilla commander (ed.).

[20]The 212th Separate Assault Brigade (ed.).

to the "Commando" Brigade. Plan to operate closely with the Soviet motorized rifle regiment that was located in the Rukha fortress.[21]

Due to the security leaks during the course of preparation for the operation, some combat missions had to be amplified and changed. The new concept required that the 2nd Afghan Battalion would exit the fortress and occupy the heights around Post 21. From there, if necessary, they could support the Soviet motorized rifle company which would independently sweep the villages of Tal'khana and Dashtak. Following this, the two units would switch roles while the Afghan battalion swept Turkha.

At the designated time, the 150-man Afghan battalion exited the fortress. It reached Post 21 in an hour and a half. The Soviet company swept the villages of Tal'khana and Dashtak. No *mujahideen* were discovered during the sweep, but a hidden *mujahideen* rest station with a small supply of food and anti-Soviet leaflets was discovered.

The battalion reached the village of Turkha on the evening of 29 October. Observers at Post 20 had seen *mujahideen* moving through Turkha the day before. On the morning of 30 October, the battalion searched the village. There, they found a few flintlock muskets and an AK-74. That evening, the battalion returned to the Bazarak fortress where they rested.

On the morning of 31 October, following joint planning between the Afghan battalion commander and the Soviet motorized rifle regiment commander, the forces set out to search the villages of Sata, Kalatak, and Kishlak. The plan was that the Afghan battalion would enter the canyon and search the villages sequentially. The canyon was controlled by two ridges which rimmed the canyon. It was necessary to put a Soviet battalion onto each of these ridges. Once they reached the crest of the ridge, the Soviet battalions would dominate the high ground and could support the Afghan battalion. The artillery was ready to open fire from protected positions within the fortresses.

At noon, the Afghan battalion began to sweep the canyon as the Soviet battalions began to mount the ridges. Combat engineers moved in front of the sweeping Afghan forces. As the Afghan battalion attempted to enter Kishlak to search it, they were met with

---

[21]Probably the 682nd Motorized Rifle Regiment of the 108th Motorized Rifle Division (ed.).

strong small arms, mortar and heavy machine-gun fire. Simultaneously, both the Soviet battalions became trapped in minefields. The enemy opened fire on the Soviet battalions from ambush and inflicted heavy casualties on them. Neither battalion was able to get into a position to support the Afghan battalion. The Afghan battalion also took heavy casualties and by nightfall was forced to withdraw to Bazarak village.

FRUNZE COMMENTARY: This combat example shows that a good plan is only as good as its skillful implementation. This opera-

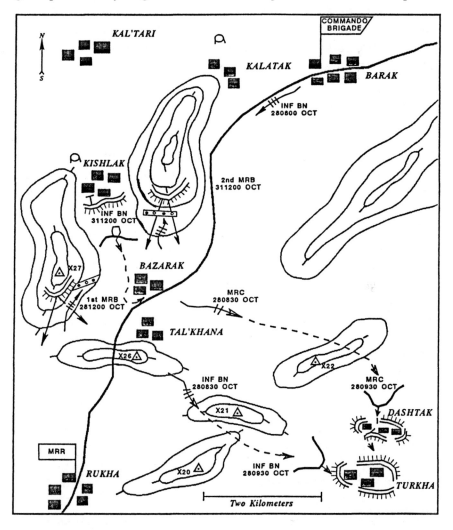

Map 8: Afghan and Soviet forces sweep villages

tion was thoroughly planned, however it was not able to overcome its inherent problems. It began with the security leaks. Further, our intelligence picture of *mujahideen* strength and their lines of communication was poorly developed. The enemy knew the scheme of maneuver for our Afghan and Soviet forces well in advance and was able to adjust the situation by maneuvering his forces into threatened sectors or away from planned strikes.

When conducting a sweep over such an extensive area, a commander cannot relax, even for a minute. The enemy lulled our forces from vigilance to complacency by secretly withdrawing from the first villages prior to our sweep. Then, they initiated combat at the time and place of their own choosing. Communications was a problem throughout the operation. This led to a loss of control and a loss of current information on the status and situation of the subunits. Coordination between the Afghan battalion and the supporting artillery was unsatisfactorily organized.

EDITOR'S COMMENTARY: The main lesson in this vignette is do not move a ground force where you cannot cover it by air or artillery fire. Radio communications are very difficult in the mountains, but uninterrupted radio communications with supporting artillery or aviation is essential for survival. Radio retransmission points on mountain tops or aircraft are a solution. The ground forces were moving without adequate flank, forward and rear security. Consequently, both Soviet battalions bogged down in minefields and left the Afghan battalion stranded. The Afghan battalion moved its main body into restrictive terrain without first clearing it and assuring that the Soviet battalions were securing its flanks and providing overwatch. The further lack of available airpower to overwatch the Afghan battalion sealed their fate.

Sweeping a potential ambush area
by Captain I. P. Tereshchenko[22]

By 1985, the *mujahideen* had become masters of stubbornly retaining highly defensible areas and attacking our forces with ambushes. This changed the combat missions of the subunits and units of the Soviet forces. Our main missions became blocking and sweeping mountain canyons and populated areas, providing convoy escort, and participating in tactical air assaults which would seize

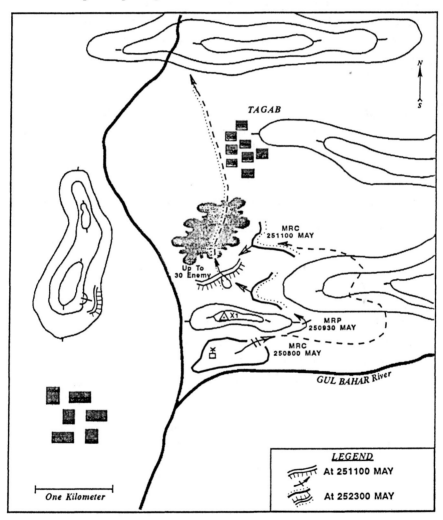

**Map 9: Sweeping a potential ambush zone with an MRC
25 May 1985**

important objectives.

Our motorized rifle battalion received the combat mission to sweep a region bordering on the village of Tagab. Intelligence reports indicated that a sizable guerrilla force was active in this area. We prepared and trained our force thoroughly for this action at our base camp. My battalion commander planned to search the region with one of our companies which would air assault into the region on helicopters.

At 0800 in the morning on 25 May 1985, the 8th Motorized Rifle Company airlanded in a area close to the village of Tagab. The company commander sent one platoon ahead as his forward patrol and moved the rest of his company around the high ground of hill #1. The patrolling platoon reached a clearing. The platoon leader reported that the area across the clearing looked like a place where ambushes might be laid. The company commander ordered him to form a platoon line and sweep forward. The *mujahideen*, thinking that they had been discovered, opened fire. The company commander decided to maneuver the rest of his company to encircle the enemy and hit him on the flank. It took the company a half hour to maneuver into position. By that time the enemy had broken contact and withdrawn. The company swept the area but was unable to find the enemy.

FRUNZE COMMENTARY: When conducting a complete sweep of unfamiliar terrain, you must have reconnaissance. All further combat actions of your subunits must be provided with reconnaissance and security elements. Further, you must seize the dominant terrain before you begin your sweep. Raiding groups are ideal for this function. Finally, in order to conduct a successful sweep, and destroy the enemy, you have to fix the enemy in place through combat to his front while simultaneously encircling or flanking him.

---

[22]I. P. Tereshchenko served in the OKSVA from April 1984 until April 1986 as the deputy commander of a battalion.

Blocking, sweeping and destroying the *mujahideen* in the Varduj Valley

by Major S. V. Krutyakov[23]

At the beginning of June 1985, the Najmuddin guerrilla force set up its headquarters near the village of Jurm in the Varduj Valley. This guerrilla force consisted of approximately 500 men and were well-armed and equipped–to include three mountain guns, eight-to-ten mortars, and communications systems. The local populace strongly supported Najmuddin and disliked the Afghan government. We received intelligence reports that a caravan had arrived at the village. The authorities decided to destroy the guerrilla headquarters, capture the caravan and seize supply caches.

My 1st Motorized Rifle Battalion was assigned the mission to insert two companies and a mortar battery on the night of 4-5 June to establish blocking positions on the east and west walls of the valley.[24] Then, my remaining company would join the 2nd Infantry Battalion of the Afghan Army and conduct a sweep north up the valley. The sweep would seize supply caches and draft young men on the spot into the Afghan army. My battalion was supported by a D-30 122mm howitzer battery and a battery of BM-21 "GRAD" multiple rocket launchers.

I supervised pre-battle preparations in our base camp. At midnight on the night of 4-5 June, my 2nd and 3rd Companies and the mortar battery moved out. The 2nd Company's mission was to take one mortar platoon and block the west wall of the valley by 0400 hours. My 3rd Company, with the other mortar platoon, was to block all exits along the east wall of the valley by 0400 hours.

My 2nd Company completed its mission and moved into position by 0300 on 5 June. The *mujahideen* did not detect their arrival. At 0345 hours, as my 3rd Company was closing onto its positions, the enemy discovered it and fired on it from the hill north of hill 246.0. Our mortar platoon returned fire and killed the enemy. Fifteen minutes later, the 3rd Company established its blocking posi-

---

[23]S. V. Krutyakov served in the OKSVA from 1985 to 1987 as the commander of a motorized rifle battalion.

[24]Probably the 1st Battalion, 860th Separate Motorized Rifle Regiment (ed.).

tions.

At 0400 hours, the 3rd Platoon of my 2nd Company was attacked by 25 *mujahideen* supported by a mortar. The enemy attacked from the east and the platoon was blinded by the rising sun. The platoon withdrew from its position on hill 224.6 and moved south to join the 2nd Platoon. At the same time, my 2nd Company command post (located on hill 246.4 with the 1st Platoon) came under attack.

As soon as I understood the situation, I ordered the 2nd Company's *bronegruppa* (which was under my control) and the *bronegruppa* of the 1st Company (my sweeping company) to join forces

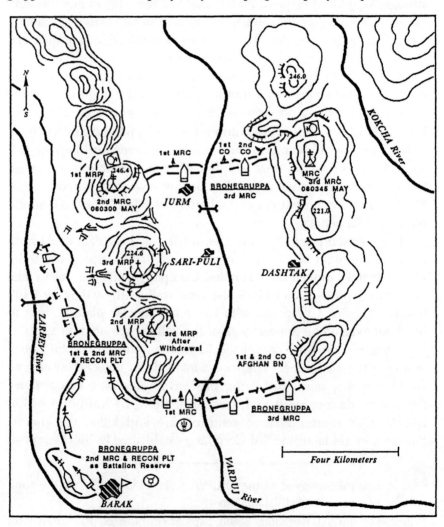

Map 10: Combat actions in Varduj Valley.

with my reserve (my reconnaissance platoon). I directed them to retake the 3rd Platoon's position on Hill 224.6, destroy the *mujahideen* who were supporting the enemy withdrawal and seal off the *mujahideen* escape route to the west. They accomplished their mission, killing seven *mujahideen,* capturing six prisoners and seizing 11 weapons. Our forces swept the valley, but made no further contact. The enemy had "melted" into the population. During the sweep we found a food cache with 90 tons of grain.

FRUNZE COMMENTARY: The following points should be noted from this action:

- the battalion commander's skillful control of the battle manifested by his rapid transfer of reserve forces and forces from inactive areas to the threatened sector;
- the lack of mutual fire support and coordination between platoons operating on the same axis;
- the inability of the junior commanders to rapidly organize and lay in a defensive fire plan;
- the lack of skill displayed by the personnel in quickly creating fighting positions and tying in their defenses with mortar fires;
- the lack of FSCs accompanying the subunits to adjust artillery fire, which lessened the effectiveness of the attached artillery.

EDITOR'S COMMENTARY: The *bronegruppa* concept is excellent for providing a quick reaction reserve and for moving fire power into a threatened sector. Mechanized infantry must train to function away from their personnel carriers.

Sequential blocking and sweeping of a mountain valley near Anushella

by Major P. A. Skovorodnikov[25]

In February and March 1986, guerrilla activities were recorded in the area of Kandahar, Kalat and Shar-e-Safa including attacks on Soviet and Afghan convoys, road mining, shellings of military camps and security outposts, and the armed protection of guerrilla caravans carrying weapons and ammunition from Pakistan.

LTC V. N. Tsarev, the commander of the air assault battalion[26] and my boss, received the following mission: "Prepare to move out in several days to conduct a block and sweep action to destroy the enemy in the valley near Anushella. The action will also involve the Brigade's 1st Motorized Rifle Battalion minus one of its companies (the 1st MRB was commanded by LTC A. G. Ivanov)."

Training and rehearsals for this action began on 16 March and concentrated on combat in mountains, clearing and overcoming minefields and boobytraps, night combat, sealing off caves and killing their defenders, evacuation of wounded from the mountains, and the destruction of supply caches by explosives (this last training was done in conjunction with attached sappers—each company had an attached sapper squad for this action). The train-up ended with a full battalion tactical exercise.

The battalion commander refined his final orders at 2000 hours on 24 March and issued them to his subordinates at 2200 hours.

"The 1st MRB (minus its 3rd Company) will establish successive blocking positions on the eastern wall of the canyon and deny the enemy a break-out to the east. The blocking force must be in place by 0600 hours on 25 March. This 1st MRB will be supported by a flight of Mi-24 helicopter gunships.

"The 3rd Air Assault Company will establish a series of successive blocking positions also running from the south to the north on

---

[25]P. A. Skovorodnikov served in the OKSVA from 1985-1987 as the Chief of Staff of an air assault battalion. He was twice decorated with the Order of the Red Star and was also decorated with the Combat Medal "For Bravery."

[26]The air assault battalion of the 70th Separate Motorized Rifle Brigade (ed.).

the west wall of the canyon to deny the enemy a break-out to the west. This blocking force must be in place by 0600 hours on 25 March.

"The rest of the air assault battalion will block the southern exit of the canyon. The battalion is reinforced with a tank platoon, an antitank battery, a flamethrower platoon, and a sapper platoon. Two self-propelled howitzer battalions, a battery of BM-22 "Hurricane" (RSZO) 220mm MRLS, a squadron of Su-25 "FROGFOOT" close-air support aircraft, and a flight of Mi-24 helicopter gunships will pro-

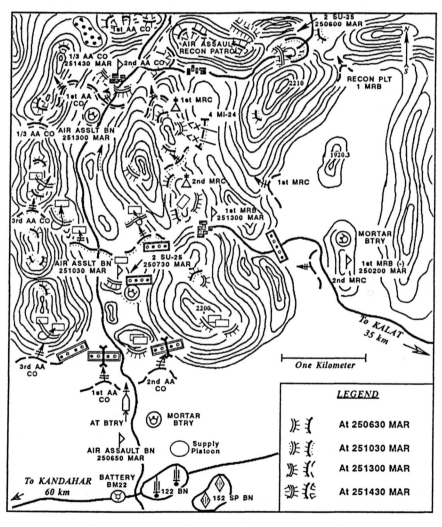

Map 11: Successive blocks while sweeping a mountain valley

vide fire support to the battalion. At 0630 hours on 25 March, following an artillery preparation, the battalion will begin to sweep north to destroy the enemy and capture his ammunition caches."

The force moved out on time and occupied their attack positions. The artillery fired a 25-minute preparation. The artillery fire plan included scatterable mines (RDM) which were fired to block any *mujahideen* withdrawal to the north. Following the artillery preparation, the battalion began its sweep.

An artillery forward observer accompanied each company of the 1st MRB as well as the 3rd Air Assault Company. An aviation combat control group (GBU) also accompanied the 1st MRB. The 1st MRB and the 3rd Air Assault Company seized the dominant terrain. They controlled the canyon walls and blocked the paths from the canyon with part of their force while leapfrogging the other part of their force north to establish the next position. In this manner, they were constantly able to support the air assault battalion in its sweep of the canyon.

By 1430 hours, the sweep had been completed. In the course of combat, we killed up to 20 *mujahideen*, captured and evacuated several weapons caches and captured and destroyed several ammunition caches.

FRUNZE COMMENTARY: We found that when conducting a block and sweep of a canyon, it was best to accomplish the approach march and get into attack positions at night. Further, close cooperation between the blocking and sweeping forces was absolutely crucial in order to maintain the tempo of the sweep and accomplish the task on time. These were done well.

However, there were shortcomings in this action. The artillery and aviation support could have been used more effectively. There were many causes for this. Too much time was wasted during a call-for-fire. The *mujahideen* had enough time to move the bulk of their force into the safety of caves while maintaining observers in the fighting positions. The enemy was able to deceive our aviation by displaying our panel markings for friendly forces on their positions. RDM mines were not delivered accurately enough and the gaps between RDM minefields allowed a significant portion of the *mujahideen* to escape to the north. Further, the enemy discovered our movement into the area in sufficient time to mine the entrance to the valley and the passes.

Finally, our study of this example shows that the block and sweep of the enemy requires an ever-larger, heterogeneous force, including the most most modern and effective combat means. This action involved only Soviet forces and excluded Afghan government forces.

EDITOR'S COMMENTARY: Airpower is great and helicopter gunships can save the day when things have gone bad. However, using standard or SOP displays of panels or pyrotechnics to mark friendly positions or communicate with pilots is risky. The enemy is quick to learn these codes and to use them against the force which needs air support. What is really needed is the capability of ground forces to talk directly to air forces.

Blocking and sweeping an inhabited region
by LTC V. V. Shubin[27]

Divisions [formations] and regiments [units] of the Democratic Republic of Afghanistan conducted operations in the province of Kandahar from March to the first days of September 1986. They inflicted such appreciable casualties on the guerrilla forces that the majority of them left for the safe haven of Pakistan.

By the beginning of September, active combat had ceased. The Afghan command decided to allow its forces the time to conduct training and to rest in their base camps. Consequently, on 6 September, the regiments of the 9th Infantry Division began moving out in march column to their camps in Ghazni Province .

The march took the division through Zabol Province, where five or six guerrilla forces with a total of approximately 500 men were located. The local guerrilla leader Pahlawan commanded these *mujahideen*. They were located near the border with Pakistan and were well-armed with recoilless rifles, mortars, rocket launchers and antiaircraft guided missile systems. They knew the local terrain very well and could quickly and secretly maneuver their forces and equipment throughout the area.

The terrain in this area is mountainous and semi-desert in places. The guerrillas used the extensive Karez underground irrigation system for ambushes. The enemy knew about the movement of the 9th Infantry Division. Since the road network in this area was poorly developed, the enemy knew at what time which forces would pass through the narrow sections on the Kandahar-Ghazni route.

At 0500 hours on 7 September, two explosions ripped apart the roadbed close to the village of Shingali-Kalay. Simultaneously, a *mujahideen* ambush opened fire with every weapon at its disposal. Within the first few minutes, they destroyed four tanks, three BTRs[28] and seven trucks.

---

[27]V. V. Shubin served in the OKSVA from 1986 to 1988. He was decorated with the "Medal for Merit in Combat", the "Medal for Personal Bravery", and the "Order of Glory".

[28]The BTR or *bronetransporter* is an eight-wheeled armored personnel carrier that can carry up to an 11-man squad. It mounts 14.5mm and 7.62mm machine guns and can carry antitank weapons as well. The BTR and BMP were the most-common infantry carriers of the Soviet Forces (ed.).

A part of the division column, including the division commander, was able to force its way through the blocked passage and escape
to the province center of Kalat. It arrived at 0520 hours. The division commander requested assistance from the commander of the
provincial "Sarandoy"[29]. The province authority agreed to dispatch
the 35th Operational Battalion reinforced with a company of the
KHAD[30] to aid the trapped subunits.

The province's plan was to draw the guerrilla main force into the
battle, hit them with aviation and artillery fire, and then simultane-

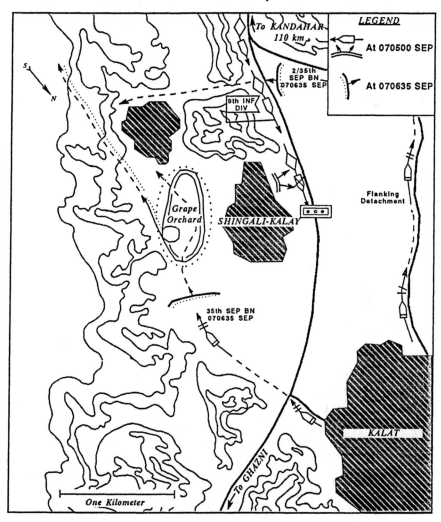

**Map 12: Blocking and destroying enemy ambushes
in an inhabited area**

ously attack them from the flank and rear to destroy them. The battalion commander formed his force into two columns. The first column consisted of the 1st and 3rd Companies of the 35th Battalion plus the KHAD company. The second column was the 2nd Company of the 35th Battalion. The columns moved out at 0600 hours.

Artillery strikes and helicopter gunships fired preparatory fires from 0610 to 0625 hours. At 0630 hours, the flanking detachment (2nd Company) radioed that it was in its designated position. A battalion subunit then gave the signal and the battalion hit the enemy in the flank and rear. The enemy abandoned their casualties, weapons and ammunition and withdrew. Enemy losses were 27 KIA and 36 WIA. The Afghan government forces captured two recoilless rifles, six mortars, two DShK 12.7 mm heavy machine guns, three RPG antitank grenade launchers, two crates of grenades and six AKM assault rifles. Losses of the 35th Operational Battalion were two killed and six wounded.

FRUNZE COMMENTARY: The successful blocking and destruction of enemy ambushes was made possible by a variety of factors;

- the rapid assembly of personnel and the readiness of weapons and equipment for combat;
- the resourcefulness and military cunning of the battalion commander;
- the thorough knowledge of the local terrain; and
- the correct determination of the probable enemy course of action.

---

[29]The Sarandoy were Ministry of Interior armed forces—a heavily armed police force. They were organized into six brigades or regiments (numbering about 6,000 men) and were based in Kandahar, Badakhstan, Baghlan, and Paravan provinces plus two in Kabul. The Sarandoy had an additional estimated 6,000 men in operational and mountain battalions (ed.).

[30]The KHAD were the secret police of the Afghan government and were responsible for detecting and eradicating domestic political opposition, subverting the mujahideen, penetrating opposition groups abroad and providing military intelligence to the armed forces through its military wing. The KHAD was patterned after the KGB and GRU and apparently reported to the KGB (ed.).

At the same time, the flanking detachment did not completely fulfill its mission to cut off the enemy withdrawal. There were several contributing factors. Reconnaissance devoted scant attention to determining the location of enemy combat outposts and early warning posts. There were isolated instances of command and control failures during the battle since the CP was located away from the battle. Finally, there was insufficient fire suppression on the withdrawing enemy.

Further combat analysis shows that the enemy studied the terrain and the convoy structure carefully and selected his ambush sites with the goal of limiting, to the maximum extent possible, the combat potential of the division march columns and especially its fire support. Combat experience clearly shows that all march columns must have air cover regardless of their ground power.

EDITOR'S COMMENTARY: Ambush sites are best assaulted from the flank or rear. Conversely, when your force is caught in a killing zone, the best immediate action is to assault into the teeth of the ambush rather than passively remaining and dying in the killing zone. Part of the Afghan division apparently tried defending in the kill zone. The total division casualties are not given, but they were probably significant.

Blocking the enemy in an area of villages and then destroying them during the sweep
by Major S. S. Gazaryan[31]

In February 1985, an intelligence agent brought us information that a guerrilla force of 100-120 men, armed with small arms, was located in the village of Karamagul'.

Our regimental commander decided to destroy this force by sealing off the area and then sweeping it to find and destroy the enemy. My battalion, the 2nd MRB, was given this mission and reinforced with the regiment's reconnaissance company and two artillery batteries. Six helicopter gunships from army aviation would be in support.

All the forces would be used for the initial blocking action. On the night of 11-12 February, two motorized rifle companies, moving out on foot, by morning had to to occupy the dominant terrain (hills 1864.4 and 1973.0) along the southern and eastern combat sectors. At 0600 hours on 12 February, our 4th MRC and the reconnaissance company had to land and secure the dominant terrain to the north and west of Karamagul' village by tactical air assaults. The 5th MRC was to establish a platoon-sized ambush to cover any attempted *mujahideen* withdrawal from Karamagul' to Batash.

Our plan was to begin the sweep at dawn only after we had seized and occupied the dominant terrain and had surrounded the enemy.

Following a 10-minute artillery and helicopter gunship preparation, the reconnaissance company moved forward and began sweeping the area. The enemy tried to break out of the encirclement through the various gullies and ravines. A group of *mujahideen* attempted to break out to the southwest. Then another group tried to break out of the encirclement. But all the enemy attempts were futile. Only a small part of his force was able to break out through a ravine in the direction of the village of Batash.

In the course of the combat, the enemy lost up to 60 killed or wounded and we captured 12. We also captured 25 weapons. The battalion's losses were negligible.

---

[31]S.S. Gazaryan served in the OKSVA from August 1984 to September 1986 as the Chief of Staff of a motorized rifle battalion.

EDITOR'S COMMENTARY: Soviet block and sweep tactics in Afghanistan differed from their own tactical encirclement methodology that they developed for war on the northern European plain. Their normal methodology called for an inner encirclement force to hold the trapped force in place while an outer encirclement force pushed out from the encircled area to put distance between the trapped forces and an enemy rescuing force. Only after the two forces were in place, would the Soviets fragment and meticulously

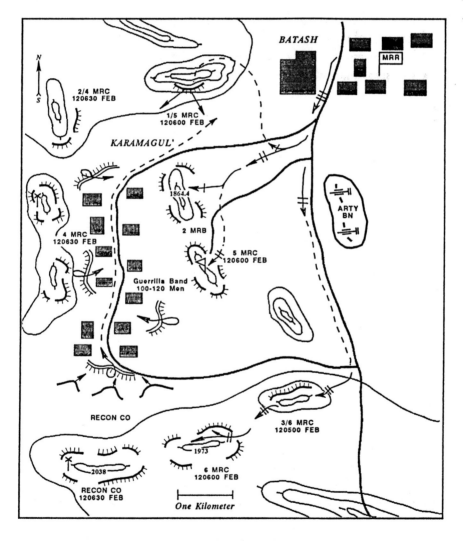

Map 13: Blocking the enemy in an inhabited region and destroying him during the sweep

destroy the trapped force. Evidently, Soviets in Afghanistan lacked the forces necessary for establishing an outer encirclement and the *mujahideen* seldom launched attacks from outside the encirclement to rescue their trapped comrades. Further, the Soviet normal methodology was designed to work against encircled mechanized forces. They really did not care about small groups of dismounted soldiers escaping from the encirclement. In Afghanistan, the enemy was normally dismounted and could usually slip through the Soviet encirclement.

The Soviets apparently showed little concern for the civilian population and started each sweep with an artillery bombardment. This did not win many hearts and minds for the Soviet forces. Often the Soviet effort seemed deliberately aimed at killing civilians or forcing them out of the rural areas.

CHAPTER 2:
THE OFFENSIVE IN POPULATED AREAS
AND MOUNTAINS

The peculiarities of this theater of military operations (TVD) called for special training for advancing in populated areas and mountains. Success was often determined by the skill of the commander and staff in the creative fulfillment of the requirements of the regulations when dealing with these particular terrain conditions; with the troop control of TO&E, attached and supporting subunits and their coordinated interaction; and with the correct determination of the enemy's strong and weak points.

Special attention was devoted to determining the place of fire support in the combat formation and its application in battle. Characteristically, the troop formation used in an advance was a function of the degree of preparation which the *mujahideen* had put into their defensive positions and whether the commander was employing assault detachments and assault groups.[32] As a rule, the offenses were launched from base camps or jumping-off areas and because of their distance from the combat zone, organizing movement became very important.

[32]An assault group is a platoon or company-size detachment temporarily created for blocking and destroying a single strong point or permanent structure(s) during an assault. An assault group typically consists of motorized rifle forces, engineers, and flamethrower operators. An assault detachment is normally battalion-sized and also has armor or direct-fire artillery attached (ed.).

Assault on the outskirts of Herat
by Major V. M. Bogdashkin[33]

The situation in Herat Province was very serious in the fall of 1984. Guerrilla forces, led by Captain Ismail, received trained reinforcements as well as new weapons from Iran. They launched raids on Soviet and Afghan convoys and struck at the Kushka-Shindand pipeline. They constituted a threat to the Herat airfield and grain elevators.

The operational group of the regiment with field post number[34] (FPN) 51883 was ordered to: block part of the southern edge of Herat city with the 2nd MRB (minus a company) and fragment the *mujahideen* force. Further, in coordination with the 2nd MRB of FPN 83260 regiment and the 3rd MRB of FPN 51931 regiment, destroy the enemy.

Preparation for this action was conducted in base camp. All company commanders and above, plus all the attached company commanders conducted coordination on a terrain model. Enemy courses of action and the sequencing of his destruction were also worked out on the terrain model. Personnel who would physically close with the *mujahideen* conducted training in a deserted village where they became familiar with the specific make-up of an assault group and gained practical experience.

At the end of October, my company (the 7th MRC) was designated part of the operational group of regiment FPN 51883 which assembled outside Herat. At 0400 hours on 4 November, our subunits were ordered into the city. By 0540 hours, the force blocked off the eastern section of the city. The east side was held by FPN 83260, the north and west sides were held by FPN 51931 and the south side by my regiment FPN 51883.

---

[33]V. M. Bogdashkin served in the Republic of Afghanistan from June 1983 through June 1985 as a platoon leader and a company commander in a motorized rifle battalion. He was awarded the "Order of the Red Star".

[34]Field post numbers (FPN) were postal numbers assigned to division and higher headquarters, regiments and separate battalions and companies. A compilation of field post numbers was considered classified. The field post numbers referred to here are probably of the 12th, 101st and 371st Motorized Rifle Regiments of the 5th Motorized Rifle Division (ed.).

At 0600 hours, FPN 51883 regiment committed its mountain motorized rifle battalion[35] to battle and it managed to cut off and surround a group of *mujahideen.* However, other *mujahideen* pounded this battalion with small arms, rocket launchers, cannon and mortars. The battalion had stumbled into a *mujahideen* fire sack. In the course of 40 minutes, the battalion lost nine killed or wounded and was forced to stop and go over to the defense.

Regiment ordered my 7th MRC to turn over our portion of the southern block to a *bronegruppa* and to move to the command post of FPN 51883 regiment. My regimental commander was LTC A. M. Budeyev. He ordered my company commander, Senior Lieutenant S. N. Bogrov, to advance along a city street to fragment the defending *mujahideen* force. My MRC had two BMP-2s[36] and a tank as part of our assault group.

Following a five-minute artillery strike, the 7th MRC went into battle at 0730 hours. It advanced 150-200 meters when it was stopped by heavy small arms fire as well as the fire from two recoilless rifles, a grenade launcher and a mortar. The small arms fire came from close range from a grape arbor and through embrasures cut in the adobe walls. One of our soldiers was wounded. The company commander was ordered to break contact and withdraw. After his professional, organized withdrawal (there were no more casualties), the company deployed along the edges of a village.

Afghan intelligence reported that there were some 800 men in the guerrilla forces which operated in this immediate territory (25 square kilometers) but we had no idea how many we were facing now. We called in ground attack aircraft[37] and artillery fire on the

---

[35] The mountain motorized rifle battalions retained most of their regular MRB TO&E equipment, but had special training, and additional equipment for mountain warfare (ed.).

[36] The BMP-2 is an upgrade of the BMP-1 (Boevaya mashina pekhoty) which first appeared in 1967. Both BMPs are tracked infantry fighting vehicles that carry a three-man crew and a squad of eight soldiers. The BMP-1 mounted a 73mm cannon, a 7.62mm machine gun and an antitank missile. The BMP-2 substituted a 30mm automatic gun for the 73mm cannon as well as a different antitank missile and launcher. The BMP-2, introduced in 1981, has a greatly enhanced elevation and depression capability over the 73mm cannon (ed.).

[37] SU-25 FROGFOOT (ed.).

encircled *mujahideen.* Three artillery battalions from division artillery fired in our support.

The company commander asked for two 152mm SP howitzers and another tank. He received these plus a sapper squad with 75 kilograms of explosive. The 1st and 2nd platoon leaders (Captain P. P. Rozhkov and Lieutenant V. I. Nikitenko were ordered to advance from the company flanks through the grape arbor and blow up the adobe walls.

LTC A. M. Budeyev, the regimental commander, requested two BM-21 "Grad" 122mm multiple rocket launchers to conduct direct

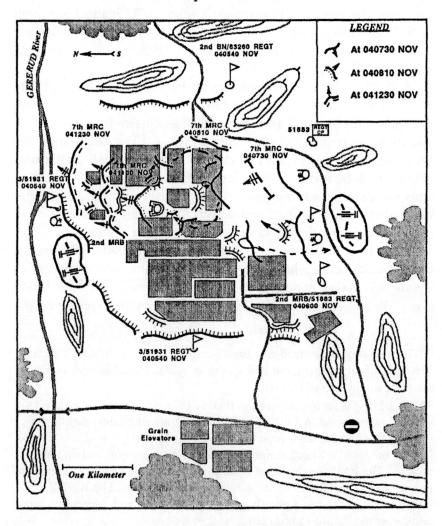

Map 14: Combat by a reinforced MRC serving as an assault group.

fire as needed by the company commander. Following an airstrike, the BM-21s opened fire. Supporting artillery simultaneously began a 10-minute artillery preparation. The company moved forward to the attack under this protective fire.

The BM-21 direct-fire salvos did not inflict heavy casualties on the enemy, but did have a tremendous effect on their morale. The company advanced 300 meters before the first *mujahideen* fired on it. *Mujahideen* fire was very weak. On signals from the company and platoon commanders, the two SP 152mm howitzers, two tanks and four BMPs opened direct suppressive fire on the enemy. The flanking platoons were able to move at the same tempo as the center and signaled their progress with signal rockets. The assault group hit a mine field at a street intersection. They defused seven mines as well as a 250-kilogram aerial bomb rigged as a mine. The assault detachment advanced 1.5 kilometers when it was stopped by strong fire from a village. The fire came from dugouts cut in earth dikes of irrigation canals. Tank and BMP-2 fire suppressed the enemy fire. The company had two more men wounded during this advance.

In all, the company accomplished its mission in an hour and a half at the cost of three wounded. They killed seven *mujahideen* in close combat. By 1130 hours, the opposing guerrilla force was shattered. However, at 1400 our attempts to destroy another guerrilla force failed. We made a second unsuccessful attempt at dusk. With nightfall, the *mujahideen* managed to slip out of the blockade.

FRUNZE COMMENTARY: In this example, a very large group of enemy was encircled, but the combat power was insufficient to destroy it. This was the result of poor intelligence which furnished insufficient information about the enemy and led to an insufficient force density in the blocking forces.

Nevertheless, good points included the rapid reconcentration of subunits from one direction to another, the powerful influence of firepower on the enemy, the proper reinforcement of the company and the skillful application of BM-21 fire to strengthen the morale of the flanking platoons which also strengthened the fighting spirit of the soldiers and officers.

EDITOR'S COMMENTARY: The Soviets used MRLS (called katyusha or "little Kathyrn") in the direct fire role during World War II. The war in Afghanistan showed that it is still an effective way to shake up your opponent. Rapid-fire antiaircraft guns are also very effective ground support weapons as are SP howitzers when used in direct fire. However, firepower is not an absolute substitute for maneuver and close combat. During the war in Afghanistan, like the United States in Vietnam, the Soviets chose to expend massive firepower in order to save Soviet lives and to compensate for their lack of infantry. It was an expensive, indiscriminate and, probably, ineffective practice.

Unlike World War II, the Soviet Army in Afghanistan does not push on despite heavy casualties. They transition to the defense after moderate casualties and call for fire support.

The Soviets assigned commands not so much by rank as by ability (or connections). Vignettes throughout this book show captains, majors and lieutenant colonels commanding battalions, senior lieutenants and captains commanding companies and captains and lieutenants commanding platoons. In this vignette, a senior lieutenant commands a company which has a captain as one of its platoon leaders. This captain could be a platoon leader as a punishment for some misdeed, or he could have been doing his normal job since wartime regulations allowed the army to carry a man in a position one grade higher than that authorized. Further, he might have just been promoted. In the peacetime Soviet Army, it was not unusual for higher-ranking officers to work for a lower-ranking officer. The position, to the Soviets, was more important than the rank. The Soviet military pay scale reflects this when it adds command or responsibility pay to an officer's pay based on rank.

The actions of a motorized rifle battalion as a raiding detachment
by Major S. A. Nikitin[38]

Besides the main mission of organizing the security of base camps and of the usual zones, the subunits of a separate security battalion were also called on to support combat in response to intelligence gathered by units and subunits.

In July 1985, our reconnaissance units in Kunduz Province determined the area from which the enemy planned to fire 122mm rockets on our division headquarters and on the base camps of its regiments.[39] Colonel Volobuev, the division chief of staff, decided to move a motorized rifle battalion reinforced with a tank company quickly into the *mujahideen* base camp, forestall his launches, hit him with artillery and seize his launchers and stores of launch bombs.[40]

One of the platoons from my company of the separate security battalion would provide security for the raiding detachment's headquarters and would move on its TO&E equipment. I was a captain at the time and took command of the platoon for the mission. Our raiding detachment moved quickly to the place where the launch bombs were stored thanks to the skilled actions of our attached sapper platoon. Within the space of a half hour and practically without incident, we found and destroyed the launch-bomb cache and several prepared launching sites. Surprise and the decisiveness of our actions guaranteed the completion of our mission.

At that time, the reconnaissance platoon of the raiding group reported that a caravan of 40 cargo-carrying camels, guarded by several horsemen, were moving from Upper Chaharasia to Lower Chaharasia. Colonel Volobuev decided to occupy the high ground dominating the road and shoot the enemy from these covered

---

[38]S. A. Nikitin served in the OKSVA as a company commander in a separate security battalion in 1985.

[39]Probably the 201st MRD (ed.).

[40]The launch bomb was a 122mm rocket designed to fire from the BM-21 MRLS. Although the resistance had access to some RPU-14 launchers, most launch bombs were simply rockets fired from a tripod or even a pair of crossed sticks. It is not an accurate weapon, but can do an effective job when fired against a city, military base or other area target (ed.).

heights. When the *mujahideen* came within range of our weapons, we opened fire at the head and tail of the caravan. An artillery subunit fired standing barrage fire in front of the enemy column. Our snatch group then moved down to the road and captured the caravan guards.

When we pulled out of the area, I commanded the rear guard which covered the withdrawal of the main body. As my *bronegruppa* was pulling out, the *mujahideen* opened fire on us from neighboring heights with a DShK heavy machine gun and small arms. Their fire

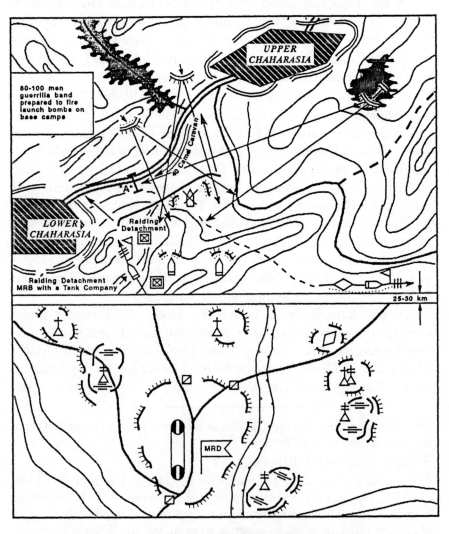

Map 15: The actions of a motorized rifle battalion as a raiding detachment

punctured the fuel tank of a combat reconnaissance patrol machine (BRDM)[41] setting if afire. We were unable to evacuate it prior to nightfall. My BRDM gave covering fire to a repair-evacuation detachment that was finally able to drag the burned-out BRDM away to a safe place.

FRUNZE COMMENTARY: Weak vigilance creates casualties.

EDITOR'S COMMENTARY: The Soviet separate security battalion was seldom discussed in print. From this vignette, the battalion's mission was to provide security for the division CP and trains. The map shows that at least a company from the battalion was involved in CP security and manning the three entrance and exit posts. It was also used as an immediate reaction force and as a reserve. It was mounted on BRDMs, which are armored cars. This implies that it was a low-strength battalion when compared to a regular motorized rifle battalion. The division had two helipads, which is noteworthy since the division did not have many organic helicopters. These helipads were most likely for material support, since the division needed significant aerial resupply at this location.

In the vignette, the captain takes command of the platoon that is sent with the raiding detachment. It was a common practice for senior commanders to take command of a subordinate's unit when the task might get challenging or fun.

---

[41]The BRDM is a four-wheeled armored car which is used primarily for reconnaissance. It has two auxillary wheels for extra mobility. In its various configurations, it carries either a 12.7mm machine gun, a 7.62mm machine gun or both. This amphibious vehicle protects the crew against small arms fire and shrapnel, so the fuel tank was probably penetrated by heavy machine gun fire (ed.).

Assaulting Xadighar Canyon and seizing weapons and ammunition caches
by LTC S. Yu. Pyatakov[42]

At the beginning of March 1986, the commander of a SPET-SNAZ detachment received information from a group of intelligence agents and staff of the Ministry of State Security of Afghanistan concerning the presence of weapons and ammunition caches in the Xadigar Canyon, Kandahar Province. In order to confirm this information, the detachment commander dispatched two SPETSNAZ reconnaissance groups to the area. He reported the resulting available information to the higher staff and requested aerial reconnaissance of the site.[43] Their data confirmed the earlier reports. The senior leadership decided to conduct an assault on the canyon.

Two motorized rifle battalions from a separate motorized brigade,[44] a SPETSNAZ detachment, a D-30 artillery battalion, a platoon of ZSU-23-4 SP AA guns, a squadron of Mi-8 helicopters, a squadron of Mi-24 helicopters and a squadron of Su-25 "FROG-FOOT" ground attack aircraft were selected to conduct the assault. The Chief of Staff of the Turkestan Military District, General-Lieutenant Yu. G. Gusev, had overall responsibility for conduct of the action.

According to the plan, two motorized rifle battalions reinforced with an artillery battalion would depart their base camp in Kandahar and conduct an 85-kilometer night road march to the canyon. The assault would begin at 0900 hours, 20 March 1986 when aviation would conduct strafing and bombing runs in the canyon. The SPET-SNAZ detachment would air assault four companies on helicopters onto mountains close to the canyon. Their mission would be to block the *mujahideen* withdrawal and call in and adjust air and artillery fire.

The "operation" began exactly as planned. At 0600 hours, 20

---

[42]S. Yu. Pyatakov served in the Republic of Afghanistan from March 1984 through June 1985 as the deputy commander of a motorized rifle battalion. He was decorated with the "Order of the Red Star."

[43]The SPETSNAZ battalion garrisoned at Kandahar airfield (ed.).

[44]Battalions of the 70th Separate Motorized Rifle Brigade garrisoned in Kandahar (ed.).

March aviation groups of 4-to-6 aircraft began strafing and bombing runs along the canyon floor and on the nearby villages which sheltered the *mujahideen*. At 0800 hours, four SPETSNAZ reconnaissance groups[45] landed on the mountain tops and occupied advantageous positions where they could observe and intercept withdrawing groups of *mujahideen*.

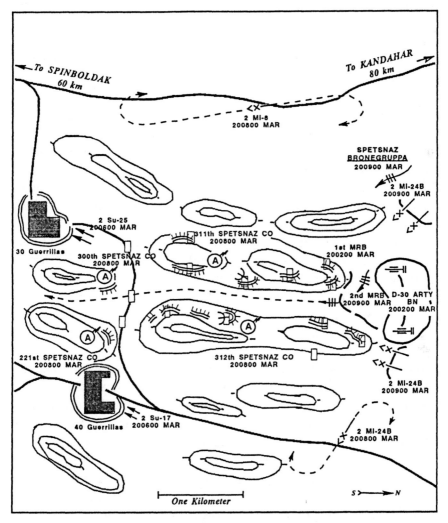

Map 16: Assaulting Xadighar Canyon.

[45]Each SPETSNAZ group consisted of 16 men armed with the AGS-17 automatic grenade launcher, two PK machine guns, an SVD sniper rifle and various other small arms.

The assault group, consisting of the two motorized rifle battalions reinforced with an artillery battalion, successfully completed an off-road night march (they traveled off the roads to avoid land mines). At 0830 hours on 20 March, they assembled prior to entering the canyon.

The artillery preparation lasted only 20 minutes. However three hours of airstrikes had preceded the artillery fire and the enemy weapons systems were either destroyed or well-suppressed. The dismounted assault was supported by BMP and ZSU- 23-4 direct fire. The combat formation had two echelons with an MRB in each echelon. A SPETSNAZ company mounted on BMPs was the reserve.

Because of the advantages in strength and speed of motorized rifle subunits, they quickly cleared the canyon without meeting any significant resistance. At the beginning of the assault, groups of five or six *mujahideen* tried to move out of the canyon over various paths, but they were interdicted by SPETSNAZ groups which cut them down in ambushes or called in helicopter gunships and ground-attack aircraft on them. Aerial reconnaissance continued to track down and destroy newly discovered targets.

The assault on the Xadighar Canyon was finished by 1200 hours 20 March. We killed 20 *mujahideen* and destroyed four DShK heavy machine guns, one mortar and two assault rifles. We captured two DShK heavy machine guns, one mortar, 20 various small arms, a large amount of ammunition, documents and combat equipment of the guerrilla groups. There were no Soviet casualties.

FRUNZE COMMENTARY: In general, this "operation" was carried out successfully. However, it did not achieve surprise. That is to say that the increased force activity and abrupt appearance of all types of reconnaissance enabled the enemy to guess in advance the start time and the direction of the advance. On the other hand, combat experience in Afghanistan shows that limiting the amount of reconnaissance assets employed lessened the effectiveness of the advance, weakened the fire support, allowed the enemy the opportunity to slip away into the mountains at the start of the offensive and led to the establishment of only a few covering forces.

The success of the assault on the Xadighar Canyon was, to a large extent, due to the direction and guidance of the senior leadership who included all necessary branches of services in this "operation". It is important when conducting similar operations to create the maximum amount of surprise. To achieve this, it is important to conduct "diversionary/decoy" actions, to take the necessary measures to disguise actions and to deceive the enemy. In a word, one must be creative when carrying out one's mission.

EDITOR'S COMMENTARY: In this vignette, a multi-battalion block and sweep is commanded by the chief of staff of the Turkestan Military District. General-Lieutenant Gusev was nowhere linked with the 40th Army's chain of command, but could field a command group which could control all the aviation required in a section of Afghanistan far removed from the 40th Army CP. It is unorthodox, but apparently worked. This demonstrates, however, that the senior leadership did not always trust their subordinates to "do it right". More cynically, this practice allowed outside senior commanders to collect combat medals while in the safety of an armored vehicle and saved them the bother of a full, uncomfortable Afghanistan tour of duty while covering their chests with symbols of glory.

This vignette also provides a good look at the employment of SPETSNAZ personnel. Unlike the U.S. Special Forces and the British SAS, SPETSNAZ were mounted on personnel carriers in Afghanistan, but when they were airdropped, the carriers functioned as a *bronegruppa*. This provided more flexibility in the employment of these rugged soldiers and gave them much more maneuverability.

Three hours of airstrikes is not a good way to achieve surprise. Again, the Soviet force seems to have engaged the rear guard and the "uninformed".

The distances and direction on this map are wrong. Spinboldak is approximately 70 kilometers southeast of Kandahar.

An airborne battalion seizes
the Satukandav Pass
by LTC A. N. Shishkov[46]

In the fall of 1987, implacable insurgents conducted combat against Afghan government and Soviet forces and practically blocked off Khost district. They cut off the lines of communication and limited the supply of weapons, munitions, and food to our forces. The high command decided to conduct Operation "Magistral'" with several divisions and regiments of the army. The main purpose was to crush the guerrilla forces on the Kabul-Gardez-Khost main route [magistral']. Further, the operation would clear mines from the route and support the resupply of material and the establishment of materiel reserves for the government forces in Khost district.

Prior to the start of the operation, the Afghan government made an attempt to resolve the problem of delivering sufficient food and other resources to the district through peaceful methods without an armed conflict. However, the field commander of the Paktia Province resistance, Mawlawi Jalaluddin Hagani, used the time to augment his guerrilla forces and, in the end, rejected this offer. They decided not to allow Soviet and government forces to enter the province. A key enemy blocking element was those guerrilla forces concentrated in the Satukandav Pass, which is, practically speaking, the only way through the mountains between Gardez and Khost. At the start of the operation, approximately 15,000 *mujahideen* operated in the area. The Satukandav Pass, which is located 30 kilometers east of Gardez, was touted in the western press as "the unassailable bastion on which the Russians will break their teeth".

The operation involved a motorized rifle division, an airborne division,[47] a separate motorized rifle regiment,[48] a separate airborne

---

[46]A. N. Shishkov served in the Republic of Afghanistan from February 1986 through June 1988 as the Senior Assistant to the Chief of the Operations Section of an airborne division. He was awarded the "Order of the Red Banner", the "Order of the Red Star", and the order "For Service to the Fatherland in the Armed Forces", Third degree.

[47]Actually, both the 201st and 108th Motorized Rifle Divisions participated in the operation, but since neither could move their entire division and temporarily abandon their base camps and the LOCs that they guarded, they

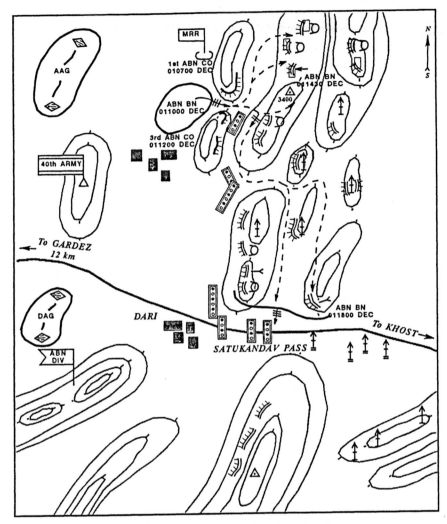

Map 17: The capture of Satukandav Pass.

formed a composite division under the 201st headquarters. The airborne division was the 103rd Airborne Division. General Gromov, in an article in *Krasnaya zvezda (Red Star)* on 30 December 1993, listed the following Soviet units participating in Magistral: the 108th and the 201st MRD, 103rd Airborne Division, 56th Separate Air Assault Brigade, the 345th Separate Airborne Regiment and other units and subunits. He also lists the following Afghan government units: 8th, 11th, 12th, 14th, and 25th Infantry divisions, 15th Tank Brigade and several special forces subunits (ed.).

[48]Either the 860th or 191st Separate Motorized Rifle Regiment, most probably the 191st. General Gromov doesn't list this unit by number, probably because of its abysmal performance (ed.).

regiment,[49] regiments and subunits of various branches and special forces of the 40th Army plus regiments of the Armed Forces of Afghanistan.   General-Lieutenant B. V. Gromov, the 40th Army commander, lead the operation.

In addition to conducting the garrison training[50] required by the regular 12-day training time, the regiments and subunits continued additional combat preparations after they moved from their base camps and concentrated in the region of Gardez city on 21 November 1987. We considered several plans to seize the Satukan-dav Pass and then to develop this success to extend our combat power deep into Paktia Province along the main highway.

Daily we increased our supplies and stockpiled ammunition and other necessary material in the area where we billeted our divisions and regiments. The division and regimental command posts and the Army Artillery Groups (AAG) and Division Artillery Groups (DAG) were positioned and dug in from 21 to 27 November. Every regimental and subunit commander began a thorough commander's reconnaissance of the area. On 28 November, following unsuccessful negotiations, the 40th Army divisions and regiments plus the Afghan regiments began the attack. General Gromov had decided to determine the location of enemy weapons systems (particularly air defense) and so he faked an airborne landing using 20 dummy paratroopers in parachutes. The enemy fired its weapons on these "paratroopers" which enabled artillery reconnaissance to pinpoint enemy strong points and firing positions. Army and frontal aviation then hit these positions. The airstrikes were followed with a four-hour artillery barrage.

---

[49]The 345th Separate Airborne Regiment part of the 105th Guards Airborne Division invaded Afghanistan and, through attrition, eventually shrunk to the 345th Separate Airborne Regiment (ed.).

[50]In the Soviet Army, maintenance, guard, work details and special projects always detracted from the time available for training. The army used to train only those people who were not on detail, but eventually realized that this was producing a very uneven quality in the readiness of the force. Therefore, they developed a program whereby regiments and battalions would pull guard and details for the division on a rotating basis and then have 12 days for training when they would not be involved in post, camp and station details. This cycle continued even in the combat zone (ed.).

On 29 November, following a short artillery preparation, the dismounted separate motorized rifle regiment (minus a battalion) started up the foothills to seize the dominant terrain along the crest. Following the capture of the crest, they were to establish a strong guard force on the east side and prevent the enemy reserve from moving into the Satukandav Pass from the northeast (from the direction of the Parachinar Salient).

Heavy enemy fire greeted the subunits. Indecisiveness and excessive fear on the part of the regimental commander bogged the regiment down in the initial stage of the operation. On the night of 29-30 November, the *mujahideen* took advantage of the commander's mistakes and errors and launched attacks on his motorized rifle battalions along several axes.

The enemy knew the territory well and was well supplied with an ample supply of first-class weapons and munitions. He used these to inflict severe casualties on the regiment.

The regiment did not succeed for several reasons. First, the regimental CP was located a fair distance from the subunits where it could not provide direct combat leadership in the mountains. Second, there was no regimental forward observation post. Third, the commander incorrectly calculated the required amount of ammunition (and by the second day of combat, personnel were down to the emergency ammunition reserve). Fourth, the combat was led in a passive and indecisive manner and the regimental leadership had a poor grasp of the situation.

General Gromov decided to continue the advance on the enemy positions with subunits of the airborne division together with subunits of the Afghan force. Therefore, on 1 December, the 1st Airborne Battalion of an airborne regiment and a battalion of the Afghan "Commandos" assembled near the CP of the separate motorized rifle regiment.

The airborne battalion commander, Major V. N. Petrov, and the Afghan "Commando" battalion commander thoroughly studied the situation and coordinated their actions. Then they began their assault on the main peak. Two airborne companies captured the nearest dominant terrain and used this lodgement to support the assault on the main peak by two assault groups. Enemy mortar and DShK heavy machine gun fire held up the advance until the airborne battalion commander called in the fires of the DAG on enemy fighting positions and firing points.

The simultaneous, headlong arrival of two airborne assault groups on the main peak took the *mujahideen* by surprise and they began to withdraw from their positions. The battalion commander called in artillery fire further into the enemy depths–primarily on the reverse slope of the peak and onto the path along which enemy reserves would be committed.

Major Petrov reported his situation and decision to the senior commander. He decided to continue the advance on the enemy in the area of the Satukandav Pass and strike the enemy on the flank and rear in order to control the pass.

Following an artillery preparation, the 1st Airborne Battalion and the "Commando" Battalion began the assault toward Satukandav Pass. The enemy had not expected the decisive attack and arrival of Soviet and Afghan forces at the main peak. The *mujahideen* lost the initiative. Part of the enemy force withdrew. The battalion advanced to the south under supporting artillery fire and did not allow the enemy to regain his composure.

The guerrilla forces defending the Satukandav Pass did not know the exact size of the Soviet and Afghan forces approaching on their flanks and rear. They began a hasty withdrawal, abandoning their crew-served weapons and ammunition at their firing positions.

Taking advantage of the panicked enemy withdrawal in the pass, the 1st Airborne Battalion captured the pass on the move and, along with the Afghan forces, dug in along their newly secured line.

This decisive and brave advance seized the prime defensive node which proved to be the key to the enemy defensive system–the Satukandav Pass.

FRUNZE COMMENTARY: Analysis of combat in the initial stage of Operation "Magistral'" (November-December 1987) leads to the following conclusions:

1. Thorough knowledge of the situation, continual analysis, decisiveness, initiative and bravery are the basis for successful and informed mission fulfillment in combat.
2. Artful distribution of forces during an advance in mountains, careful coordination between combined arms subunits, and the constant support of artillery fires are the most important steps in such a successful operation.
3. Proper use of the protective characteristics of mountains along

with constant reconnaissance will allow one to accomplish his mission with a minimum of personnel casualties.

4. Success in mountain combat under constantly changing conditions demands continuous troop control.

EDITOR'S COMMENTARY: The dummy airborne drop was a masterful use of deception to discover enemy firing positions. Operation Magistral' was the largest operation of the war and eventually involved large air assaults, attacks on different axes and the successful lifting of the siege of Khost. In this vignette, Operation "Magistral'" massed the fires of an AAG and a DAG for a four-hour artillery preparation during the fight for the Satukandov Pass. The goal was complete destruction of the area by air and artillery and is far outside any Soviet artillery norms. This extensive artillery preparation still did not do the job. Nor did Magistral'. After the costly Operation Magistral', the *mujahideen* once again cut off Khost and again put it under siege (a constant feature since 1981).

Storming Spinakalacha village
by LTC V. D. Vlasyan[51]

From 21-26 December 1987, a strong enemy force overran a series of security outposts in the Daman region. This area was the responsibility of an Army Corps of the Army of the Republic of Afghanistan.[52] As a result, the enemy began freely moving arms and weapons into the Kandahar region. Two battalions of a Soviet Separate Motorized Rifle Brigade were unable to restore the situation.[53]

At 2000 hours on 27 December, our division commander, General-Major Uchkin, called me in and gave me my orders. At the time, I was a major and commanded a motorized rifle battalion. He ordered me to take my battalion on a 500-kilometer road march to Kandahar.[54] My battalion had to be in the Spinakalacha combat area by the morning of 31 December. I was to seal off the Spinakalacha village from the major supply bases and create conditions which would allow the Separate Motorized Rifle Brigade to recapture lost positions. In the course of preparing for our road march and ensuing combat, I added extra ammunition, water, fuel and rations to what we usually carried and picked up some reinforcing subunits. At 0400 hours 29 December, my battalion moved out to accomplish its mission.

At 1600 hours 30 December, we arrived in Kandahar. There, I was met by General-Major R. K. Pishchev, the Deputy commander of the 40th Army. He gave me specific orders. We were to enter the contested area at 1100 hours 31 December and assault and capture Spinakalacha village by 1500 hours. We were then to seal off the canyon and hold this area until 7 January 1988. During that time, an

---

[51]V. D. Vlasyan served in the Republic of Afghanistan from October 1986 through June 1988 first as a deputy commander and then as the commander of a motorized rifle battalion. He was decorated with the "Order of the Red Banner" and the "Order of the Red Star".

[52]Afghan 2nd Army Corps headquarted in Kandahar (ed.).

[53]70th Separate Motorized Rifle Brigade (ed.).

[54]The battalion could be from the 5th MRD if it came from western Afghanistan (Shindand area) or from the 108th MRD if it came from eastern Afghanistan (Kabul area) (ed.).

Afghan regiment[55] would fortify the area and assume responsibility for the area defended by my 2nd MRB.

At 1100 hours, I put my battalion on the road flanked by security patrols. As we entered the area, we began battle and I lost two KIA and three WIA. By 1210 hours, I assembled the bulk of my battalion 1.5 kilometers south of Spinakalacha. From 1220 until 1240, I

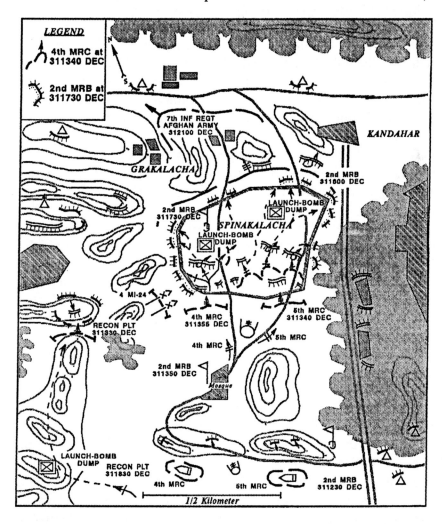

Map 18: Storming Spinakalacha village, 31 December 1987.

[55]The Afghan Army had both a brigade and a regiment force structure. This regiment was from either the Afghan 7th MRD or 15th MRD stationed in Kandahar (ed.).

conducted a personal reconnaissance, finalized my plans for the assault groups and finalized air and artillery coordination. I reported my plan to the senior commander at 1240.

Ten minutes later, my reconnaissance platoon began to climb mountain ridge from the west to destroy enemy security outposts on dominant terrain and on the canyon approaches and the approaches to Spinakalacha village. During their advance, the reconnaissance patrol uncovered a launch-bomb cache with 150 launch bombs and two launchers. The patrol rigged the cache for detonation and preceded up the hill where they could secure the left flank of the assault detachment. At 1320 hours, the patrol attacked and destroyed an enemy outpost and established solid communications with me.

At 1320 hours, I signalled the start of an artillery preparation. A 152mm SP howitzer battalion, a separate 122mm SP howitzer battalion and a MRLS battalion participated in a 10-minute artillery preparation. This was immediately followed by a bombing and strafing attack by two squadrons of SU-25 FROGFOOT ground-attack aircraft.

At 1335 hours, my 5th MRC moved out to it's jumping-off point some 250 meters from the village. The 5th MRC was commanded by Captain B. M. Mikul'skiy. The 5th MRC was configured as Assault Group #1. It had 46 men, including a squad of sappers, and eight BMP-2s. I added a tank with a mine plow and an Afghan infantry company of 40 men to this company. As the 5th MRC moved out, I covered its movement with the fires of a sniper squad, a flamethrower platoon, an AGS-17 platoon and a mortar battery. At 1340 hours, I had the MRLS battalion lay down a smoke screen to blind the enemy.

At 1340 hours, my subunits attacked Spinakalacha. We met strong resistance on the right flank and the Afghan army company withdrew to the jumping-off area. I was not able to get them to come back and they did nothing further toward accomplishing our mission. The enemy began to shift his forces to his left flank in order to put flanking fire on the 5th MRC. For awhile, we were held back by the thick adobe walls of the village. Then, however, my troops were able to blow gaps in the adobe walls and my platoons burst through these gaps in three-man groups on the attack. My 5th MRC faced the enemy main force.

At 1355 hours, my 4th MRC (Assault Group #2) attacked on the battalion's left flank. The 4th MRC, commanded by Captain Yu. A.

Shalkin, broke the enemy defense and destroyed his covering forces guarding the entrance to the canyon. One of his platoons was able to hit the enemy in the rear which helped the 5th MRC's fight. Two more 4th MRC platoons grabbed the western edge of the village and established blocking positions. At 1500 hours, these platoons got into a fire fight with *mujahideen* who were retreating into the mountains.

By 1600 hours, the 5th MRC completed the destruction of the enemy in the eastern part of the village and established blocking positions against the access points from the neighboring green zone. The surviving enemy had fled into the green zone. At 1800 hours, I organized the defense of Spinakalacha and provided fire support to an Afghan infantry regiment which attacked north to seize the southern slope of Grakalacha.[56]

FRUNZE COMMENTARY: Analysis of the organization and conduct of combat in this advance in a village shows:

First, the totally successful march and concealed concentration of the battalion near Kandahar was possible due to the thorough and complete preparations for the march and follow-on combat.

Second, prior combat experience allowed the subunit leaders to correctly use initiative during combat in the village.

Third, the battalion commander's actions merit attention, particularly when you consider how he coordinated actions and rapidly conducted his personal reconnaissance and arranged the necessary fire support to destroy the enemy and then decisively used their results to conduct the advance of his subunits.

Finally, the battalion commander's interesting maneuver of his reconnaissance platoon's supporting fire on the enemy from dominant terrain, his skillful use of snipers and portable flamethrowers, and the actions of his platoons' three and five-men sections during the assault on the village are all worthy of study.

---

[56]According to his map, the 7th Infantry Regiment (ed.).

A motorized rifle battalion offensive at night in the mountains of the Andarab Canyon
by Major V. G. Tarasyuk[57]

After the end of February 1988, my regiment returned through Kabul from the successful completion of Operation "Magistral'" (the opening of the road to Khost) to our base camp in Kunduz.[58] After we negotiated the Salang tunnel, the division commander ordered our regiment to halt in the Andarab Canyon. With his orders came the following important information: exactly 24 hours earlier, the *mujahideen* kidnapped the governor of Baghlan Province and his commander of the Ministry of Security Forces in Andarab Canyon.

Our regimental commander, LTC V. V. Telitsyn, received orders to move to the borders of a zone controlled by Afghan government forces, gain contact with the enemy, punish him with massed fires and create the conditions necessary to free the province leadership.

The regimental commander was able to muster two motorized rifle battalions, the reconnaissance company, and the SP artillery battalion (minus one battery) for this mission. In addition, two artillery batteries supported this force with illumination missions from positions along the Salang-Puli-Khumiri highway. Each motorized rifle battalion was down to two motorized rifle companies, the battalion reconnaissance platoon and the mortar battery (in reduced strength). In all, the regiment consisted of 40-45 BMPs, 25-30 howitzers, six *vasilek* (cornflower) automatic mortars, four 82mm mortars (*podnos-*"tray") and about 300 men.

The regimental commander decided to advance to the border of the Afghan controlled zone at night and drive to the foot of the mountain on BMPs with one MRB and the reconnaissance company. At the base of the mountains, the subunits would dismount and begin the ascent in three company-sized groups (two motorized rifle companies and the reconnaissance company). They would advance about a kilometer or a kilometer and a half to establish contact with

---

[57]V. G. Tarasyuk served in the OKSVA from April 1986 through April 1988 as the Chief of Staff of a motorized rifle battalion. He was awarded the "Order of the Red Star".

[58]Either the 122nd, 149th or 395th MRR from the 201st MRD (ed.).

the enemy and accomplish their mission.

Fire destruction during the approach, deployment and ascent would be provided by the regiment's artillery battalion, the mortar batteries of the battalions, the two supporting artillery batteries and the BMP-2 automatic guns of the trail battalion.

The reconnaissance company moved out an hour before the motorized rifle battalion in an attempt to deceive the enemy and conducted a reconnaissance sweep along the opposite canyon wall.

The 1st MRB was ordered to move out, under the cover of artillery fire and the 2nd MRB, which would be firing over the heads

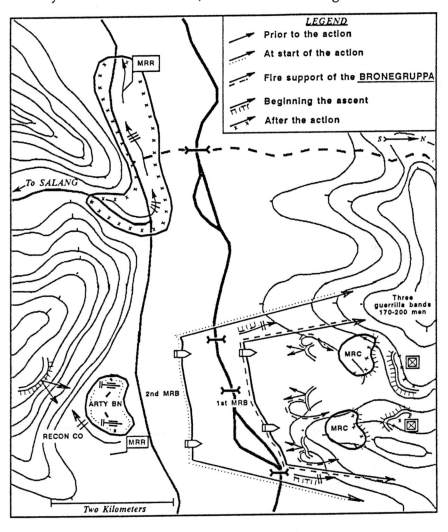

Map 19: Advance of a MRB in the mountains at night.

of the advancing column as it broke into company columns. Then, the 1st MRB was to cross the dry river and deploy into a combat line at the base of the mountain. At this point, the 1st MRB would dismount the 1st and 3rd MRC and the reconnaissance company plus the recon platoon of the battalion. The battalion would form into two groups. The first group was the 1st MRC commanded by Captain A. V. Ribakov. The second group was the 3rd MRC plus the recon platoon. I was the battalion chief of staff and I commanded this second group. We were to climb the mountain, find the enemy and cut off his escape. The battalion *bronegruppa* would support us with BMP-2 30mm automatic gunfire into the gap between our two groups.

The 1st MRC dismounted group consisted of 36 people, one 12.7mm *utes* (cliff) machine gun, one 30mm AGS-17 automatic grenade launcher, and two 82mm *podnos* [tray] mortars plus small arms. My dismounted group comprised 49 people, two *utes* machine guns, one AGS-17 automatic grenade launcher, two *podnos* mortars plus small arms. The dismounted reconnaissance company had 38 men, two *utes* machine guns, one AGS-17 automatic grenade launcher and one *podnos* mortar plus small arms.

Intelligence reports told us that there were supposedly three guerrilla forces with a total of 170-200 men in this area.

We prepared for combat during 10 hours of daylight. The troops pulled vehicle maintenance and cleaned their weapons. There were essentially no material reserves to replenish since we had restocked our combat loads when we left Kabul and had not used them during the march.

The subunit commanders received their orders and formulated their own plans. Particular attention was paid to coordination. The way this was done is particularly instructive. The regimental commander took all commanders from platoon leader up on a personal daytime reconnaissance. This group moved to the reconnaissance site in two stages mounted on two BMPs. The majority of the commanders were hidden inside the BMPs and practically all were dressed as ordinary soldiers (without rank and commanders' accoutrements). The officers had the chance to scrutinize their entire march route and coordinate their movement to the depth of the mission.

At 2100 hours on 25 February, the regiment moved out. At first, the movement and deployment of the 1st MRB went according to plan. Then, however, the ascent was delayed by an hour and 15 minutes. There were two reasons for the delay. First, a BTR-70 from the movement support detachment hit a mine. The driver was shell-shocked and the regimental assistant engineer was wounded. This was a result of the imperfect reliability of our mine detectors when used in the mountains. Second, no one had reckoned on the intervening natural obstacle-the dry river bed. The bank of this river bed was impassable, it was practically sheer and was from one-to-three meters high. Therefore, we had to jockey our BMPs around and zigzag by some 50-to-100 meters to enter and exit from the stream bed. This also ate up the time.

The approach was done by platoons traveling by bounds. Each successive height was occupied by a platoon which would then cover the advance of the other platoon with his on-board weapons. The success of the advance was also supported by covering fire from the artillery group and supporting BMPs. The 1st MRC advanced up the mountain some 800 meters and the 3rd MRC with the recon platoon some 1,300 meters. The 1st MRC fulfilled its mission at 0130 hours while the 3rd MRC fulfilled its mission at 0330 on 26 February.

During the climb up the mountain, we found several abandoned defensive works and campfires with smoldering embers. We disarmed two explosive devices. However, the delay during our approach and deployment kept us from cutting off the enemy's withdrawal. At the same time, the guerrilla forces did not succeed in getting out of the area completely since the other side of the canyon was controlled by Afghan government forces.

At dawn, we were able to establish visual reconnaissance. We discovered signs of enemy activity and called artillery fire in on the area and also shot it up with fire from the *utes* machine gun and AGS-17 automatic grenade launcher. However, the enemy knew the terrain well and was well versed in the art of camouflage. Therefore, the rounds mainly impacted on the ground and effects of the fire were minimal.

With the approach of darkness, we were ordered to come down from the mountain and rejoin the regiment. We travelled on to our base camp, but later learned from agent intelligence that during the time of our action, enemy losses were up to 30 KIA or WIA in that region.

FRUNZE COMMENTARY: This vignette shows that thorough coordination is necessary when functioning under unusual conditions (night combat, conduct of fire above and between friendly forces). The commander used a variety of means to deceive the enemy (the reconnaissance sweep in the opposite direction, the secret conduct of the commanders' reconnaissance). The unit also made mistakes. There was insufficient consideration given to the impact of terrain on the combat approach by the subunits , which led to the unforeseen jockeying about to cross the dry river bed. Further, reconnaissance of the march route and mine detecting were poorly done.

EDITOR'S COMMENTARY: The Soviet infantry carried some incredible weights. Carrying a 58-pound heavy machine gun, its tripod and ammunition up a hill at night is a challenge. The AGS-17 and 82mm mortar are not any easier. How the commander expected his infantry to cut off the enemy escape route, when the nimble *mujahideen* already had an uphill advantage, is questionable. Air-landed blocking forces seems to be an answer to cutting off escape routes.

The Soviets adopted bounding overwatch in this vignette and apparently throughout the Afghanistan War. Bounding overwatch was not in the European battle book since it slowed down movement tempo. However, bounding overwatch is essential when moving over rough terrain or when your enemy is not totally occupied with your artillery and air strikes.

In this vignette and others, the Soviets had no problem assigning a staff officer as a temporary commander. Here, the recon platoon was attached to a MRC and the battalion chief of staff was put in field command. This was a normal field practice and does not necessarily mean that they were having problems with the regular company commander.

As the vignette demonstrates, mine clearing in mountains is a difficult proposition-particularly against some of the non-metallic mines. Soviet equipment was frequently not up to the job. The Soviet Army lost 1,995 KIA and 1,191 vehicles to mines during the course of the Afghanistan War.

From the entire book, it is apparent that Soviet forces were spread very thin. Vignette 14 required a battalion each from three different regiments from a division spread over 400 kilometers. They could not assemble a single regiment, which would have been more effective, since they had to secure bases and LOCs. Vignette 18 required an understrength battalion to conduct a 500 kilometer road march on BMPs prior to entering combat. Operation "Magistral'" (Vignette 17) pulled most of a division out of the northeast part of Afghanistan to combine with part of another division, but there are indications that KGB border troops came south into Afghanistan to help hold the area during the division's absence. The Soviets did not commit sufficient force to win the war. They committed forces to bolster the Marxist-Leninist government of Afghanistan and hoped that they could buy enough time for the Afghan government to build up its own forces to fight its own war.

This is not to say that the Soviets did not try to win the war militarily. The 40th Army was much larger that the Afghan Peoples Army and Afghan government security forces and was reinforced by Air Force units and reserves located just across the Amudarya (Oxus) river in the Soviet Union. The Soviets controlled the country and were able to effectively intervene at any point in Afghanistan at any time they desired. However, such intervention was effective only as long as they remained in the area. They could not conquer the country. General Secretary Gorbachev directed that the military achieve victory in 1985 and casualty figures on both sides reflect this effort. This effort failed and Gorbachev finally decided that the Soviet Union must withdraw with dignity from Afghanistan.

Why did the Soviets fail to achieve military victory in Afghanistan? First, they were unable to seal the border with Pakistan and Iran to prevent the *mujahideen* resupply of their forces. Second, they were unable to bring enough force into the country due to public opinion (particularly in the third world) and their inability to provide the logistic support necessary with a larger force. Third, Afghanistan is a country of strong beliefs and traditions and the population opposed the Soviets and the hostile communist ideology of the government of Afghanistan. The communist ideology directly attacked the ethnic structure, community structure and religious beliefs of the people and the people violently rejected this ideology. Fourth, the Soviets had little respect for the people of Afghanistan. They used the Afghan Peoples Army, Sarandoy, the Khad and the local militias ("Defenders of the Revolution") as cannon fodder. These demoralized and inefficient forces regained some of their lost respectability only when the Soviets left. Further, the Soviets conducted indiscriminate air and artillery attacks against the rural population in order to force them out of the countryside in order to dry up the *mujahideen* supply lines. Finally, the Soviets were reluctant to accept the casualties necessary for such a victory and tried to substitute fire power for infantry close combat.

What is equally apparent from the book is that the Soviet Union failed to maintain adequate personnel strength within its units. The battalion in Vignette 18 is short an entire company. The regiment in Vignette 19 is short two battalions and each battalion is short one company. Even these companies are at one-third strength. Granted, this regiment was returning from hard fighting during operation "Magistral'", but the personnel strength of the regiment is less than that of a full-strength battalion. These are skeleton figures. A MRR should have 2,315 men. An MRB should have 455 men. An MRC should have 103 men. An MRP should have 28 men. Soviet forces were badly understrength and Afghan forces were in even worse shape. Other sources describe the significant Soviet problems with disease which cut into units' present-for-duty-strength in Afghanistan. From 1/4 to 1/3 of a unit's strength was normally sick with hepatitis, typhus, malaria, amoebic dysentery, and meningitis. Guard, details and LOC security cut further into the strength. Units were filled twice a year from the spring and fall draft call-ups. Conscripts sent to the Turkestan Military District had 6-12 month's training before going to Afghanistan for the rest of their service. Further, military districts and Groups of Forces were levied for troops twice annually. These levies were quite significant. Yet, the unit strengths are appallingly low. Apparently, units need to be filled well in excess of 100% in some regions of the world if one hopes to field a reasonable fighting force.

CHAPTER 3:
THE APPLICATION OF TACTICAL AIR ASSAULTS

The study of combat experience in Afghanistan allows us to perfect the theory and practice of tactical air assaults. Afghanistan practice demonstrated that tactical air assaults were successfully employed for independent, surprise attacks against guerrilla forces and base camps in remote locales or difficult terrain. Air assaults were also employed in joint actions involving other subunits and regiments, advancing along the front.

Air assaults were normally conducted to seize dominant terrain and road junctions. They would land directly on the target or adjacent to it. As a rule, prior to landing the first lift and the main body, we would use air, artillery and even small-arms fire to suppress the enemy.

Tactical air assaults in Nangarhar and Laghman Provinces
by Major S. A. Urban[59]

In February 1983, the brigade intelligence section reported that approximately 150 enemy were functioning in groups in the brigade area of responsibility (AOR).[60] They were shelling security outposts and civilian facilities with 81mm mortar fire and were mining roads.

The brigade commander decided to eradicate these groups in our AOR. He planned to attack the enemy in the village of Kama (located in Nangarhar Province about 12 kilometers from our base camp) and the village of Ghaziabad. He would air-land two companies, one into the area near Kama and would later follow this landing with one against Ghaziabad. The *bronegruppa* of the participating motorized rifle battalion and airborne company would move out from Jalalabad to Ghaziabad in support. The air landing would be preceded with a 10-minute artillery preparation. Captain Kostenko, the acting battalion commander, would command the air landing. Major Ermolaev, the deputy commander for technical support, would command the *bronegruppa*. The first lift would consist of an air assault platoon, an engineer squad and a flamethrower squad.

On 12 February, the air landing took place near Kama. The 2nd AAslt company swept through the green zone, but did not find any enemy. The *bronegruppa* moved toward the village of Ghaziabad.

On 13 February, we conducted an air landing with the 1st AAslt company, this time near Ghaziabad to seize the crest of the southern mountain and block the enemy withdrawal. However, before the *bronegruppa* reached Ghaziabad from the north, the enemy withdrew into the mountains. On the morning of 14 February, the battalion commander decided to pick up the two air assault companies and air land them near the village of Charbagh (in Laghman Province). From there, they would advance across the mountains to Bailam village. According to preliminary intelligence, the *mujahideen* stored ammunition and had a hospital in Bailam. The advancing compa-

---

[59]S. A. Urban served in the Republic of Afghanistan from December 1981 through April 1984 as a platoon leader and then a company commander in an air assault battalion. He was awarded the "Order of the Red Star".
[60]The 66th Separate Motorized Rifle Brigade (ed.).

nies would work with the *bronegruppa* to seal off Bailam and destroy the enemy inside it. We had 24 hours to accomplish our mission.

The area around Bailam was well-fortified and had reinforced security. The enemy observed our air landing and the battalion lost the element of surprise. We lacked the necessary combat power to take the village. Finally, toward the end of 17 February, our brigade commander gave us the necessary air and artillery support to take the village. The battalion lost 25-30 men.

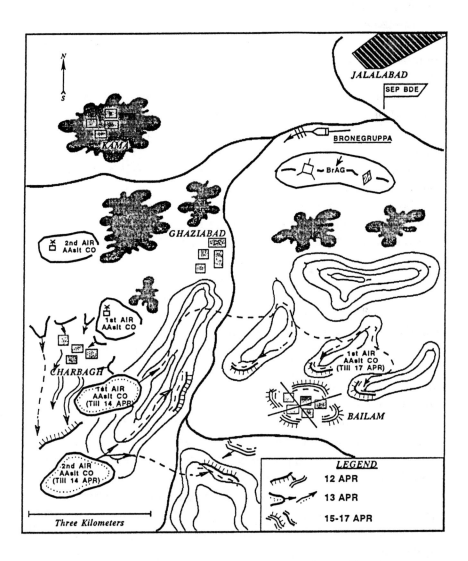

Map 20: Air assaults in Nangarhar and Laghman Provinces.

FRUNZE COMMENTARY: This action shows that the first requirement for a successful air landing is surprise. Without surprise, it is impossible to dislodge the enemy unless you have sufficient aviation and artillery support.

EDITOR'S COMMENTARY: The 66th and 70th Separate Motorized Rifle Brigades were forces created especially for counterinsurgency. They were composed of two-three motorized rifle battalions, an air assault battalion, an artillery howitzer battalion, a reconnaissance battalion, a tank battalion and support troops. There are also some indications that a MRLS battalion might have belonged to this organization. In this vignette, a MRLS battalion is part of the Brigade Artillery Group (BrAG) of the 66th. Evidently it was not brought in just for this action. In Vignette 18, an MRLS battalion supports an attack in the 70th's AOR. The 70th was located in Kandahar and it was over 400 kilometers from Kandahar to the next major Soviet force. Perhaps the Afghan forces in the area had MRLS, but there is also the possibility that a MRLS battalion was part of both separate brigades.

Soviet military vocabulary is very precise when it differentiates between tactics and operations in the European theater. Tactics are the business of platoons, companies, battalions, regiments and divisions while operations are the business of armies and fronts. When the 40th Army conducts Operation Magistral (Vignette 17) it is an operation. When divisions and regiments fight, it is tactics. However, whenever the 103rd Airborne Division, the 56th Air Assault Brigade, the 345th Separate Airborne Regiment, the 66th Separate Motorized Rifle Brigade, or the 70th Separate Motorized Rifle Brigade fight, it's an operation. This is probably due to the unique combined arms mixes of the separate brigades and the level of impact of the airborne and air assault forces.

In this vignette, the actions of the *bronegruppa* spook the enemy before the air assault element is in a position to deal with them. Apparently, there were problems with the coordination and communications between the two elements.

It would also appear that intelligence for this operation was very poor. This may be a reflection of poor performance by the reconnaissance forces and a demonstration of an inability to identify enemy positions.

An air assault in the area of Rumbasi village
by Major V. V. Kovalev[61]

At the start of January 1985, the commander of our motorized rifle brigade[62] received an intelligence report that the enemy planned to hold a conference on 25 January near the village of Rumbasi (located southwest of Kandahar). The meeting would involve the leaders of the main guerrilla forces in a three-province area and was being held to coordinate their future actions. The decision was made to destroy the enemy at this meeting.

The brigade commander decided to conduct an approach march to Rumbasi on 25 January, cut up the guerrilla forces during the approach, launch a tactical air assault to block the enemy in the village and then destroy the enemy. The following morning, the brigade would continue the advance to the southwest and complete the destruction of any enemy in the region. The brigade would move in a single echelon and use the brigade's air assault battalion[63] for the air assault.

Our air assault battalion's mission was to seize an LZ to the southeast of Rumbasi, destroy any enemy in the vicinity of the LZ, establish blocking positions to the east and southeast of Rumbasi and hold these positions until the arrival of the brigade's main force. Then, we would link up with the brigade and join its subsequent advance.

We prepared our battalion for combat at our base camp from 23 to 25 January. Our preparations included outfitting our soldiers, preparing our weapons and equipment for combat, and conducting air assault training for our soldiers. The battalion staff prepared the load plans for each helicopter and each lift, as well as the assault plan and the materiel and armaments transport plan. The aerodrome was located near our base camp. At 1100 hours on 25 January the battalion began moving to the aerodrome, loading the helicopters and finalizing the lifts. Embarkation was finished by 1300.

---

[61]V. V. Kovalev served in the Republic of Afghanistan from June 1983 through July 1985 as a platoon leader, company commander and battalion chief of staff. He was decorated with the "Order of the Red Star" and the Republic of Afghanistan order "For Valor".

[62]The 70th Separate Motorized Brigade (ed.).

[63]The 4th Air Assault Battalion (ed.).

The first lift went in flying low in a single column. A flight of fighter-bombers and two flights of Mi-24 HIND helicopter gunships prepped the LZ and our Mi-8 HIP transport helicopters also hit the LZ with their on-board armaments and door guns. As our lead group of four helicopters set down, the enemy opened up with grenade launchers and small arms fire. Therefore, the LZ location for the main body was slipped one kilometer to the southeast of the first lift's landing site. The first lift courageously and decisively destroyed the enemy in their LZ and established blocking positions around Rumbasi. During this combat, they killed a large number of enemy

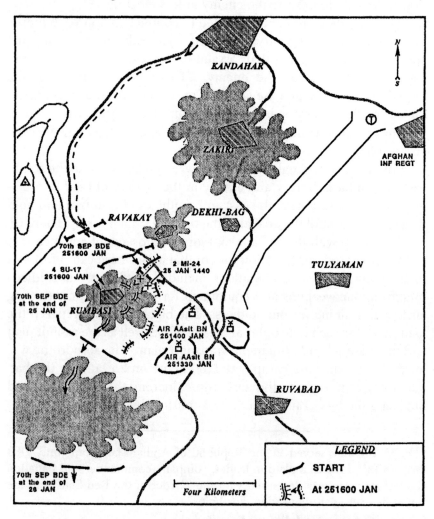

Map 21: An air assault in the area of Rumbasi village.

and captured over 30 modern, automatic weapons and grenade launchers as well as ammunition.

As the main body was closing up to their first lift, the enemy opened up with interlocking, integrated small arms fire which did not let the main body approach the village. Two Mi-24 HIND helicopter gunships helped support the first lift after the landing, but since we did not haul any artillery along with our assault, we had no way of suppressing the enemy until the brigade closed to within firing range. When the brigade artillery moved to within firing range, they were able to put fire on the enemy and the battalion main body moved forward to take up blocking positions. *Mujahideen* who tried to withdraw out of Rumbasi to Ruvabad were cut down by fire from our first lift.

Our battalion lost two killed and three wounded. Enemy casualties were over 100 men. We captured a large supply of weapons and ammunition. Our success was due to our achieving surprise, deception measures we took to deceive the enemy (we prepared a feint into another area), and the courageous and decisive actions of our first group.

However, our battalion did not fulfill its entire mission. We had not coordinated fully with the supporting aviation and this resulted in an insufficient amount of aviation ordinance being fired to soften up the LZ. Further, we operated out of the range of the brigade's artillery and had not considered using smoke or remotely delivered mines (RDM).

FRUNZE COMMENTARY: Combat experience shows that, depending on the type of mission and the anticipated enemy counteraction, a single lift should consist of a complete, reinforced, air assault (or airborne) company or even up to a reinforced battalion. As a minimum, a company should be reinforced with a mortar platoon, an AGS-17 platoon and a sapper squad. As a minimum, a battalion should be reinforced with a mortar battery, two or three AGS-17 platoons and a sapper platoon. A supporting artillery battalion and a supporting battery of BM-21 MRLS must be within range of the landing. Army and frontal aviation must support the landing. It is better to fly in one air corridor where the enemy air defense posture is weaker and where the terrain facilitates an undetected approach. Helicopter gunships must precede and flank the landing force to soften up the LZ and then circle the LZ and use its on-board weapons if necessary. Air assault troops must be trained to fire small arms from the lift helicopter doors while in flight.

EDITOR'S COMMENTARY: The above commentary appears to be a "cookie-cutter" solution to an air assault's fire support problems. Instead of specifying the number of required BM-21s, mortars and AGS-17s, perhaps the realistic solution is to remind planning officers that an air assault needs accompanying and supporting indirect-fire support. Despite all the photos showing D-30 artillery pieces being carried by helicopters to an action, the air assault forces and airborne forces seem to have gone on operations without accompanying artillery on numerous occasions. Perhaps this was the result of the limited availability of lift ships.

Air assaulting and blocking the enemy in the Lar-Mandikul' Valley

by Major V. G. Chabanenko[64]

On 16 March 1985, our intelligence organs received reports of a concentration of guerrilla forces in the Lar-Mandikul' Valley, some 30 kilometers northeast of Kabul. The division commander ordered my regimental commander to destroy them[65]. My commander decided to air land the regiment some six kilometers away from the guerrillas and then sneak up to the valley, block off its exits and then conduct a hunt with part of the regiment, while the rest would cover their movements. Aviation would provide fire support as would some MRLS located some 15 kilometers from the valley with our *bronegruppa*. Illumination support would be planned and on call and be furnished by illumination flares, artillery illumination rounds and air-delivered flares. After accomplishing our mission, the regiment would walk to our *bronegruppa*.

On 19 March, we hit the LZ and were immediately spotted by the enemy. The enemy opened up with a heavy volume of fire and began rapidly pulling his units out from under our air and artillery strikes. Only the forward subunits of our 1st and 2nd battalions managed to reach their blocking positions and they did not have sufficient combat power to stop the enemy main body. During the next 48 hours, our search groups found and destroyed weapons and ammunition caches. Our covering subunits managed to occupy the dominant terrain, support the search groups, and repulse enemy attempts to clear away the blocking forces.

Over in an adjacent valley, a similar situation had developed. The enemy managed to extricate his subunits away from the strike of the regiment and conduct a march through the valley. This was because we landed at the tail end of the enemy column and we could not get to the blocking positions designated by the regiment. In addition, once again our landing had been discovered and we had been put down in the wrong place. This was because rather than landing at the designated sites, we landed in places safe from enemy fire and

---

[64]V. G. Chabanenko served in the Republic of Afghanistan from December 1983 through June 1985 as a battalion commander.

[65]The 103rd Airborne Division (ed.).

large enough (2x2 kilometers) for easy landing. It took two hours to assemble my battalion's subunits and, consequently, I was unable to move to the correct positions in an organized fashion in time. The enemy escaped.

FRUNZE COMMENTARY: This operation underscores the necessity of conducting continuous reconnaissance of the enemy and, depending on the existing situation, fine-tuning your plans and

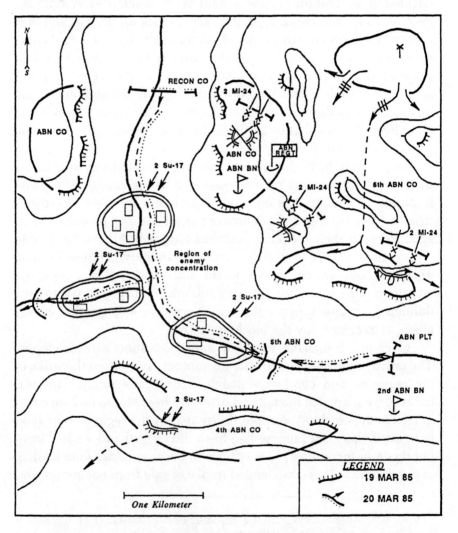

Map 22: Air assaulting and blocking the enemy in the Lar-Mandikul' valley.

if necessary changing your LZ. A company should have one LZ, a battalion should have two or three LZs which are no further than a kilometer or a kilometer and a half apart. LZs need to be shielded from enemy fire. It goes without saying that there must be a reserve LZ as well.

Combat action in Afghanistan, and, in particular this operation, demonstrate that evacuating the assault force after mission accomplishment requires particular attention, since it is during this stage of the operation that the subunits receive their most significant casualties. During the return to the assembly areas on helicopters, pay particular attention to ensuring that the enemy has not placed weapons around them. In order to keep the enemy away from evacuation points, use air-delivered or MRLS-delivered RDM on enemy approach routes. When covering a region from dominant terrain, evacuate the force by establishing a series of perimeter posts around the LZ. After evacuating the main force, evacuate the posts simultaneously. When moving the assault force to seize an evacuation zone, cover the movement with overwatching forces and aviation, move in precombat formation and lead with reconnaissance.

Start helicopter load plans immediately upon receipt of the evacuation order and refine them when at the pick-up point. Pull mortar crews and mortars out first and riflemen last. The air assault commander directs the evacuation and is on the last helicopter out along with the last part of the perimeter security posts. Supporting helicopter gunships are held in full readiness or fire on the enemy along their climbing paths. Air assault troopers, once on board the helicopters, must be ready to conduct small arms fire through aircraft openings.

Experience shows that helicopters should spend the minimum possible time at the air evacuation point as personnel and equipment are already concentrated there as a tempting target. Helicopters can spend a maximum of one and one-half minutes on the ground.

Airborne and air assault forces can return to their initial assembly area, after mission accomplishment, on board helicopters or on board their armored vehicles. In this operation in the Lar-Mandikul' Valley, the regiment withdrew mounted in their *bronegruppa* after fulfilling their mission. They pulled out at night. In order to navigate at night, commanders used compasses and parachute flares. During the day, they could have used route reconnaissance. The regiment's various *bronegruppa* moved by bounds as subunits provided overwatch for the main body. Once the main body had passed through a covered segment of the route, the overwatching forces would rejoin the main force and other subunits would move forward to the next overwatch positions. In this manner, the regiment maintained a high tempo of movement and suffered minimal casualties during encounters with the enemy.

EDITOR'S COMMENTARY: Pulling out the mortars prior to the infantry is a commander's call and depends on the tactical situation, but there are times when the mortars will be the final system a commander wants to evacuate.

Many commanders prefer forming an uninterrupted "collapsing ring" for evacuation zone security. This ring gets tighter with each lift-off. The collapsing ring has a better chance of preventing enemy infiltration of the perimeter and evacuating the security personnel than establishing a series of far-off posts as this vignette recommends.

The withdrawal of the force mounted in its *bronegruppa* appears to be a withdrawal under pressure. Night movement of a mechanized column through the Pandshir valley using parachute flares and compasses seems to be an option that a commander would adapt only under pressure.

Destruction of a guerrilla force by a tactical air assault into Lowgar Province
by Major V. V. Selivanov[66]

The enemy increased his activity in Lowgar Province in August 1985. Guerrillas shelled Kabul from the southeast, attacked military and civilian convoys and attacked Soviet and Afghan outposts. According to intelligence reports from the Afghan security service,[67] guerrilla forward detachments were located in the area bordered by the villages of Khurd-Kabul, Malang, Kala and Malikheyl'. A total of 500 to 600 men in 10 to 15 guerrilla units were located here. The main concentration of guerrilla forces was located some 15-to-20 kilometers further to the southeast of this area. There, in the village of Tizini-Khas, they had created ammunition and armaments caches which were guarded by some 300 men armed with DShK heavy machine guns and mortars. The Afghan government decided to stop the shelling of Kabul from Lowgar Province by establishing a base camp in the Lowgar Valley manned by a "Sarandoy" battalion.

The airborne division[68] was ordered to go after the guerrillas. The airborne division commander decided to move his units for this operation into the area secretly from 9 to 11 August. Then, from 11 to 18 August, he would surround and destroy the enemy forward detachments and prevent their retreat into their major base area.

Two airborne regiments were selected for this operation. One of the regiments was short a battalion and the other was short two battalions. The division commander reinforced this force with the reconnaissance company of the remaining regiment, a separate reconnaissance company, a sapper battalion, a tank battalion and an artillery regiment (which was short a battalion). Two reconnaissance groups were formed—one from the reconnaissance company of the remaining regiment and one from the separate reconnaissance company. Their mission was to conduct a 50-kilometer deep raid on 13 August to block two canyons south of the Lowgar Province valley. The main body of the force (three airborne battalions) would air

---

[66]V. V. Selivanov served in the Republic of Afghanistan as the Chief of Intelligence of an airborne regiment.

[67]KHAD (ed.).

[68]The 103rd Airborne Division (ed.).

assault into an area north of the village of Khurd-Kabul, attack the enemy, and prevent his withdrawal to the south. Then, in cooperation with the reconnaissance groups, the main body would complete the destruction of the enemy.

However, this operation plan was upset by the guerrilla forward detachments which attacked the new Afghan base camp of the "Sarandoy" battalion. The battalion did not put up any fight but fled from the base in a panic. The division commander then decided that rather than having the recon groups move out to the planned areas, he would combine the two reconnaissance groups into one and add

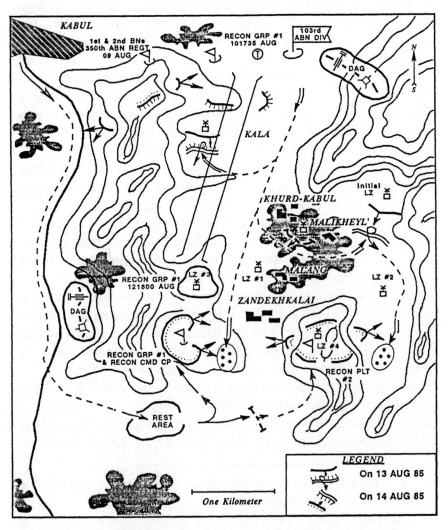

Map 23: Destroying guerrilla forces in Lowgar Province.

a sapper squad to it. This new recon group would air land to the east of Malikheyl' village and establish a blocking position of the canyon.

The reconnaissance detachment command group and the regimental recon company were on the first lift. The second lift consisted of the separate recon company and the "Sarandoy" Battalion. Retransmission helicopters would stay on station over the battle area all day to insure constant communications.

The assault flight took 30 minutes. The two lifts landed on the west slope of the canyon and moved south under heavy enemy DShK and mortar fire. They escaped without any casualties thanks only to nightfall. They could not receive any artillery support since they were out of artillery range and, since it was dark, they could not get any air support. The enemy held the dominant terrain and fired at them from the surrounding heights from three directions. This fire pinned them down while the enemy moved a guerrilla force of approximately 600 men out of the canyon. The reconnaissance company shot at the withdrawing guerrillas, but the plan was to have the entire force down in the canyon blocking this very withdrawal. However, the heavy enemy fire kept the reconnaissance group commander from moving his force into the canyon and he dug them in along a high ridgeline instead. On the next morning, 14 August, the first regiment of the division landed following an artillery preparation of the LZ. The enemy suffered some casualties, however the goal of the operation was not achieved. The air assault came too late and the enemy had already managed to withdraw his main force out through the canyon and away from our strike.

The division commander, General-Major Yarygin, received some more detailed information on the enemy and decided to salvage the operation by preceding to the next stage and capturing the weapons and ammunition caches and also destroying guerrilla forces in the villages of Tizini-Khas and Zandekhkalai.

The remaining tactical air assault force consisted of an airborne regiment commanded by LTC Solov'ev and a reconnaissance group which I commanded. The reconnaissance group was the separate recon company and the Afghan "Sarandoy" regiment which was not inserted the previous night.

The division commander's plan was that at 1445 hours on 14 August, the force would lift out of the area near Malikheyl' on Mi-8 helicopters. The force would air assault into the area around Tizini-Khash using three lifts and four LZs. The first lift would establish blocking positions by 1830 and by 1900 would have an integrated fire plan organized and implemented. The main body would follow and be used to destroy the enemy in the region and prevent the enemy main body from withdrawing. After the blockade was established, every company would send a platoon forward to search. The first lift included the 2nd battalion (180 men on 18 Mi-8s)and the first battalion (120 men on 12 Mi-8s) of the 350th Airborne Regiment. The second lift included the division CP, the regimental CP, the regimental recon company, a company of the 1st battalion (180 men on 18 Mi-8s) and the reconnaissance group (120 men on 12 Mi-8s). The third lift consisted of the transferred recon group (180 men on 18 Mi-8s). The landings were distributed so that the 2nd battalion landed at LZ #1, the first battalion (minus a company) landed at LZ #2, the recon group on LZ #4 and the rest at LZ #3. Artillery would prep the LZs from 1412 until 1428. Then airstrikes would pound the LZs from 1430 until 1500. Aviation support would be on station from the completion of the landing until 1800.

The commander of the air assault group made a mistake and set all my groups down six kilometers west of the planned LZ. We had to cross the mountains to get to our correct LZ. The factor of surprise was lost. We did not find any arms and ammunition caches in the village of Tizini-Khas. However, an Afghan guide's explanation cleared this up. What map names are printed for tiny villages are not necessarily what the villages are actually called or how the locals refer to them. Thus it was with the so-called village of Tizini-Khas. On the map, it is actually named the village of Zandekhkalai. I pushed on to Zandekhkalai, seized it and concentrated my force there. We dislodged the enemy security forces on the approaches to the village and on the dominating heights which sealed off the approaches to the canyon. Then the recon group searched for caches while an airborne company and the Afghan "Sarandoy" regiment covered us.

As a result of this fluke, our recon group killed approximately 150 *mujahideen* and captured seven weapons caches. The skilled actions of the recon group contributed to the completion of the division's mission.

FRUNZE COMMENTARY: The first and second stages of the operation were filled with mistakes: During the first stage, they landed at the end of daylight so that their aviation could not support them. Further, there was no artillery within range to provide fire support. Intelligence did not tie their information to an actual map location. Finally, the flight route and LZs were poorly planned for the second phase of the operation.

EDITOR'S COMMENTARY: Soviet artillery theory occasionally allows Division Artillery Groups (DAG) to be split to provide wider coverage. In reality, in the European theater, this never happened. In Afghanistan, it became necessary to spread the coverage and this vignette shows a split-DAG doing fire support.

The Soviets had no difficulty in taking the reconnaissance elements from one force and putting it in support of another. Most western commanders would not willingly surrender their reconnaissance element. This vignette shows a typical example of the redistribution of TO&E reconnaissance forces to another unit.

Map reading and terrain navigation from an aircraft is tough in a region without hard-top roads, powerlines, major rivers and permanent bridges. It is not any easier on the ground. Map reading is particularly difficult in the mountains. The Soviet performance in this area seems about average.

Seizing and holding a *mujahideen* training center with a tactical air assault

by LTC V. G. Istratiy[69]

In October 1985, we received intelligence reports that an enemy training center, which was built to train gunners for shoulder-fired surface-to-air missile systems, was located southwest of Kandahar.

On the basis of this intelligence report, my battalion commander gave me his concept of battle.[70] My 12th Air Assault Company would conduct an air assault landing and secure an LZ near the training center on 13 October. Then, when the rest of the battalion arrived, we would join it and help capture and destroy the training center.

We prepared our force for combat at our training grounds. We emphasized the organization for the air assault to include a detailed analysis of past combat actions which we went over in detail with our personnel and then assessed the missions of the platoon and company commanders. We used aerial photographs to work out the details of the plan. From these photos, we identified "dead space" in the approach to the objective, likely enemy firing positions and areas of fire concentration, and targets that we wanted to destroy with air and artillery fire.

We had 48 hours to prepare prior to the beginning of the operation. The battalion commander carefully planned each platoon's mission on the map and "wargamed" various contingencies. He devoted special attention to balancing the subunit's firepower and that of the supporting aviation. At the same time, the battalion commander personally designated the firing positions of the mortars and the AGS-17 as well as the site for the company CP/OP. While wargaming each of the contingencies, he paid particular attention to the actions of my forward group as we seized and secured the LZ.

My 12th Air Assault Company air landed onto the LZ on the morning of 13 October. Despite the careful planning, we were cut off

---

[69]V. G. Istratiy served in the Republic of Afghanistan from 1984 through 1986 as a company commander.

[70]The 4th Air Assault Battalion of the 70th Separate Motorized Rifle Battalion (ed.).

from the main force of the battalion. After a full day of combat, the situation became critical as our ammunition began to run out and attempts to resupply us by helicopter failed. My men had to fire single shots on semiautomatic instead of bursts of automatic weapons fire. I continually called in air and artillery fire on the enemy.

The battalion's main force tried to break through to me, but it became apparent that they would not make it before the morning of 14 October. We could not hold out that long. So, after reviewing the situation, I decided to attack at nightfall. The 3rd platoon would take

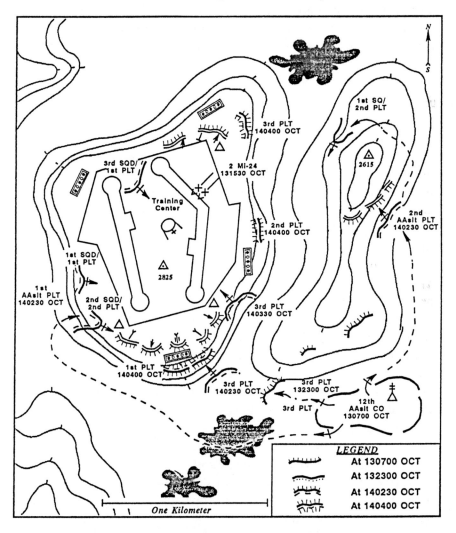

**Map 24: Seizing and holding a training center
with an air assault company.**

the southeast slope of hill 2825 and, together with the covering force, distract the enemy. The 1st and 2nd platoon would envelop the enemy from the west and the east and at 0230 hours 14 October, they would simultaneously attack from two directions to seize the base, capture ammunition and then hold the base until the arrival of the battalion.

My plan worked and by 0400 we took the base without casualties. We captured three DShK heavy machine guns, two recoilless rifles, 17 individual small arms and ammunition. At 0600, the enemy tried to retake the base, but we drove him off. In the course of combat, my troopers used the weapons and ammunition that they had captured from the enemy. When the main body of the battalion arrived, they punished the enemy badly and forced him to withdraw, denying him the opportunity to retake the base.

FRUNZE COMMENTARY: This combat example shows that the proper equipping of air assault personnel, including sufficient ammunition, rations, water, and radio batteries is essential. Further, one must insure that there is uninterrupted resupply and access to safe LZs. Resupply can determine the course of battle in the mountains. And as important as resupply and evacuation of the wounded are, the length of time needed to complete the entire military mission depends on how well direct coordination is done with the aviation. Weather conditions are a major factor in employing combat aviation, as is the effectiveness of the enemy's air defense. The closer the LZ is to the objective or fewer the number of available LZs, the harder it will be to resupply forces and conduct timely MEDEVACs.

During another battle (on 21 July 1985) in the vicinity of Alikheyl' village, a battalion had to take part of its force to quickly clear an area of trees, brush, and large boulders to create an LZ to evacuate the wounded, since their original LZ was under enemy fire. Sometimes, during the course of this battle, the only way to resupply their unit was to throw the supplies out of the helicopter. They put food and drinking water in bags and rubber bladders from their chemical defensive equipment stores prior to dropping them. Thus, without the proper containers for drops, about half of the food and water was destroyed in the drop.

In order to fight independently for three or four days, each air assault trooper needs to carry the following: two or three combat loads of ammunition for his assault rifle, four hand grenades (two of them defensive grenades), one RPG-18 antitank grenade launcher[71] for every two personnel, two 200-gram blocks of TNT with blasting caps, five smoke pots and five parachute flares (or orange smoke grenades which can be used for signalling or laying down smoke), four 82-mm mortar rounds (if there is a mortar section) or a canister of ammunition for the AGS-17, enough rations for three-to-five days, two-or-three canteens of water or tea, a poncho or shelter-half and one blanket for two people or a sleeping bag. The weight of all this kit is 35-to-40 kilograms, so if regular resupply is guaranteed, this considerable load can be lightened.

EDITOR'S COMMENTARY: In this vignette, an air assault company runs out of ammunition in a day's combat. This is partially due to the Soviet philosophy that small arms fire suppresses enemy fire and eventually may kill the enemy. The West wants to kill the enemy with small arms fire and uses crew-served weapons to suppress enemy fire. The standard Soviet assault rifle's fire selector switch goes from safe to full automatic to semiautomatic. The standard Western assault rifle's fire selection switch goes from safe to semiautomatic to full automatic. The West sees semiautomatic fire as the norm. The Soviets saw full automatic fire as the norm. Perhaps the Soviets needed to devote more time to rifle marksmanship for a guerrilla war. It saves on ammunition consumption. In the mountains, a bolt-action rifle with range and accuracy is frequently of more use than a rapid-firing assault rifle (though not in an ambush).

---

[71]Similar to the U.S. LAW (light-antitank weapon) (ed.).

An airborne battalion lands in Islam-Dara Canyon and seals it off
by LTC S. I. Pariy[72]

In 1985, having suffered a series of major set-backs in the provinces of Kabul and Kunar, the enemy markedly stepped up the intensity of combat. He shelled military bases and outposts and shot up civilian convoys. There was a particularly unpleasant situation along the southern border of the country in Kandahar Province. One of their largest guerrilla bases was located 150 kilometers south of Kandahar. This base trained guerrilla forces and provided weapons and ammunition for combat deep inside Afghanistan. The base was located in Islam-Dara Canyon and consisted of several camps, a hospital, a large bakery, and weapons and ammunition stores.

The division commander ordered my airborne regimental commander to air land a battalion at the northern mouth of the canyon and air land another battalion at the southern mouth of the canyon.[73] They were to block the enemy inside the canyon and then participate in his destruction when the other regiments of the division arrived to capture and destroy the base. My battalion, the 1st Battalion, was to initially load an airborne company plus the reconnaissance platoon on eight Mi-8 helicopters and, escorted by four Mi-24 helicopter gunships, conduct an air assault to seize LZ #1. By the end of 18 November, they were to seize the dominant heights (hill 2300 and 2100) and the pass. On 19 November, they were to support the insertion of the rest of the battalion and the regiment. We would then block the canyon in the north and prevent the enemy from withdrawing in that direction.

During our preparations for this combat, the subunit commanders paid particular attention to studying the objective area with aerial photographs, coordinating their actions, and directing radio com-

---

[72]S. I. Pariy served in the Republic of Afghanistan from September 1985 through October 1987 as the chief of staff of an airborne battalion and as a airborne battalion commander. He was awarded the "Order of the Red Star" twice and the Afghanistan "Order for Bravery."

[73]The 103rd Airborne Division (ed.).

munications training. The troops were put through a seven-day training program which finished with a company exercise emphasizing issues closely related to the upcoming operation: seizing and holding high ground, sealing off an area and supporting a helicopter landing. By 18 November, the mission of the first lift and the battalion main force had been worked out in detail. The battalion commander would command the first lift.

At 1500 hours on 18 November, our first lift (forward group) was airborne. During our approach to the LZ, the enemy shot down four of our helicopters. Seven of our troopers were wounded as a result.

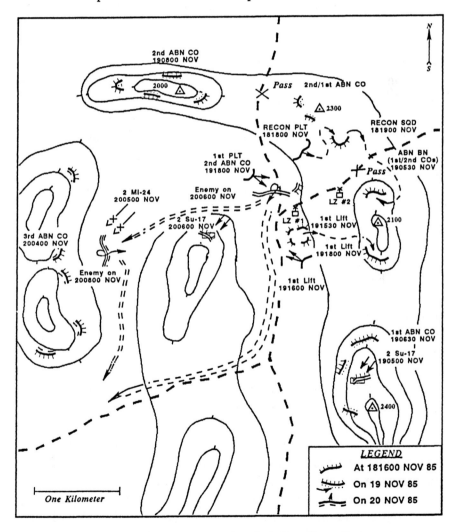

Map 25: An airborne battalion in Islam-Dara Canyon.

The surviving helicopters were unable to set down and returned to base. The first lift's mission had to be fulfilled by a much smaller group of survivors on the ground. The air assault survivors came under enemy fire. Senior Lieutenant V. V. Serdyukov commanded the reconnaissance platoon, which was in a better situation. He led his men up the heights to seize hill 2300 and cover the withdrawal of the survivors. He hit the enemy on the flank, destroyed two firing points and captured hills 2300 and 2100. The recon platoon provided covering fire which enabled the survivors to withdraw into the pass and dig in on high ground.

On the morning of 19 November, air strikes and artillery fire rained down on the enemy firing points which reconnaissance had identified. Then, the rest of the battalion, followed by the regiment, landed at LZ #2. The first lift covered this insertion successfully. By 0800 on the 19th, the 2nd Airborne Company seized the heights which blocked the northern approach into the canyon. By 0400 on 20 November, the 3rd Airborne Company seized the dominant terrain along the west wall of the canyon. Two platoons of the 1st Airborne Company drove off the surviving enemy on hill 2400 and by 0630 hours on 19 November, they had occupied it. In this way, by 0400 hours on 20 November, the northern exit to the canyon was completely sealed. Consequently, the enemy had to try to withdraw to the southwest. By this time, other subunits of the division had captured the heights and sealed the canyon. They completed the destruction of the enemy.

Our battalion had no irrevocable losses. We had seven wounded—all from the first lift on the first day. We had three men badly bruised and shaken up from an accident with a BTR on the second day. Four Mi-8 helicopters were shot down. The enemy lost approximately 35 men KIA.

FRUNZE COMMENTARY: The enemy concentrated the bulk of his combat power in the southern section of the canyon. We deceived him as to the location of the main strength of the Soviet force which led to his defeat. Attention must be paid to the well-organized air defenses which the enemy fielded. His air defense firing points were interconnected and well-protected. They proved to be safe from artillery fire and airstrikes. Because we did not have any intelligence data on the location of the enemy air defense weapons, our supporting helicopter gunships indiscriminately shot up the mountain tops, but the machine guns which downed the lift ships were located at the base of the mountains.

After examining the mistakes, we can draw the following positive experience from this operation: The success of the entire operation depended, to a great deal, on the courageous and decisive actions of the first lift. Every group, landing on a single or several LZs, must be ready for independent action, since follow-on lifts into the same LZ may not be possible. How helicopters are used will vary with the height of the mountains. An Mi-8MT helicopter can carry six-to-eight troopers with all their kit at 2000 meters altitude, but only four-or-five at 3000 to 4000 meters altitude.

EDITOR'S COMMENTARY: Guerrilla warfare is a platoon leader's and company commander's war.   Lower level initiative is essential for survival and success. This vignette shows a good example of how the Soviets were developing junior leader initiative in the airborne and air assault forces. Motorized rifle forces seemed to continue to suffer from top-driven lack of initiative.

Success in guerrilla war is hard to define and body count is certainly a poor criteria.   However, example after example shows blocks, sweeps and raids into areas supposedly containing hundreds of guerrillas. At the end of a battle or operation, the *mujahideen* casualties are in the dozens and the action is termed a success because the guerrilla force has been smashed. From Vietnam experience, a guerrilla force is very difficult to destroy. After very rough handling, the majority of them seem to bounce back. It seems that what the Soviets were normally engaging were the rear guards and the slow or uninformed guerrillas. The Soviet block seemed very porous (especially at night) and the sweep seemed to miss a lot.

The lack of a professional NCO corps really hurt the Soviets during these block and sweep actions. According to interviews I have conducted, a conscript NCO was normally in charge of a blocking post. Time and time again, the Soviet troops would either go to sleep on post or fail to engage the enemy for fear of getting killed in the firefight. The NCO should have corrected this, but was often the instigator.

Conducting a tactical air assault in the "Melava" fortified region
by Major N. G. Ten'kov[74]

In the spring of 1987, intelligence reports stated that the *mujahideen* had constructed a fortified region near Jalalabad in Nangarhar Province. The so-called "Melava" fortified region contained huge stores of weapons, ammunition, medicine and foodstuffs which had been brought over from Pakistan. The dominant heights in this area were well-fortified with dense minefields and with deep trenches and dugouts dug into the rocky strata. Each mountain had been turned into a self-sufficient strong point, prepared for defense in all directions. Each mountain fortress had an antiaircraft weapon, and 82mm mortar and a heavy machinegun. According to intelligence reports, about 500 men, armed with automatic weapons and sniper rifles defended the region. The enemy correctly manned his defenses around the clock.

The Separate Air Assault Brigade[75] was commanded by LTC V. A. Raevskiy. He received orders to conduct a 120 kilometer road march with two reinforced airborne battalions, an artillery battalion and some of the specialized subunits of the brigade to Kabul. Once there, he refueled his equipment and rested his men before he conducted a 170 kilometer roadmarch from Kabul to Jalalabad. At Jalalabad, he moved his brigade into an assembly area and prepared for action.

The plan for destroying the enemy in the fortified region was as follows: Conduct a 32-kilometer road march in the early hours of 12 April and in the morning air assault two battalions close to the enemy strong points. The battalions would destroy the enemy security elements and then, exploiting success, would engage the reserve; capture the stores, strong points and firing positions; and then blow up the enemy fortifications.

The day before the operation, the brigade commander and his assistants diligently studied the map and aerial photographs of the

---

[74]N. G. Ten'kov served in the OKSVA as the Deputy Chief of the Operations Section of a Separate Brigade. He received the order "For Service to the Fatherland in the Armed Forces of the USSR" Third Class.

[75]The 56th Separate Air Assault Brigade stationed in Gardez (ed.).

objective, determined the more expedient flight path, determined the LZs and calculated the time necessary to carry out the mission. The troopers who would participate in the operation trained in air assaults, taking out sentries and capturing supply caches. During preparations, special attention was given to coordination and command and control.

In accordance with the plan, the brigade moved out on its road march at 2030 hours on 11 April under black-out drive conditions. Due to the heavily mined roads, the brigade arrived three hours late at the staging area. They immediately began to load the helicopters.

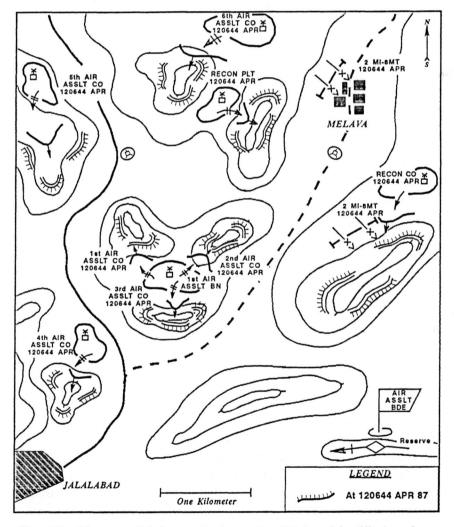

Map 26: Air assault brigade destroys the "Melava" fortified region.

Thanks to the skillful actions of the Deputy Brigade Commander, Colonel A. V. Maslov and the high level of training of the commanders of the 1st and 2nd Battalions (Captain A. V. Andreev and Major A. I. Samusev), the helicopters were ready for flight at the appointed time—0630 hours. Using nap-of-the-earth flying, the helicopter pilots flew undetected to the mountain side of the strongpoints and landed the force at 0644 hours on 12 April. Mi-24 helicopter gunships supported the insertion while artillery fire closed down the enemy firing points. Simultaneously, two pair of Mi-8 MT helicopters hit the DShK heavy machine gun and the guards' barracks.

The fight for the dominant heights lasted 17 minutes. Our force lost two KIA and three WIA, while the enemy, caught totally unawares, lost several dozen men. The next 24 hours were spent rooting out the survivors of the guerrilla forces. We captured a huge supply of arms and ammunition. The number of captured launch bombs alone surpassed 1,000.

FRUNZE COMMENTARY: The success of the operation was achieved by thorough preparation, a high state of training for the troopers and helicopter crews, and a penetrating analysis of the enemy situation. The qualitative study of the enemy and terrain led to a correct understanding of the situation, defined the probable enemy courses of action, and resulted in a superior combat plan for our forces. The successful actions of our units and subunits at night allowed us to seize the enemy mountain positions with minimal casualties. The mountains should have been the enemy's ally in battle. Instead, they were ours. Finally, the careful coordination and all-encompassing support of our combat allowed us to carry out the assigned task on time.

EDITOR'S COMMENTARY: The force failed to clear the roads ahead of time and was three hours late. This appears to be a failure to conduct proper reconnaissance. Throughout this chapter, units are getting lost and getting surprised. Helicopters are being shot down. No one appears to be looking into these areas before the main force arrives. Apparently, the Soviet Army did not always employ pathfinder-type units prior to air assaults. Perhaps it should have. Most of the difficulties encountered seem to be due to a failure to use reconnaissance forces properly.

Why did the force perform the night march to a field helicopter staging site anyway? Jalalabad has a perfectly good airfield. The 56th Separate Air Assault Brigade could have flown from Gardez to Jalalabad and then staged out of the Jalalabad airfield. Apparently, they could have flown the same nap-of-the-earth route and achieved the same surprise.

Soviet air assault tactics and techniques evolved rapidly in Afghanistan. The Soviets relied on helicopter maneuver to replace the mobility that they were unable to realize from their tanks and armored personnel carriers on Afghanistan's rugged terrain. Armored vehicles were restricted to the roads and valley floors. Soviet infantry were uninspired conscripts who were generally reluctant to close with the dedicated and motivated *mujahideen.* The Soviet advantage was found in the skies. The Soviet helicopter gunship was a very significant system in the war. Their Mi-24 HIND . was the most dreaded and effective weapons system employed against the *mujahideen* until 1988, when "Stinger" portable surface-to-air missiles limited their ability to range freely over resistance-controlled areas. The Soviet military would have liked to employ far more helicopters in Afghanistan, however, the lack of maintenance facilities, the increased logistics demand and the lack of secure operating bases prevented this. The Soviets were unwilling (or unable) to make a larger logistic and psychological commitment to the war.

CHAPTER 4:
DEFENSE AND OUTPOST SECURITY

The Soviet and Afghan government forces seldom went over to the defense in Afghanistan, so we have little defensive experience from the Afghanistan war. This was the result of several factors: there was no continuous front line; our assigned mission was to defeat the guerrilla forces; the nature of the *mujahideen* forces was to hit and run; and we enjoyed a qualitative and quantitative superiority in units, equipment and weaponry over the enemy. When we defended, most often it was subunits (platoons, companies and battalions) that went over to the defense.

But combat experience showed us that good, organized security actions were vital for protecting the day-to-day activities of entire regions, cities and our garrison base camps in Afghanistan. Effectively organized security yielded positive results in the battle with the *mujahideen* and helped in keeping convoys secure and in sweeping *mujahideen* from the areas around garrisons, airfields, electric power plants and transfer stations, mountain passes, tunnels and other important sites.

[76]The Soviets see a big difference between a defensive position and a security post. They defend when they are in immediate danger of being overwhelmed and when the correlation of forces is against them. A security outpost is a control measure which incorporates defensive measures as combat multipliers (ed.).

A motorized rifle platoon
defends outside Jurm village
by Major S. V. Milyuk[77]

In August 1980, a large guerrilla force was gathering in the area near Baharak village. Baharak village is located near Faizabad in Badakhshan province. A separate motorized rifle regiment was garrisoned in Faizabad and in the surrounding area. The regiment's subunits provided stability and control in the province. Due to the large area the regiment had to control, it was split into two bases—one in the fortified village of Baharak (60 kilometers from Faizabad) and the rest in outskirts of Faizabad. The regiment's tank battalion stayed behind in the Soviet Union.[78]

The regimental commander decided to destroy the enemy in the hills surrounding Faizabad and then move on the village of Jurm, surround it and then destroy the guerrilla forces which were gathering there. In order to support the timely entry of the regiment into the combat zone, my platoon was sent to fix several sections of road and a bridge over the Kokcha River which had been destroyed. [My entire platoon was not available for the mission, since all my dismounted motorized rifle soldiers were taken for other duties.] I was left with my three BMPs and their crews. I was reinforced with 20 Afghan soldiers on two trucks and a bulldozer. In preparing for this mission, I paid particular attention to the maintenance of my vehicles and their armaments. I loaded 72-hours worth of supplies on these vehicles.

On 3 August, I guided my rag-tag force into the area located two or two and one/half kilometers west of Jurm where the destroyed bridge stood. A quick scan of the countryside revealed that the enemy had constructed a well-prepared defense on the probable

---

[77]S. V. Milyuk served in the OKSVA from January 1980 through June 1981 as a platoon leader. He was awarded the medal "For Excellence in Military Service" First Class.

[78]The 860th Separate Motorized Rifle Regiment was garrisoned in Faizabad. Its 1st Battalion was garrisoned in Khamrabad (Baharak) and, later, its 3rd Battalion was garrisoned in Kishim. The action takes place in the 1st Battalion area (ed.).

approaches to the village. I decided to establish a perimeter defense and ordered the force to begin digging-in the vehicles and individual fighting positions. I used the bulldozer to help in this effort. But the bulldozer operators and the local inhabitants who were employed in repairing the road [and bridge] categorically refused to stay with me overnight and returned to Baharak village.

We dug our individual and vehicle fighting positions within four hours and I dispersed the Afghan soldiers between the BMPs. Our fighting positions were circular and looked like wells. This design permitted firing throughout 360 degrees and also provided a place

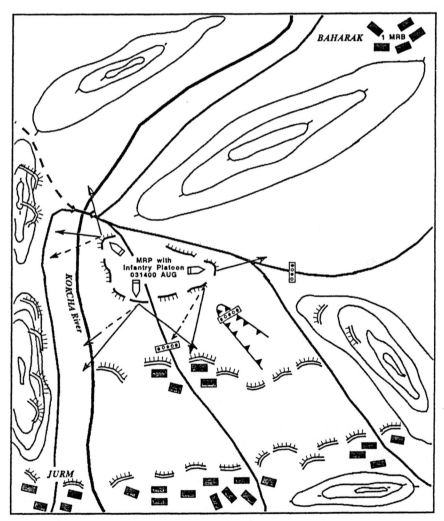

Map 27: A motorized rifle platoon defends outside Jurm village.

for the soldiers to rest. We reinforced the breastworks with stones and clay.

My BMP crews had been in battle before and, therefore, when the enemy began to shell our positions at dusk, they knew how to conduct night fire and were prepared to do so. My drivers started up their tracks at the right time and helped my gunners.[79] My vehicle commanders stood outside the tracks and adjusted fire from the strike of the tracer rounds. They talked to the gunners on the intercom by linking the issue 10-meter extension cables to their tanker's helmets and the intercom sets. They talked by toggling on the helmet's breast-level switch. The attacking enemy finally withdrew at sunrise, but had not given up his intention to overrun my position. He proved this on the following night when he resumed his shelling.

The time which we were able to gain gave me the opportunity to give detailed orders to my subordinates and arrange coordination. During the daylight, we put out mines and trip flares[80] on the approaches to our position and also worked on repairing the road and bridge.

The enemy employed various ruses against our defense. For example, on the next day Private Tagirov noticed that a small group of men, disguised as local natives, was crossing the bridge carrying some kind of material on donkeys. He saw that a thin stream of some kind of liquid was spilling out from one of the packs onto the wooden bridge. We investigated and found that the liquid was gasoline. We washed part of it off with water and covered the area with sand. That night, the enemy fired many tracer rounds at the bridge, but were unable to set it on fire.

---

[79]When in use, the electrically-powered turret of the BMP rapidly drains energy from the vehicle. Therefore, during alerts and combat, the BMP engine must be kept running in order to keep the battery charged and provide adequate voltage to the turret (ed.).

[80]Soviet trip flares are not merely ground flares which illuminate the area. Soviet trip flares contain multiple green, yellow and red rockets which fire into the air and produce a whistling sound. These trip flares (more precisely signal mines–signal 'nye miny) draw the sleepiest sentry's attention with repeated lights and sounds (ed.).

FRUNZE COMMENTARY: The proper organization of the security force and the timely undertaking of necessary measures allowed a motorized rifle platoon to successfully defeat the *mujahideen* attack.

EDITOR'S COMMENTARY: Bridge and road repair is a mission that western armies would normally give to an engineer unit. Here, a motorized rifle platoon leader is put in charge of some Afghan troops and civilians and is expected to accomplish this mission. He apparently does so.

Usually, in a defense, the *bronegruppa* serves a mobile reserve, capable of rushing to a threatened sector. Here, the *bronegruppa* is the basis of the defense.

In this vignette, the platoon leader does not incorporate high ground into his defense, but leaves a significant piece of high ground immediately outside his perimeter. He may have done so because he could not position his vehicles onto that ground or, when there, his vehicles would not have been able to support each other. Still, it is remarkable that he apparently did not even put a security post or observation post on the dominant terrain.

Organizing a security outpost
in the suburbs of Kabul
by Major S. V. Mos'kin[81]

At the end of May 1982, enemy diversionary/reconnaissance groups conducted actions against Soviet Army base camps. In particular, they fired directly on the 40th Army headquarters. The leadership of the guerrilla forces announced that they would destroy the headquarters in the near future. Therefore, the high command decided to upgrade the defense and security of the army headquarters.

As a result, Major Avramenko, my battalion commander, decided to establish a new security post which would be manned by my motorized rifle platoon which had three BTR-70s and 28 men.[82] My platoon was reinforced with two AGS-17s and three PK machine guns with night sights. We also received some night vision devices for night observation. An engineer excavator came to the site and within 72 hours, dug the primary and reserve fighting positions for my BTRs and men and then connected all the positions with deep fighting trenches. We dug secret forward redoubts on the flanks of the security outpost for our machine gun crews.

We also built an observation post for a long-range field of vision over our area. We established visual communications between the secret dugouts and the observation post to assist in coordinating fires. We built two barbed wire fences all around the security perimeter. Between the two rows of barbed wire fence, we put in an antipersonnel minefield (using both pressure and tension-release mines). On the far side of the wire, we laid in trip flares. A land-line was installed to give us telephone communications with the battalion commander, a neighboring tank platoon and the duty officer at army headquarters. I organized my post to have two-thirds of my men manning their posts at night and one third during the day. Every soldier had

---

[81]S. V. Mos'kin served in the OKSVA from September 1980 through November 1982 as a platoon leader.

[82]The 2nd Platoon, 2nd Company, 1st Motorized Rifle Battalion, 180th Motorized Rifle Regiment of the 108th Motorized Rifle Division. The 1st and 2nd Battalions were mounted on BTRs while the 3rd Battalion was mounted on BMPs (ed.).

his combat crew assignment and instructions in case of an alert.

In September 1982, we intercepted an attempt by an enemy reconnaissance/diversionary group to penetrate to the army headquarters. The *mujahideen* preceded this provocation by shelling our positions with mortars and launch bombs. On the day before the attempt, they did a reconnaissance of our obstacles by driving a large flock of sheep into our mine field.

And on the next night, the *mujahideen* attempted to penetrate to the army headquarters using a dry river bed and irrigation canal. We killed two of these who wandered into our mines. We recovered

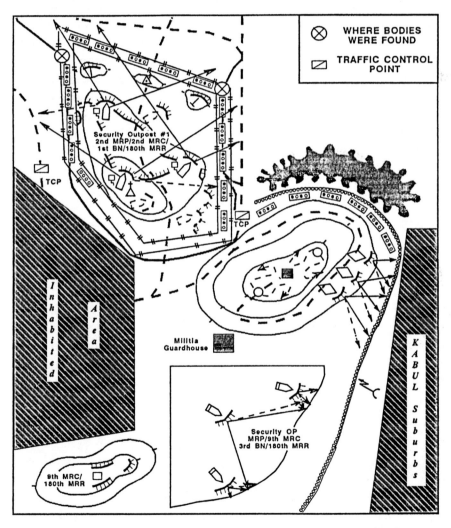

Map 28: Layout of a security outpost in the Kabul suburbs.

weapons and documents from their bodies.

FRUNZE COMMENTARY: Following repeated, unsuccessful *mujahideen* attempts on the army headquarters, future attempts by their reconnaissance/diversionary groups were thwarted by thorough, well-thought out measures to protect the army headquarters including the establishment of a new security outpost on the enemy approach route.

EDITOR'S COMMENTARY: Due to the preeminence of the offense in Soviet military training, the Soviets rarely trained for the defense.   There seems to be a hunker-down-and-wait mentality in their defenses, whereas one would expect to see patrols, moving ambushes, mechanical ambushes, and aggressive reconnaissance. This is particularly true at night.   The only night patrols done in this vignette are done by the Afghan police.   After a unit has gone to ground so thoroughly, it is hard to imagine putting it into an aggressive action without some serious readjustments and retraining.   The unit seems to have bunker mentality.

Repelling a raid on a security post
by Major I. A. Egiazarov[83]

During the second half of June 1982, the high command decided to strengthen and expand Afghan government power around the city of Rukha in the Panjsher valley. They decided to do this during the course of an operation in the Panjsher valley which involved Afghan government forces and a SPETSNAZ detachment. The Afghan Army had a series of security outposts on the dominant heights surrounding Rukha. These posts were poorly fortified, there were not enough soldiers and heavy weapons to hold them and the Afghan soldiers' morale was low. The high command decided to reinforce the existing posts and to add additional outposts by assigning men from a SPETSNAZ detachment to man them.[84]

Thus on the 13th of June, I received orders to take my 31st SPETSNAZ Group and occupy the heights opposite the rest of the force across the Panjsher River.[85] I was a lieutenant at the time. My commander wanted me to establish an observation post and look for *mujahideen* activity in the area of the hamlet of Marishtan. This would also deny the enemy the opportunity to conduct his own reconnaissance and launch a surprise attack on our battalion.

There were 15 men in my 31st SPETSNAZ Reconnaissance Group. Besides small arms, we had two AGS-17 automatic grenade launchers, one DShK heavy machine gun and one 82mm "tray" mortar. We were supported by an artillery battery [that belonged to the SPETSNAZ detachment]. We expected enemy action in the region on 15 or 16 July, and that action might include an assault on the security outposts.

---

[83]I. A. Egiazarov served in the OKSVA from 1982 through 1984 as the commander of a SPETSNAZ group. He was awarded the medal "For Military Merit."

[84]A SPETSNAZ detachment is equivalent to a battalion command, although its personnel strength was less than 100. They are sometimes called SPETSNAZ companies. SPETSNAZ groups were equivalent to company commands, but had a personnel strength of 15-16 men or less. Some were four-man groups. They were sometimes called SPETSNAZ platoons (ed.).

[85]The 31st SPETSNAZ Group of the 177th SPETSNAZ Detachment (ed.).

We occupied our assigned peak on 15 July and began fortifying the position. This was our order of work. First, prepare firing positions and establish an integrated, comprehensive firing plan. Second, fortify the positions with local materials to blend in with the natural terrain and build covered shelters for the troops. Third, build tiered observation posts out of stone and clay. Fourth, mine the approaches to the post. Fifth, on a nearby terrace, build a hidden, tanglefoot obstacle.[86] Sixth, organize an uninterrupted schedule of observation and security. Three men were always on guard during the day and seven men were always on guard at night. The detachment resup-

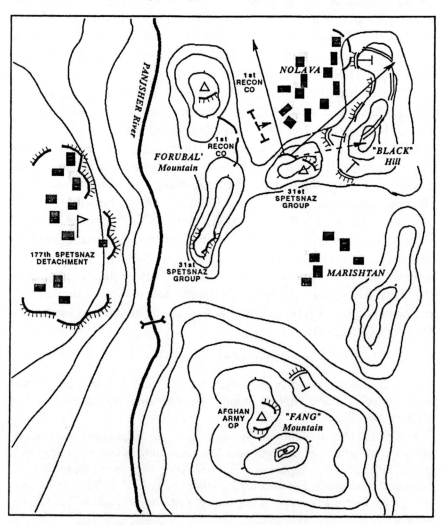

Map 29: Repelling a raid on a security outpost.

plied us with ammunition and food every three days.

About 1830 hours on 18 July, we were eating dinner and observation was lax. [Probably my lookouts had also decided to eat without my authorization]. During this time of relaxed vigilance, the enemy snuck onto our high terrace, climbed to within 10 meters of our defensive position and simultaneously opened fire with three DShK heavy machine guns from "Black hill" and "Fang mountain". My men, with the exception of two look-outs, dove behind the walls and in the dugouts for shelter. The guerrillas had resolutely seized the initiative and pushed their attack forward, throwing grenades as they came. The *mujahideen* having climbed onto our high terrace, ran toward our defenses, but were caught in our tanglefoot. This broke their attack and we were able to destroy them with fire from our dugouts. The enemy left four corpses on the terrace. The rest withdrew under the cover of DShK fire. We had no casualties.

EDITOR'S COMMENT: Even, and sometimes especially, in elite forces, the commander must stay on top of his personnel and ensure that they maintain vigilance and perform other routine soldiers' duties. Soldiers' carelessness almost led to the destruction of this OP.

This vignette indicates that an artillery battery may have been part of a SPETSNAZ detachment. In this particular vignette, the detachment was operating within MRLS range, since part of the artillery plan is for MRLS.

The Soviet tanglefoot obstacle appears to be a most effective obstacle. It has not been adopted by western armies. Perhaps these armies ought to consider doing so.

---

[86]This Soviet tanglefoot obstacle is different than that used in western armies. It is a large, compressed, banded spring made of high-quality wire. It is similar to an uncontrolled "Slinky" toy. When unbanded during set up, it uncoils wildly in every direction. It will stop dismounted soldiers, animals, vehicles and even tanks. It is almost impossible to extricate anything from this without heavy-duty wire cutters, pliers and lots of time. These obstacles are called MZP (malozametnye prepyatstviya) or concealed obstacles (ed.).

A mobile security patrol in combat
near the village of Chandaran
by LTC F. V. Zhitoryuk[87]

In April 1985, the 1st Motorized Battalion, which I commanded, was detailed to perform guard and security duties within my regiment's 65-kilometer stretch of the Termez-Kabul highway. I was reinforced with a tank company and an artillery battery. My mission was to secure the unimpeded movement of Soviet and Afghan convoys in my area of responsibility and to prevent the demolition of the pipeline, bridges and sections of highway.

My regimental commander[88] constituted 14 mobile security patrols and 23 security posts for the mission. A reinforced motorized rifle platoon usually functions as a mobile security patrol. A motorized rifle company usually constitutes two-or-three mobile security patrols and five-or-six security posts. I designated my share of the patrols and posts and constituted a reserve in case I suddenly had to do battle with the *mujahideen.*

Mobile security patrol #31 was my largest mobile security patrol since I had integrated my CP/OP in that grouping. The patrol had 193 men including my battalion command group, a signal platoon, the 1st firing platoon of my mortar battery, a tank company (minus one platoon), the artillery battery (minus a firing platoon), and the battalion's recon platoon.

A guerrilla force of about 500 men operated in my battalion's area of responsibility. They were armed with 82mm mortars, recoilless rifles, heavy machine guns, launch bombs and many small arms.

From 16 to 21 April, our division participated in an operation to destroy guerrilla forces in this region. After the operation, the participating units and subunits returned to their base camps. Guerrilla activity quickly picked up. Agent reconnaissance reported that a wounded miner [i.e. one who emplaces land mines] was located in Chandaran village. This miner had been trained by foreign services. Two renegade Russian soldiers who had gone over to the *mujahideen* in 1981 and 1983 were guarding the miner.

---

[87]F. V. Zhitoryuk served in the OKSVA in 1985 as a battalion commander.
[88]Most likely the 177th MRR of the 108th MRD (ed.).

I decided to seal off the village on the night of 22-23 April and destroy the enemy. I assembled my recon platoon, the 1st platoon of my 3rd MRC, and a force from a battalion of Afghan "Sarandoy" for the mission. The group consisted of 73 men, four tanks, eight BTRs, and two "*Vasilek*" automatic mortars. We were supported by the artillery battery.

At 0100 hours on 23 April, two groups of five men each set out along the pipeline. They were disguised to look like pipeline work-ers and carried pipeline equipment as they walked and checked the

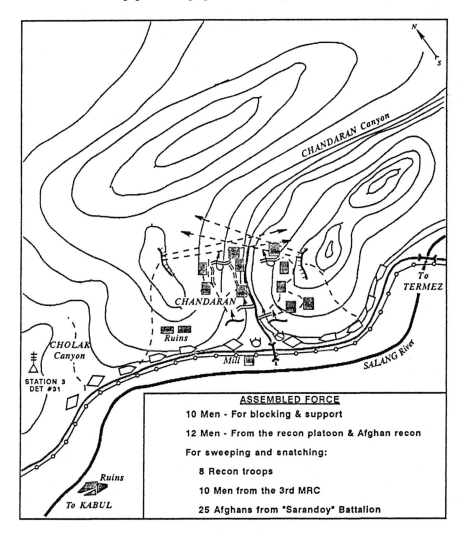

Map 30: Blocking and sweeping Chandaran village.

pipeline and worked their way into the target area. Under the cover of night, they crept into place and took up firing positions. At 0400 hours, mobile security patrol #31 quickly moved through the fog cover to Chandaran. They blocked the canyon mouth and entrance to the village, dismounted, formed a line and began to sweep the village.

Precise coordination between the Soviet subunits and the Afghan armed police allowed the battle to precede with minimum casualties. We killed three *mujahideen* and captured 16. Among the prisoners were the bodyguards of Said Mansoor, an important guerrilla ringleader in the northern provinces, and the wounded miner. We found out later that the *mujahideen* were resting in the village and because of the sudden and unconventional nature of our subunits actions, they were unable to offer any resistance.

EDITOR'S COMMENTARY: This was a heavy force to go after a minelayer and his renegade guards. Probably the main impetus for the mission was to capture or kill the renegades. It is interesting that their fate is not mentioned.

A mobile security patrol destroys a guerrilla force in Khinjan Canyon
by LTC F. V. Zhitoryuk[89]

One of the more characteristic actions of a mobile security patrol is illustrated by the destruction of the Naima guerrilla force. This force had 15 men armed with two RPG-2 antitank grenade launchers, a DShK heavy machine gun, a sniper rifle and several AKM assault rifles.

On 12 March 1986, my battalion was pulling security duty when I received a report that a BRDM belonging to the local "Sarandoy" battalion was firing in the Khinjan canyon. This was not far from where my mobile security patrol #32 was working. I ordered my 2nd MRC commander, Captain V. P. Yusov, to take the reserve (eight soldiers on two BTRs) and move on the enemy. Forty minutes later, Captain Yusov reported that the enemy was indeed doing battle in Khinjan canyon and was firing small arms and grenade launchers.

My reconnaissance platoon was on alert and I had them road march on their vehicles to the combat site. My plan was to have Captain Yusov and the reserve block the *mujahideen* in the canyon, while my recon platoon would split into two groups and skirt the canyon on two sides to hit the enemy in the rear and destroy him when he tried to withdraw. This plan required a thorough knowledge of the local terrain, the availability of two Mi-8 helicopters (which were in the area) to fly over the battle and report on the composition and location of the enemy, and the availability of the necessary combat power to block and destroy the *mujahideen.*

Twenty to twenty-five minutes after the pursuit began, Major A. G. Kravets, my political deputy, reported that we had overtaken the enemy and joined battle. As a result we killed 13 men and captured two. Additionally, we captured two grenade launchers, one machine gun, eight assault rifles, and two rifles.

---

[89]F. V. Zhitoryuk served in the OKSVA in 1985 as a battalion commander. [This is the same author of the last vignette.) (ed.)].

FRUNZE COMMENTARY: This example shows that decisive, unconventional action, a good knowledge of the terrain, and the correct organization of reconnaissance will lead to success.

EDITOR'S COMMENTARY: The last two vignettes show positive, aggressive action on the part of a battalion commander as he finds, fixes and finishes his enemy. These are classic examples of how to do it right. The Soviets seem to have enjoyed some success when cobbling together a mixed force at the spur of the moment and

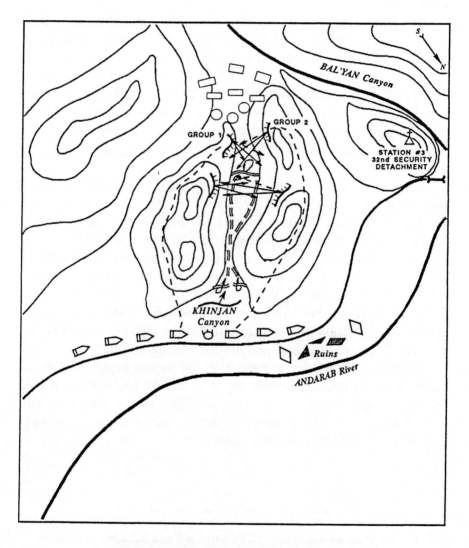

Map 31: Destruction of the Naima force.

then making it work. This shows a great deal of tactical flexibility on the part of the Soviet battalion commanders to even attempt such solutions. The cynic might say that it shows what a Soviet commander can really accomplish when the generals are absent.

The road security elements seemed to do a lot of moving and were a lot more aggressive than their counterparts in the stationary outposts. Apparently, the commander should rotate his mobile and stationary elements frequently in order to maintain an aggressive attitude.

Repelling a *mujahideen* attack on a security detachment in the Panjsher Valley

by LTC V. G. Serebryakov[90]

In August 1986, my battalion was assigned road security duty in the Panjsher Valley. To accomplish this mission, I broke my battalion down into mobile security patrols and security posts and distributed them along the route. One of the mobile security patrols was commanded by Lieutenant Yu. B. Tyubekin. He put his force in a perimeter defense, dug it in and fortified it to the extent that his resources allowed, laid in an interlocking and coordinated fire plan, and laid mines on the near and far approaches to Post #13. In all, he had 13 men in the mobile security patrol.

The *mujahideen* knew that the mobile security patrol consisted only of a small group of draftees and attempted to overrun the position. At 1715 hours on 4 August, they began shelling the detachment. The *mujahideen* fire knocked out an 82mm mortar, a 12.7mm "*Cliff*" heavy machine gun, and an AGS-17 automatic grenade launcher. Sniper fire from the surrounding heights pinned down the force and made it difficult to move personnel from one sector to another. Capitalizing on the reduced fire from our patrol, the *mujahideen* were able to move a recoilless rifle up to a position to blow a path through the minefield. [Minefield not shown on map.]

The enemy moved within hand grenade range. A howitzer battery commanded by Captain S. A. Ivanov, plus a platoon of self-propelled howitzers, had been firing in support of the detachment. Now, however the fog and twilight restricted observation and their supporting fire became much less effective. One of my company commanders, Captain Lavrent'ev, was bringing up the reserve of four BMP-2s, when Lieutenant Tyubekin called in fire on his own position. We fired air bursts on the post killing 23 *mujahideen* and wounded approximately 30 others. They withdrew. The security detachment lost its leader and six soldiers were wounded.

---

[90]V. G. Serebryakov served in the OKSVA from May 1986 through June 1988 as an airborne battalion commander. He was awarded the "Order of the Red Banner", the "Order of the Red Star", and the Afghan "Order of the Red Banner".

FRUNZE COMMENTARY: Only the act of calling artillery fire on his own position, permitted the lieutenant to save the mobile security patrol.

EDITOR'S COMMENTARY: Apparently, the mobile security patrol lost its BMPs (and mobility) to a *bronegruppa* when they occupied the defensive position for a night lager. There were no armored vehicles incorporated in the defense. The force became a stationary security post. The soldiers had to shelter in open-topped foxholes when the artillery hit their position.

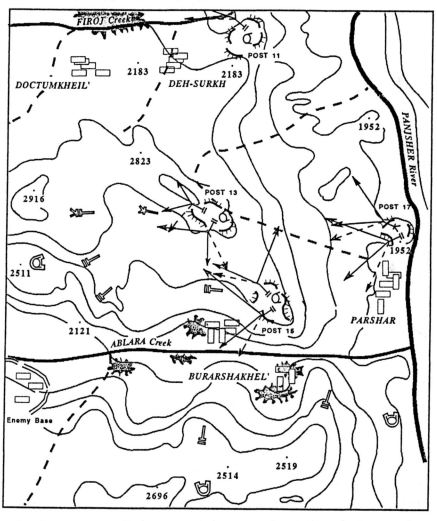

Map 32: Lieutenant Tyubekin's last battle.

Securing a base camp
by LTC A. Yunakov[91]

My battalion was part of a separate brigade based in Kandahar and Helmand provinces.[92] The brigade had three motorized rifle battalions, an air assault battalion, a signal company, a radio-electronic warfare company, an artillery battalion, a helicopter squadron and a brigade headquarters. The battalion's mission was three-fold: first, to provide security to a base camp near Lashkargah in Helmand Province, second, to escort convoys two-or-three times a week along an 80-kilometer stretch of road, and finally to fight guerrilla forces in the immediate vicinity. My battalion was reinforced with a battery of D-30 122mm howitzers and two tank platoons. A 12-kilometer perimeter encompassed our base camp. I had seven fighting positions spaced around the perimeter. Each position was occupied by one or two motorized rifle platoons. When providing convoy security, I usually dispatched one or two motorized rifle platoons with one or two 82mm mortars. When fighting guerrillas, I usually dispatched a motorized rifle company, with the artillery battery, reconnaissance platoon, and two mortar platoons.

The guerrillas began firing launch bombs at my base camp shortly after we created a security zone. These attacks were launched from the green zone along the Helmand river. In early 1987, we conducted an operation, in conjunction with the Afghan Army to clean out the guerrilla forces from Lashkargah and to establish observation posts in the green zone for a Sarandoy battalion. After the operation, we established another security outpost in the Qala-Bust fort in order to control the green zone adjacent to the observation posts. We gar-

---

[91]This and the following vignette are not part of the Frunze book. They are extracts from P. Alexseev's "Okhranenie" [Security], *Voyenny vestnik* [Military herald], April 1994, p. 42-46. Colonel Alexseev is on the faculty of the Frunze Department of the History of Military Art. He apparently used LTC Yunakov's report that was in the Frunze Afghanistan archives. Although both examples lack the element of combat, they show how base camp and LOC security were organized (ed.).

[92]Probably the 5th Motorized Rifle Battalion, 70th Separate Motorized Rifle Brigade. The article (which is riddled with typographical errors) says the 2nd Battalion, but this is unlikely (ed.).

risoned this outpost with another Sarandoy battalion. We maintained close coordination with the Sarandoy through a liaison officer.

In order to protect my men from mortar and light machine-gun fire, I paid a lot of attention to digging in and fortifying the positions. Every squad was completely dug in. Every firing position was linked to it's platoon positions by communications trenches. Each fighting position had a dug-in sleeping quarters (where possible), ammunition point, platoon command post, dining room, water point, wash room and latrine. In order to improve observation, I established forward security posts which consisted of a BTR machine-gunner, a driver

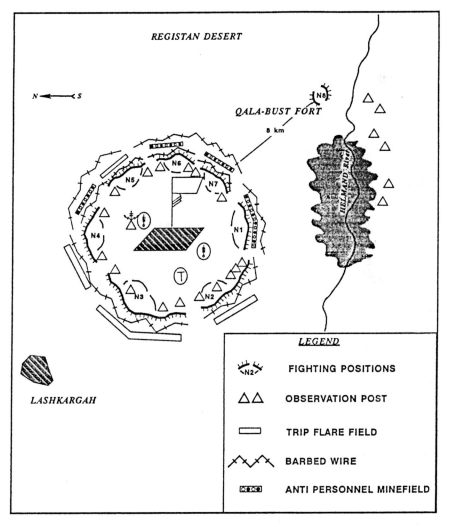

Map 33: Base camp defense.

and a rifleman. These were placed in position at 1800 hours following the issuance of the combat order and challenge and password. They were checked every two hours and changed every four hours by the platoon leader or his assistant. During the night, these posts were only allowed to fire on semiautomatic as a warning or probe. If they fired a burst on full automatic, the entire force would occupy its fighting positions. Artillery fired scheduled harassing and interdicting fires and had fires planned throughout the area. We were also able to open fire without warning when a target appeared in my AOR at night. At daybreak, I pulled all my forward posts back and fired on any person, convoy or caravan that we discovered in the Registan Desert within four kilometers of my camp. None of my personnel was allowed to withdraw from a fighting position.

Every six months, the battalion commander ordered rotation of subunits. The rotation occurred during daylight. Subunits coming off base camp defense were assigned to convoy security duties. In preparation for these duties, we trained the subunits in procedures for clearing roads of mines, checking and clearing bridges, defeating enemy attacks and evacuating vehicles under fire.

EDITOR'S COMMENTARY: The 70th Separate Motorized Rifle Brigade was headquartered in Kandahar, while this schematic shows a brigade headquarters in the Lashkargah base camp—some 150 kilometers away. Despite the text, this headquarters is that of one of two Soviet SPETSNAZ brigades. The brigade also had a battalion and supporting elements in Lashkargah. The sketch shows the brigade headquarters, three battalion headquarters, two artillery batteries, a helipad and a radio-electronic warfare company in the base camp. The motorized rifle battalion provided security for the SPETSNAZ elements. The area of this base camp is only a little over 11 square kilometers. This must have been very cramped and a tempting target for *mujahideen* gunners.

LOC Security
by LTC M. Tubeev

The first priority of *mujahideen* commanders was to disrupt the movement of convoys travelling on the main roads of Afghanistan. Motorized rifle subunits were usually responsible for route security. Normally, a motorized rifle battalion would be responsible for a 40- to 150-kilometer stretch of road, whereas a company would cover from two- to 10-kilometers. In February 1986, my 3rd Motorized Rifle Battalion, reinforced with a tank company and two artillery batteries, was responsible for the security of a 102-kilometer stretch of road along the Puli-Charkhi to Jalabad highway as well as the security of the Naghlu power dam site.[93] I could field 11 tanks, 42 BMPs, twelve self-propelled howitzers, 27 82mm mortars, nine twin-barrelled anti-aircraft guns[94], and 23 AGS-17 automatic grenade launchers. I decided to split the area into three sections. My 7th MRC had a 32-kilometer section, my 8th MRC had a 40-kilometer section and my 9th MRC had a 30-kilometer section. I determined the length of each section after considering the terrain, key sites, enemy activity and the line strength of my subunits. I considered several solutions, before I selected the one which seemed to best concentrate combat power in critical sectors.

My LOC security was based on a series of security outposts running the length of the road. An outpost was usually occupied by a motorized rifle platoon, one or two AGS-17 automatic grenade launchers, one or two heavy "*Utes*" or DShK machine guns, one or two 82mm mortars and a tank. These could be combined into a security detachment (a motorized rifle company or battalion reinforced with artillery, tanks, and engineers).

The security outposts functioned around the clock. During the day, one man per squad or tank was on watch while a two-man patrol worked the area. At night, every security outpost would send out one or two security points. These four-man points were located 500 to 800 meters from the security outpost and had wire and visual com-

---

[93]The 3rd Battalion of either the 180th or 181st Motorized Rifle Regiments, 108th Motorized Rifle Division (ed.).

[94]The ZSU-23-2. These 23mm machine guns could fire 2,000 rounds per minute and could be mounted on a truck bed or BTR (ed.).

munications with the outpost. The outpost could cover the point with fire.

Each security outpost had a full perimeter defense in order to defeat a *mujahideen* attack from any direction. Each platoon had a primary and alternate sectors of fire with interlocking fields of fire with adjacent units. Crew-served weapons had reserve positions and reserve sectors of fire. Artillery fire planning was carefully done. Artillery subunits were usually collocated in the security outposts with the motorized rifle subunits. The artillery was positioned in order to effectively support all the security outposts. Artillery fires

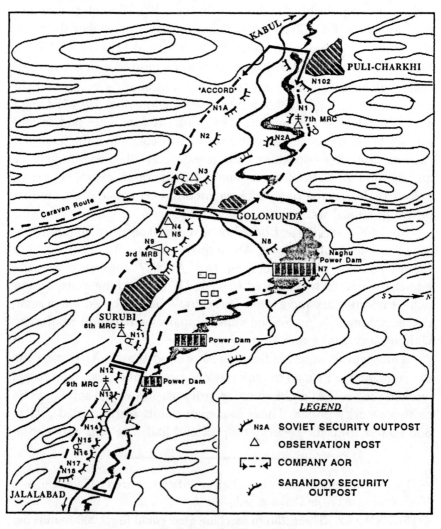

Map 34: LOC security

were planned on all likely axes on which the *mujahideen* could move. Targets were registered and numbered. The targets, and their coordinates were maintained by the security outposts, artillery guns crews and by the battalion headquarters. Fires could be adjusted from pre-planned targets by the security outpost commander or, if he could not communicate directly with the artillery subunit, through the battalion commander. Normally, it took not more than two-to-four minutes to bring artillery fire onto a group of *mujahideen.*

We selected the position for the outposts carefully and fortified them thoroughly. We piled up earth and stones to make complete trenchworks, bunkers, and ammunition, food and water points. We ran two rows of barbed wire fence around each outpost and put antipersonnel mines between the fences. We put trip flares and sensors at remote and concealed approaches to the outposts. The entrance and exit to the security outposts were closed and mined at night. Rules of conduct were posted at the perimeter of the security zone and outside the security outposts. The signs were in the Afghan, Russian and English languages.[95]

Every security outpost had five combat loads of ammunition[96], and 10 days worth of food, water and fuel. Night-vision devices, "Blik" binoculars, night scopes, parachute flares and tracer ammunition were available for night-time employment.

Each security outpost maintained the following documents and maps:

- the combat mission of the outpost and the sequence of mission fulfillment:
- the commander's map marked with positions, fire plans and known enemy situation;
- a diagram of the strongpoint;
- orders from the battalion commander;
- combat orders of the security outpost commander;

---

[95]There is no single Afghan language. Pushtu and Dari are the official languages, while Tadjik, Uzbek, Kirghiz, Baluchi, Turkmen, and Arabic are also spoken (ed.).

[96]The combat load [boekomplekt] is a logistic planning term which differs from the U.S. "basic load". Five combat loads is a significant amount—probably enough for six good fights (ed.).

- an observation schedule;
- a patrol schedule;
- a duty weapon schedule and sectors of fire[97];
- signal tables;
- observer's journals, combat journals and journals of enemy activities.

The battalion produces the security plan which shows the number and composition of each security outpost, the quantity of vehicles, weapons and ammunition at each security outpost, the security belt at each outpost, the defensive plan for key sites, the coordination measures between elements, the defensive fire plan, the signal plan for communication between garrisons, convoys, dispatch posts and the fire support elements. In addition, the battalion had a shift schedule for its subunits and also the battalion commander's order for organization of the security zone. Subunits had their TO&E equipment plus additional radios, telephones and cable communication gear for command and control.

Radio is the primary mean of communications in LOC security. All armored vehicles, TO&E and attached subunits and passing convoys monitor a common channel. The battalion reconnaissance platoon is located close to the battalion command post. It's function is to cut off and destroy any groups of *mujahideen* in the battalion AOR. They usually do this by setting up ambushes on sites where *mujahideen* could approach the highway. Their ambush site is coordinated with the regiment's ambush plan and usually lasts one night. There have been times, however, when the ambush party has stayed on site for three days.

EDITOR'S COMMENTARY: The Soviet concept of LOC security appears to have been to establish a series of fortified positions, man them and then sit back and wait. This is a very passive, reactive posture. There is no aggressive patrolling or reconnaissance. Again,

---

[97]Duty weapons were manned, crew-served weapons in temporary positions. Only these weapons would engage enemy reconnaissance or probing elements while the rest of the force moved to battle positions. The duty weapons would then move to battle positions. Enemy return fire would be on the temporary position and the enemy knowledge of the locations of defending Soviet crew-served weapons would be faulty (ed.).

the Soviets used their reconnaissance force as a primary combat force and not for gathering intelligence. There seems to be no attempt to shift forces, occupy temporary sites and take actions to deceive or "wrong-foot" the enemy. The *mujahideen* could easily collect against this scheme and take appropriate actions to avoid or overcome it.

CHAPTER 5:
MARCH AND CONVOY ESCORT

Side by side with the mission of destroying guerrilla forces, the Soviet forces had a mission of delivering cargo and escorting convoys. Analysis of enemy tactics shows that during the first years of the war, the enemy hit convoys mainly by mining isolated stretches of road. During the later years of the war, the enemy became far more focused on the convoys and used special diversionary groups to attack the convoys physically .

The enemy's attacks on the convoys were characterized by: a maximum effort to achieve surprise; a skillful selection of ambush sites; well-prepared, excellently fortified and masterfully concealed ambush positions; a well-prepared route of withdrawal; a process for mining the roads which included the shoulders and detour routes; and the simultaneous destruction of equipment in several locations of the convoy to prevent maneuver and the movement of the convoy out of the kill zone.

Escorting a truck convoy from Kabul to Gazni
by Major V. I. Rovba[98]

At the end of 1981, guerrilla forces were very active in the province of Gazni. Especially bitter combat was fought along the Ghazni-Kabul and Ghazni-Kandahar highways. The enemy paid special attention to mining the roads where convoys would pass.

The 9th MRC was stationed six kilometers west of Ghazni with our parent regiment.[99] On 5 September, our company commander was ordered to provide an escort on the next day for an 80-vehicle convoy from Ghazni to Kabul. On 7 September, we would offload the cargo and would return on 8 September. Two motorized rifle platoons were detailed to provide security and convoy escort. The company commander would command the detail on an R-142 radio set from the regimental communications company.[100] The route is 160 kilometers long.

The only preparation that the troops had for the mission was drawing their ammunition and cleaning their individual and crew-served weapons. The drivers pulled maintenance on their vehicles by themselves.

My company commander decided to keep the convoy together in one single column. He put a BTR in the lead of the convoy and two at the tail. He spaced the remaining BTRs between every 15 or 16 trucks in the convoy. Altogether, he committed seven BTRs to the mission. In the event that the *mujahideen* would attack a motorized rifle squad, each squad's BTR would pull over to the side of the road from which the enemy was firing and return fire with all its weapons. Thus, it would provide covering fire for the trucks driving out of the kill zone. Once the convoy was clear, the BTRs would rejoin the column and reoccupy their positions in the march column. Under no

---

[98]V. I. Rovba served in the OKSVA from 1981 to 1983 as the platoon leader of a motorized rifle platoon. He was awarded the medal "For Bravery".

[99]The 9th MRC, 3rd Battalion, 191st Separate Motorized Rifle Regiment (ed.).

[100]The R-142 radio system is actually an R-130 shortwave radio, two R-111 medium-range FM radios and one R-123 short-range FM radio mounted on a GAZ-66 truck. The R-142 can communicate over distance and with helicopter aviation (ed.).

circumstances were we to allow the enemy to stop the column.   It would be very difficult to get the convoy going again should it be stopped.

The road march to Kabul passed without incident.   However, there was a delay in refilling the fuel trucks that constituted the bulk of the convoy back to Ghazni.   The return trip was supposed to start at 0600 hours and finally got started at 1030 hours.   We had sat on the outskirts of Kabul for four hours waiting for all of the fuel trucks. While we were waiting, individual Afghan trucks loaded with men and cargo continually passed by the entire convoy.

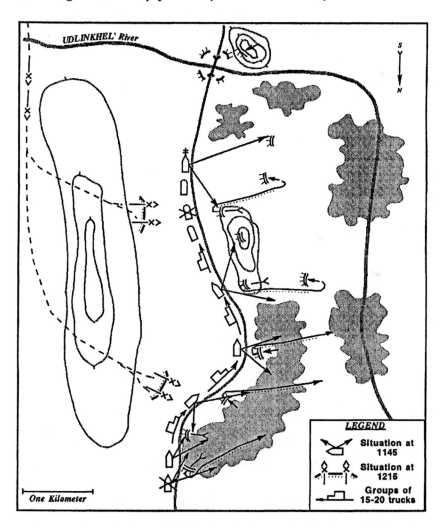

Map 35: Defeating an enemy attack on a convoy.

When the loaded fuel tankers finally arrived, they took their place in the convoy. The commander gave the order and the march began. After driving for an hour and a half, we entered the minor Kabul-river canyon and traveled through a green zone. Three kilometers ahead of us was an Afghan Army post which guarded a river bridge. The presence of this post had a certain psychological effect and we relaxed our vigilance as we approached the post. The company commander's BTR and the truck with the R-142 radio set traveled at the front of the column. Right behind them was a fuel truck towing a broken-down fuel truck. Once the entire convoy was flanked by the green zone, the enemy opened fire on the lead vehicles with grenade launchers at a range of 25-to-30 meters. The fuel truck towing the other fuel truck was hit. Simultaneously, the enemy opened fire on the tail end of the convoy and knocked out a trail BTR with a RPG.

The escort vehicles reacted as they had been briefed and returned fire. The truck column began to drive out of the kill zone while the enemy was rattled by the return fire. The company commander radioed for air support and 30 minutes after the battle began, helicopter gunships arrived. They hit the enemy and supported the motorized riflemen in their battle. The enemy ceased fire and began to withdraw to fall-back positions. In this combat, we lost one soldier KIA and seven WIA.

FRUNZE COMMENTARY: This vignette shows insufficient preparation for the convoy duty and further insufficient preparation in its accomplishment. On the day before the mission, the company commander did not conduct training with his personnel including training on coordination of actions in the event of enemy attack. The prolonged wait along the road side permitted the enemy to closely study the convoy as he drove by the column. The use of helicopter gunships to cover the column from the air did not come soon enough to ward off the enemy attack. Reconnaissance was not used during the course of the march. Nevertheless, the high psychological preparation of the drivers and the selfless actions of the motorized rifle soldiers allowed the column to rapidly exit the kill zone.

EDITOR'S COMMENTARY: In this vignette, the commander is taken to task for not carefully supervising the preparation of his troops for the march. Part of this criticism is based on lack of trust of subordinates and the lack of a Soviet professional NCO corps.   The commander is expected to personally conduct all training. In armies with a professional NCO corps, such training and preparation is done by trained, seasoned sergeants who understand the unit missions and train their forces to meet them.   The commander checks his sergeants, but does not have to get involved in training to the extent that his Soviet counterpart had to.   This leaves more time for carefully planning the action.   The Soviet system overburdened the company grade officers and limited individual training opportunities.

The *mujahideen* learned to take out command vehicles early in the battle.   Command vehicles were always distinguished by extra antennae and convoy commanders usually rode in the first vehicle of the main column.   This is the case throughout this chapter.   Other Soviet writings talk about strapping extra antennae on all vehicles before going into action and varying the commander's position in the column.   This did not happen.   Consequently, when the commander's vehicle was hit, communications were usually lost and the commander, if he survived, could not control the fight.   In this vignette, the essential communications were in a soft-bodied truck, instead of an armored vehicle.   The Soviets used radio almost exclusively to control the battle.   Although the *mujahideen* had little jamming capability, once they knocked out the Soviet vehicles with the multiple antennae, they usually had disrupted the tactical control net.

An air assault company escorts a convoy
in Kunduz Province
by Major A. M. Portnov[101]

Enemy activity was a problem near Imam-Sahib in Kunduz Province at the end of October 1981. The enemy would launch diversionary attacks against Soviet bases, while simultaneously trying to prevent the export of cotton from the cities of Shekravan and Imam-Sahib.[102]

On 26 October 1981, I received an order to provide escort to a convoy of 70 trucks hauling cotton. My 7th Air Assault Company was to provide escort along the 114-kilometer route from Shekravan to Shirkhan. My company had two air assault platoons and was reinforced with a mortar platoon, a machine-gun squad, and two AGS-17 automatic grenade launchers mounted on BTR-D carriers.

While preparing for the mission, I brought in all my officers, sergeants and drivers and we went over the route on a terrain model in detail. We developed several courses of action for each vehicle in the event of an enemy attack on the column. In my forward security patrol, I had two BMDs[103] and a BTR-D mounting the AGS-17. They moved at one-kilometer intervals in front of the main body.

---

[101]A. M. Portnov served in the OKSVA from 1979 through 1982 as the assistant company commander of an air assault company and then as the company commander of an air assault company. He was awarded the "Order of the Red Star" and the medal "For Military Valor".

[102]Both cities bordered the Soviet Union and cotton was one of the commodities with which the Afghan government paid the Soviet government for their aid. Afghan export of cotton to the Soviet Union started with an agreement in the 1930s in exchange for Soviet gasoline and manufactured goods. Cotton was only a small part of Afghan exports to pay for Soviet arms. Natural gas, uranium, precious stones, fruit, and other resources were also sent north (ed.).

[103]BMD or *boevaya mashina desanta* is an air-dropable, armored personnel carrier that carries up to nine men (usually a maximum of seven). It has the same turret as the BMP, so the BMD-1 has the 73mm cannon of the BMP-1, while the BMD-2 has the 30mm chain gun of the BMP-2. They both mount three 7.62mm machine guns. They were widely used by Soviet airborne and air assault forces (ed.).

After the cotton was loaded, the convoy left Shekravan at 1200 hours on 27 October. I augmented my Soviet security force by putting three or four Afghan armed police from the "Sarandoy" company on each cotton truck. In the event of an attack on the convoy, the Afghan armed police would act under my command.

When our column approached Basiz village, the enemy fired on the forward security patrol with grenade launchers and blew up a command detonated mine.[104] The enemy was trying to destroy the bridge across the canal and the BTR-D that was on it. Thus, they hoped to stop the convoy. Thanks to the skilled handling by the dri-

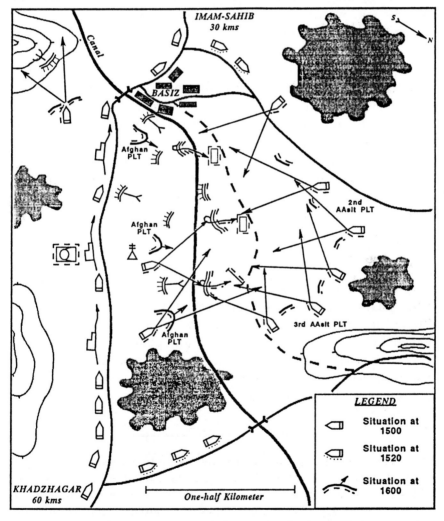

Map 36: The 7th Air Assault Company destroys the enemy.

ver of the BTR-D, it was not damaged. However, at the same time, the enemy was firing rifles and grenade launchers at the column from 70-100 meters away and knocked out four cotton trucks.

I ordered my forward security patrol (the 2nd Air Assault Platoon) and the 3rd Air Assault Platoon to maneuver behind the enemy and take him from the rear. The fires from one BMD, the AGS-17 crew and the mortar platoon were sufficient to pin down the enemy and allow the Afghan police company to deploy.

Having failed their mission, the enemy began to withdraw from prepared positions and came under fire from my platoons which had encircled them from the rear. The trapped guerrilla force continued to resist and we destroyed them. I had one air assault trooper wounded in my company.

FRUNZE COMMENTARY: Combat experience shows that when preparing for a march, it is necessary to conduct coordination not only with your officers and sergeants, but with your armored-vehicle drivers as well. Your forward security patrol must not only have a route reconnaissance mission, but must also be instructed as to what actions to take when necessary in order to fight in coordination with the rest of the subunits. When combat is joined, it is necessary to maneuver subunits boldly to take the enemy on the flank and in the rear.

EDITOR'S COMMENTARY: The column deployed a forward security patrol, but their reconnaissance effort seems lacking. Although they went over the route on a terrain model, it appears that simple map reconnaissance was neglected and choke points and potential kill zones were not identified and planned for. The bridge is an obvious chokepoint and a place for a reconnaissance elements to dismount and check for mines. Flank security is never discussed and evidently seldom deployed.

104The Russian here is *fugas*, similar to the western word *fougasse*. The Russian term means a large explosive charge buried in the ground and covered with rocks and debris. The western term describes a flame weapon that is a buried 55-gallon drum of thickened gasoline with a propelling explosive charge at the base (ed.).

Convoy escort and combat
in the village of Daulatabad
by LTC A. A. Agzamov[105]

At the end of 1981, enemy attacks against convoys mounted along the Termez, Shebegan, Andkhoy, Maimana route. It was particularly difficult in the region of Daulatabad. Intelligence reports indicated that a guerrilla force of 25-to-30 men armed with rifles operated in this area. Acting secretly, the enemy would attack a single vehicle or column. Their goal was to paralyze resupply into the area.

On 2 December 1981, the 2nd Reconnaissance Company, which was garrisoned in Maimana, was ordered to escort a 120-vehicle convoy loaded with supplies from Andkhoy to Maimana. The distance was 110 kilometers. The company reinforcements included a sapper squad, a flamethrower squad armed with the RPO flamethrowers, a ZSU-23-4 self-propelled air defense gun, and a BTS-4 towing vehicle.[106]

We had two days to prepare for the mission. During this time we studied data which we received from the high command and resolved issues of rear support and maintenance support. We paid particular attention to readying the vehicles for the march and to preparing our weapons for combat. The troops drew rations and ammunition.

The convoy commander was the deputy commander of a SPETSNAZ detachment, N. Beksultanov. He decided to conduct the march from Maimana to Andkhoy on a single route and precede this with a forward security patrol. At 0500 hours on 4 December, the column moved out and 11 hours later closed into the assembly area some three kilometers northeast of Andkhoy. The truck convoy, already loaded with supplies, joined us. We then had to arrange the march column, distribute our combat power throughout the convoy,

---

[105]A. A. Agzamov served in the OKSVA from 1981 through 1983 as the commander of a reconnaissance group of a reconnaissance company. He was awarded the "Order of the Red Star".

[106]The BTS-4 *bronirovanyy tyagach sredniy* is a turretless T-55 tank equipped for towing tracked vehicles (ed.).

agree on coordination measures, and arrange for our night rest stop. We planned to leave on the morning of 5 December, move for five or six hours covering 80 kilometers with one rest stop. Following an overnight rest, we would close into Maimana the following day. The company had a platoon serve as the forward patrol.

The column moved out at 0500 on the morning of 5 December. By 0900, the forward patrol reached the village of Daulatabad. They reported back that the village was deserted. This report put us on our guard, and the convoy commander ordered us to increase our observation. When the lead vehicles of the convoy began to exit

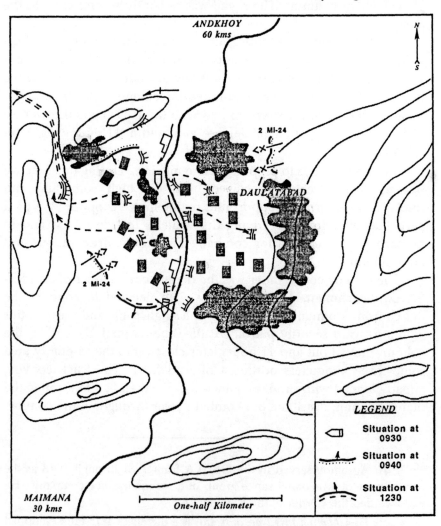

Map 37: Defeating an enemy attack in a village.

Daulatabad village, the enemy opened fire with a grenade launcher and destroyed a BMP-2KSH[107] and a fuel tanker. A fire broke out and the vehicles immediately behind the conflagration were stuck in narrow streets.

The enemy opened up with small arms fire. Two more BMPs were knocked out and, as a result, the convoy was split into three sections. We returned fire, but it was not controlled or directed. The convoy commander lost control over his subunits since his communications were gone. Individual vehicles independently tried to break out of the kill zones. The FAC called in helicopter gunships and directed their fires. The helicopters began gun runs on the enemy in the village. In the meantime, the trail platoon received the mission to sweep the western part of the village. The dismounted troopers moved under the cover of BMP and helicopter fire to carry out their mission. The enemy withdrew when faced with this decisive action.

In the course of this three-hour battle, four of our soldiers were killed (all drivers), six were wounded, three BMPs were destroyed and five trucks were burned up.

FRUNZE COMMENTARY: This example shows poor decision-making, inadequate preparation for battle and inadequate troop control during the course of the battle. None of the commanders involved had been briefed on the probable sites of enemy contact and the likely enemy courses of action.

EDITOR'S COMMENTARY: In this vignette, the recon element reports that all the people in a village, which is a traditional trouble spot, have left. This leads to increased observation, but the commander does not dismount a force and have them probe the village for ambushes. This appears to demonstrate a basic lack of field craft on the part of the commander.

Again, the company commander muddles through a three-hour battle with a lightly-armed platoon and only manages to extricate himself when airpower is brought to bear. There seems to be a strong reluctance to dismount and close with the enemy. There is an over-reliance on firepower.

---

[107]The BMP-2KSH is the the command version of the BMP-2 series (ed.).

Finally, Afghan government forces and Afghan civilian drivers are never part of the equation. Losses are strictly in terms of Soviet men and material and trucks from the convoy. Either the Afghans never suffered casualties, or they were considered of no account. If it is the latter, it demonstrates a mindset that is counterproductive when trying to assist another government in winning a guerrilla war.

Convoy escort and battle near Maliykhel'
by Major A. I. Guboglo[108]

During the winter of 1982, several guerrilla detachments worked near the village of Maliykhel' on the Kabul-Ghazni highway. The guerrillas would launch attacks on Soviet military convoys.

On the 11th of December 1982, the commander of the 7th Motorized Rifle Company received orders to escort a truck convoy from Ghazni to Kabul and return.[109] They were to insure the unimpeded movement of the convoy in both directions on the 170-kilometer stretch.

The road march to Kabul went as planned and the enemy did not try to attack the convoy. After loading the trucks, we were prepared for our return trip to Ghazni. My company commander decided to place two BTRs at the head and two BTRs at the tail of the column and then intersperse five BTRs within the truck column. He put a BTR between every eight trucks. He had the 1st MRP serve as a reconnaissance platoon and move ten kilometers in front of the convoy. The average road speed of the convoy would be 35-40 kilometers per hour. There would be one rest stop at the end of three hours driving.

In case the enemy would attack the column with small arms, the BTRs and helicopter gunships would place maximum firepower on the enemy while the convoy moved out of the kill zone. As a variant, should the terrain permit, the BTRs would roll right over the ambush sites of the attacking enemy.

At 0730 hours on 13 December, my company commander gave the order and the convoy moved out. After 30 minutes of travel, one of our heavy-transport trucks broke down. My company commander had another transport truck link up with this vehicle and tow it right behind his command BTR at the front of the column. At 1115 hours, the lead vehicles of the main body approached the green zone near the village of Maliykhel'. As the vehicles crossed the river

---

[108]A. I. Guboglo served in the OKSVA from 1981 to 1983 as a motorized rifle platoon leader. He was awarded the "Order of the Red Star" and the medal "For Valor".

[109]The 7th MRC, 3rd MRB, 191st Separate Motorized Rifle Regiment (ed.).

bridge, the enemy activated a radio-controlled, command-detonated mine which damaged the towing vehicle. The passage was blocked. At that instant, the enemy opened fire on the convoy from positions on the dominant heights.

Attempts to push the trucks off the bridge failed. The company commander decided to have his 2nd Motorized Rifle Platoon flank the bridge site through a gully. However, the enemy had mined the exit from the gully. The 2nd platoon's lead BTR hit a mine. Attempts to extricate this BTR failed, and while they were trying, another BTR hit another mine. Taking stock of his increasingly

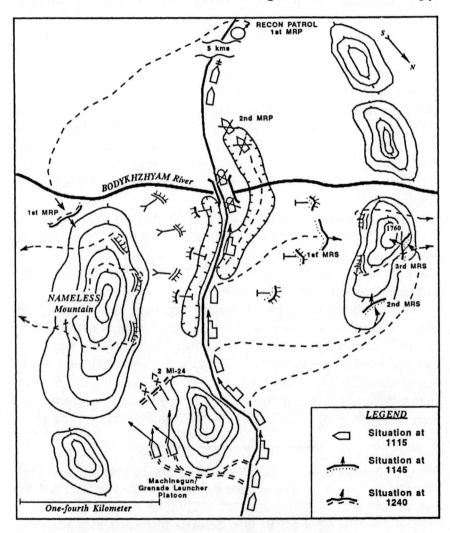

Map 38: The 7th MRC defeats an attack.

untenable situation, the company commander ordered the 3rd Motorized Rifle Platoon to dismount and take hill 1760. This was my platoon. I maneuvered my first squad into a position where they could pin down the enemy with fire from the front. Then, I took my 2nd and 3rd squads to flank the enemy and hit him from the flank and rear. By 1145, we had successfully accomplished our mission and hill 1760 was ours.

During this time, our force continued attempts to retake the road and move the convoy to a safe place. However, due to the intense fire from "Nameless" mountain, we were unsuccessful. The approaches to the mountain were wide-open and a flanking attack did not appear possible. Despite our heavy small arms and BTR fire plus the repeated gun runs by helicopter gunships on the height, we were not able to take it.

Finally, the company commander's radio requests resulted in an additional flight of helicopter gunships. The commander decided to attack the enemy with the 1st platoon, which had originally acted as the recon platoon. At 1240 hours, the 1st platoon attacked. It was supported by fire from the machine-gun/grenade-launcher platoon and a flight of helicopter gunships. It took the hill. The convoy could now resume its march.

FRUNZE COMMENTARY: This vignette shows that it is always necessary to "wargame" several variants for your subunits in the event of an enemy attack. Further, sapper subunits should always be a part of a convoy escort along with the motorized rifle force. And, again we see how good combat training of the troops leads to success in battle, regardless of how difficult the situation is.

EDITOR'S COMMENTARY: The companies in this vignette and the first vignette in the chapter (#35) are from the same battalion. There is a year's difference between the two incidents. It would seem reasonable to check for improvements and a learning curve. There appears to have some tactical improvements made in this time. The force now moves with a reconnaissance force forward and with more responsive air cover. But, the commander still rides in the lead vehicle, bridges are not checked for mines, and likely ambush sites are not probed by dismounted forces. Broken-down convoy vehicles are still towed at the front of the column right behind the command vehicle. There is no apparent attempt to control dominant terrain or check it before the convoy's advance. There is no discussion of using air assault forces to leapfrog from one dominant height to the next to cover the convoy's movement. Apparently, not all the lessons on convoy escort had been learned.

This chapter started out by saying that the *mujahideen* attacked convoys with mines during the early stage of the war and, as the war progressed, they began to conduct full-scale attacks on convoys. All these examples are from 1981 or 1982–the early stage of the war and, yet, the *mujahideen* seem well advanced in convoy attack by this point. In these vignettes, however, the Soviets are not taking steps that are standard in western armies. There seems to be no road-opening force on these routes. Evidently, there are no "bait-and-hunt" decoy convoys. Rapid reaction forces supporting the convoy escorts are not apparent. There is no evidence of any planning to use airmobile forces on likely guerrilla escape routes. Artillery fire support planning also seems absent. These examples fail to show map and terrain work to identify chokepoints, kill zones and ambush sites in advance. Reconnaissance forces seem road-bound. The effort appears passive and reactive.

CHAPTER 6:
CONDUCTING AMBUSHES

Combat experience in Afghanistan shows that not only is the ambush an accepted form of reconnaissance, but it is also one of the more widely used methods of combat practiced in the areas of responsibility of regimental-sized and division-sized units. Reconnaissance, air-assault, airborne, and SPETSNAZ subunits routinely conduct ambushes and motorized rifle subunits may also conduct them once they receive special training.

Ambushes are widely employed in all types of combat. This is conditioned by the fact that the tactics of the guerrilla forces were very different from those of regular forces and more closely resembled those of partisan warfare. Therefore, it was necessary for Soviet forces to find more effective ways of combatting the *mujahideen* under these circumstances.

A reinforced motorized rifle company conducts an ambush in Kandahar Province
by Major V. I. Pavlenko[110]

Our separate motorized rifle brigade completed its road march to its new base camp in March 1981.[111] Its movement was covered from the air by a squadron of helicopter gunships. At the same time, the squadron began reconnaissance of enemy forces located along the Kandahar-Shindand road.

The squadron commander reported that at 1820 hours, a truck convoy carrying supplies entered Musa-Kala village. Further, a number of enemy was concentrated at Musa-Kala, which is located about 20 kilometers from Kandahar. The brigade intelligence officer also confirmed this information.

We could not waste any time. The village of Musa-Kala is located close to the border with Pakistan and was a rest stop and a staging point for the *mujahideen* bases. Weapons and ammunition were brought through this village for distribution throughout the country. Our brigade commander, LTC Yu. P. Shatin, devised the following plan. He would seal off the village from the north and the southeast with two motorized rifle battalions. Then he would use the air-assault battalion and some Afghan Army subunits to sweep the village. At the same time, in order to halt the northwest movement of the enemy convoy, he would fly a reinforced motorized rifle company ahead of the convoy to establish an ambush.

My battalion commander, S. V. Antonov, designated my 8th Motorized Rifle Company as the ambush company. I was a Senior Lieutenant at the time and the company commander. My brigade commander personally gave me my mission. My company had three motorized rifle platoons. The brigade commander reinforced my company with three AGS-17 automatic grenade launchers with their crews, three sappers with twenty mines, and two RTOs with two

---

[110]V. I. Pavlenko served in the OKSVA from 1980 through 1982 as a motorized rifle company commander. He was awarded the medal "For Bravery". [This medal was given to enlisted men and junior lieutenants only (ed.).]

[111]The 70th Separate Motorized Rifle Brigade (ed.).

radios. Seven Mi-8T transport helicopters were to deliver my company close to the ambush site. I had two hours to prepare my force for the mission.

At 2055 hours, my company was loaded on the helicopters and at 2130 hours we landed five kilometers from the ambush site. The landing took place 15 minutes before dusk. After the landing, I assembled my company at the rally point which was located 500 meters from the LZ. We waited for the cover of darkness before moving out. I pushed out a patrol squad in front of the company. I had each platoon split into two groups and move side-by-side in two

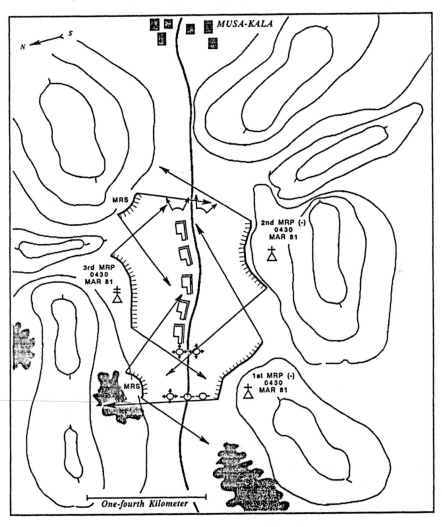

Map 39: An ambush in Kandahar Province.

columns where they could be controlled by hand signs and visual signals. I had a patrol move in front of and behind each platoon. I had every squad and platoon conduct all-around observation and stop periodically to get their bearings. At 0020 hours, my forward patrol reported that they were at the ambush site and 20 minutes later, my entire company had closed into the area.

I put my platoons and squads into position. I placed forces to block the entrance and exit to the ambush site and concentrated the bulk of my force in the center of the ambush site. All-around observation was maintained on the site entrance and exit while my troops dug in and fortified their firing positions and then camouflaged them. The sappers mined the road at the ambush site. By 0430 hours, my company ambush was ready.

At 0500 hours, brigade subunits sealed off the village of Musa-Kala and began the sweep at 0530. The enemy, shooting at the Soviet forces in the village in order to slow them down, put their ammunition-truck convoy on the road and headed toward our ambush. At 0620 hours, my sentry reported that five trucks were approaching the site. The trucks entered the site and the lead truck hit a mine. The 1st and 3rd platoons immediately opened fire on the enemy. Two trucks turned around and tried to leave. We killed one with a command detonated mine and the 2nd platoon killed the other. The enemy was confused and his return fire was wild and disorganized. Some of the *mujahideen* tried to break out, but we cut them down. The battle was short.

The results of our ambush were 26 enemy killed and 20 captured. Eight of the captives were wounded. We destroyed five trucks loaded with ammunition and food. I lost one soldier KIA and five WIA.

FRUNZE COMMENTARY: The success of this combat was determined by the rapid decision to employ the ambush; the short time taken to organize the action; the rapid, concealed movement into the ambush site; the initiative and bravery displayed by all commanders, the uninterrupted control of the subunits and their fires, and the support and continual coordination with the subunits which were carrying out the block and sweep of the village.

EDITOR'S COMMENTARY: This book does not discuss the problem of fratricide, but this particular ambush seems to set the conditions for fratricide. Forces on low ground are positioned across from forces on high ground. The forces on the high ground fired through the convoy and maybe into friendly forces. The account states that the *mujahideen* return-fire was wild and disorganized, yet the Soviets lost one killed and five wounded. Some of these Soviet casualties may have been from fratricide. Further, if the *mujahideen* had entered the ambush at night, the force on the low ground would have fired into the force on the high ground, since night firing is inevitably high unless bars and elevation blocks are constructed at each firing position. These field firing aids are hard to put in at night.

Although this ambush worked, there are still some troublesome details. There was apparently no control on traffic entering the kill zone from the west and inadvertently setting off a mine, spoiling the ambush. Further, the use of conventional mines on the road takes control away from the ambush commander. If the *mujahideen* had sent a patrol vehicle ahead of the main convoy, it might have triggered a mine and ruined the ambush. Command-detonated mines seem appropriate here.

An airborne group ambushes a bridge site
by LTC V. P. Gladishev[112]

Weapons and ammunition that were furnished to the *mujahideen* came into Afghanistan from Pakistan and Iran. Much of this cargo came into Helmand and Kandahar provinces. Our airborne division commander decided to establish ambushes along the likely routes that these armament caravans would travel.[113] In July 1982, my battalion commander ordered me to prepare a reconnaissance group

I had 10 days to select and prepare a 20-man group for the mission. I selected battalion officers, sergeants and soldiers who were in exceptional physical shape, and had combat experience. My group consisted of two officers, a warrant officer, five sergeants and 12 soldiers. The soldiers included two RTOs, two sappers, a medic and an interpreter. I also received an officer from the Afghan KHAD to accompany the mission.

My group's equipment included six machine guns, 14 AKS-74 assault rifles, and an AKMS automatic rifle with a silencer. We carried two combat loads per weapon, four hand grenades per man, four RPG-18 antitank weapons, five mines, seven radios (two of which could link with helicopters), seven pair of binoculars, one night vision device, and a flak jacket for every man. The group wore camouflage smocks and tennis shoes.

Our target was a bridge over which, according to Afghan counterintelligence, enemy trucks, motorcycles and tractors had crossed on previous nights. At the end of July 1982, my group boarded two Mi-8TV helicopters. We were inserted some five kilometers from the bridge one hour prior to sunset. Four Mi-24 helicopter gunships covered our insertion. The insertion was timed to allow the helicopters to return to the battalion base camp during daylight. We waited for darkness and then moved stealthily to the bridge. My patrol, which

---

[112]V. P. Gladishev served in the OKSVA from February 1982 through June 1984. He served as the deputy commander and then the commander of an airborne battalion. He was awarded the "Order of the Red Star".
[113]The 103rd Airborne Division (ed.).

moved 200 meters in front of the group, discovered an enemy observation post which consisted of two men, military rifles and a motor-
cycle. We slipped around their observation post and surreptitiously
moved to the bridge. There, we split into our designated subgroups
and deployed according to my plan. My ambush subgroups were a
fire support group, a security group, a snatch group and a support
group. By 2130 hours, my ambush was established and my troopers
were ready for battle.

Every 15-20 minutes, the enemy sentries would signal the nearby
villages with some flashlight signals. From this, I understood that

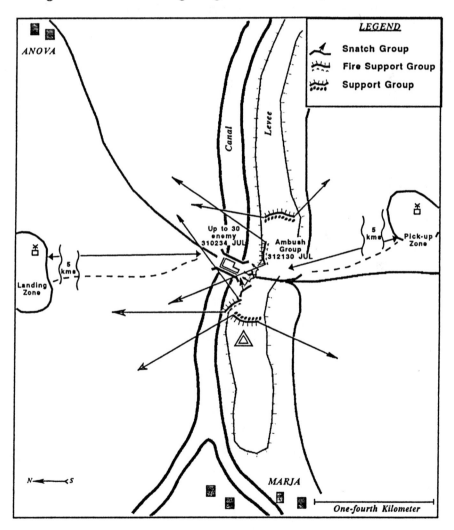

Map 40: An airborne group ambushes a bridge site.

they had not discovered our presence. This continued until 0230 hours. According to our plan, I had to withdraw my ambush force and start moving to the pick-up zone at 0300 hours. However, at 0235 hours, a medium truck moved from Anova toward Mardzha and was crossing the bridge. I gave the command to detonate two MON-50 mines and to open fire. Simultaneously, two troopers from my security force threw grenades into the enemy OP.

The enemy never got a shot off and it was all over in one or two minutes. The enemy was completely destroyed. After the snatch group and the fire support group ceased fire, we gathered enemy weapons, ammunition and documents. We killed 28 enemy, captured 32 weapons of varying types as well as their ammunition. I had no casualties. We quickly reassembled and moved out to the pick-up zone. The helicopters had us back to our base camp by 0700 hours.

From the end of July to the end of September, we conducted 18 similar ambushes. We had positive results from 14 of them. During this time, we had three soldiers wounded. Our ambush groups killed approximately 200 *mujahideen* and captured about 20. We captured approximately 200 various weapons, a large amount of ammunition, and a large sum of money. There were about 50,000,000 Iranian rials, Pakistani rupees and Afghanistan afghans. This money was destined to pay for their Iranian and Pakistani advisers.

FRUNZE COMMENTARY: The successful accomplishment of all these ambushes was due to the careful selection of the personnel for the mission, the well-thought-out training, the clearly defined duties during the organization of the ambushes, the detailed coordination between the subgroups, the superb physical conditioning of the troopers and the use of specialized clothing and shoes.

EDITOR'S COMMENTARY: The Soviets did not stress unit integrity to the same degree as in the west. Time and again, scratch units are assembled without any apparent regard for maintaining unit integrity and habitual relationships. This ambush group was apparently drawn from throughout the battalion.

A motorized rifle platoon conducts an ambush in the area of Aibak

by Major V. N. Popov[114]

The 3rd Motorized Rifle Battalion secured the road between the town of Tashkorghan and Aibak.[115] A pipeline ran through the battalion's area of responsibility, bringing fuel from the USSR to the Republic of Afghanistan. The battalion's mission was to prevent attacks on the pipeline, insure the uninterrupted movement of truck convoys, and to safeguard and defend important facilities within our area of responsibility.

In April 1984, the city of Aibak was subjected to systematic enemy mortar fire. Their main target was the 9th Motorized Rifle Company which was garrisoned there. The constant enemy shelling interfered with the company's ability to perform its missions and damaged civilian property and created panic. We tried to destroy the enemy with our artillery, but these attempts failed. The enemy knew his terrain like the back of his hand. He would fire five-to-eight mortar rounds and then change firing positions so that he would not be caught under our return fire.

Agent intelligence reported that the group of eight-to-ten men who conducted the mortar attacks on Aibak had left for the village of Kakabulak to rest and replenish their ammunition supply. The group would be resting there for two days. We knew the route that the *mujahideen* would use. The 3rd MRB commander decided to ambush this route with a platoon backed by the rest of the 8th MRC.

The battalion commander decided to establish an ambush site at night before the *mujahideen* returned west. The 8th MRC, mounted on BTRs, would support the ambush site with direct fire if necessary and would provide the ambush platoon. The ambush platoon would be reinforced with an AGS-17. In order to deceive the enemy, we conducted our reconnaissance in the Aibak area and coordinated our actions with the Afghan subunits.

The ambush platoon's mission was to dismount from moving

---

[114]V. N. Popov served in the OKSVA from February 1984 through March 1986 as the assistant to the chief of staff of a motorized rifle battalion.

[115]The 3rd Motorized Rifle Battalion, 122nd Motorized Rifle Regiment, 201st Motorized Rifle Division (ed.).

vehicles which were conducting a patrol along the pipeline and, at the turnoff point, walk to the ambush site, occupy the site, and eliminate the enemy.

The 7th MRC, which was located about 40-kilometers away, would provide the site and training for the ambush platoon from the 8th MRC. The company commander trained this 8th MRC platoon for the mission on a piece of ground that was similar to the actual ambush site. On the first day of training, several alternate courses of action were devised depending on the way that the *mujahideen* would approach the ambush site. In the event that the enemy discovered

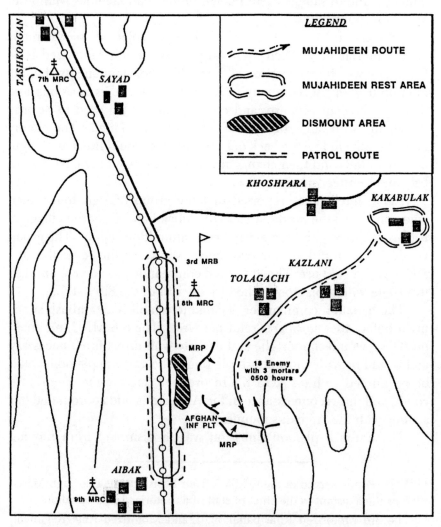

Map 41: A motorized rifle platoon conducts an ambush.

the ambush, the commanders coordinated their plans so that the rest of the 8th MRC would provide fire support to their ambush force. The platoon paid careful attention to coordinating the actions between the fire support group and the snatch group. It also worked out procedures for dismounting from the moving BTRs. On the second day, the troops prepared their weapons and equipment for combat. In the afternoon, the platoon rejoined the 8th MRC.

The platoon moved to the ambush area on two BTRs of the 8th MRC. We normally used two BTRs for conducting road patrols. At 2100, the *bronegruppa* set out on patrol. At 2230 hours, as the patrol was coming to an end, the personnel of the ambush group started jumping out of the moving BTRs. They lay spread out in a ditch along a 500 meters stretch of the road waiting for the platoon leader's signal. They lay there for 30 minutes until the platoon leader knew that they had not been discovered. Then he gave the signal for the platoon to assemble. He sent out two patrols in front of the platoon and they all moved to the ambush site. The platoon took four hours to get to the site. At 0230 hours, they arrived at the site some three kilometers east of Tolagachi. After putting his platoon into their firing positions, the platoon leader fine-tuned the missions of each group on the ground. At the appointed time, the platoon leader "broke squelch" twice on his radio set to signal the battalion commander that the ambush was ready for battle.

At 0500, we saw the enemy approach. The platoon leader let their forward patrol pass through the site and waited for their main body. When the main body came into the kill zone, we called out and demanded that they surrender. The *mujahideen* did not surrender, but began firing small arms at us. Their fire was intense. The battle began. The platoon leader immediately reported the events to the battalion commander by radio. The battalion chief of staff led the 8th MRC to blocking positions to prevent the enemy withdrawal and to support the ambush party. As the fire fight raged, the *mujahideen* realized that they were in a trap and tried to breakout of the encirclement. However, the 8th MRC arrived at that point and blocked their exit route. Close coordination between the ambush party and their supporting MRC insured that the enemy did not escape.

We killed 14 enemy and captured four more. We also captured three mortars, plus small arms and ammunition. We had three WIA.

FRUNZE COMMENTARY: The positive points of this example are the training given to the soldiers on a site similar to the actual site, but at a place removed from enemy observation, the development of variants of the ambush plan for the ambush party, and the undetected movement of the subunit to the ambush site. On the other hand, they did not develop a variant plan to deal with a possible larger force than they expected. Further, it is not always a good idea to demand that your enemy surrender. Surprise, sudden, close-range fire demoralizes an enemy and significantly lessens your own casualties.

EDITOR'S COMMENTARY: The platoon's mission was to kill or capture the enemy force. Why they would challenge the enemy and demand their surrender is puzzling. Their specific mission did not require prisoners, and yet, if they wanted prisoners, combat experience shows that there are usually prisoners (wounded or otherwise) left at the end of any ambush. There seems to be no reason to challenge the enemy and lose surprise. To challenge a force that is roughly equal in size seems foolhardy and a risk to your own force.

A motorized rifle company conducts an ambush in the Loy-Karez region

by Major A. V. Van'yants[116]

During the time that Soviet forces served in Kandahar province, guerrilla forces systematically attacked convoys, pillaged the local population, torched schools and attempted to seize Kandahar city.

The 2nd Motorized Rifle Battalion of a separate motorized rifle brigade was garrisoned in the city of Kandahar.[117] This battalion was the most experienced and combat-hardened subunit of the brigade and had participated in all the brigade operations. The battalion was particularly skilled in ambush techniques and was equally adept at moving to the ambush site on helicopters or on our assigned BMPs.

We prepared for ambushes in a very exacting and thorough fashion. We would prepare and check our personnel, their weapons and gear, and the night-vision devices. In the event that the ambush would involve a helicopter insertion, the battalion commander or his chief of staff would personally train the ambush party. We selected the soldiers and sergeants for our helicopter-borne ambush groups based on their superior physical conditioning, their combat experience, and their skill with various types of weapons and communications equipment. When we travelled to the ambush site on our BMPs, we took everyone in the subunit.

On 12 June 1984, my fully-equipped motorized rifle company moved on BMPs to the Loy-Karez region to conduct ambushes. Captain V. Patrushev, the battalion chief of staff, was in charge of the mission. My company was divided into four ambush groups. One of these groups moved to a small river to block a fording site. The ambush group commander gave his orders, organized his lookouts and put the rest of the soldiers to work digging their firing positions.

After 0200 hours on 13 June, the look-outs spotted truck headlights as a truck drove down from the heights. In a few minutes, a

---

[116]A. V. Van'yants served in the OKSVA from 1982 to 1984 as a platoon leader and company commander and from 1987 to 1988 as a battalion chief of staff. He was awarded the "Order of the Red Star".
[117]The 70th Separate Motorized Rifle Brigade (ed.).

13-truck convoy followed the lead truck. They stopped about 300 meters from the fording site. With our night-vision device, we could see about 30 dismounted *mujahideen* moving in a cautious manner into our ambush site. The *mujahideen* observed the area carefully. The group commander decided to withdraw since the enemy action would preclude a successful ambush, the enemy force outnumbered the ambush force by 30 to 14 and the BMPs were seven kilometers away from the ambush site and unable to provide fire support.

At dawn, the ambush party arrived at the company assembly

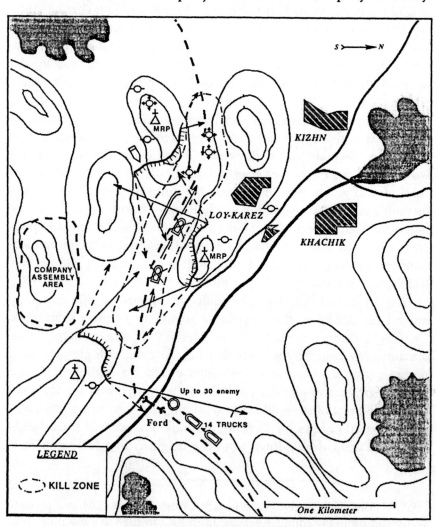

**Map 42: A MRC conducts an ambush near Loy-Karez,
12-13 June 1984.**

area. They posted look-outs and the personnel rested. After some time, one of the lookouts reported that the *mujahideen* were in a near-by valley strung-out in a column and heading our way. It appeared that the enemy had set out to search for our ambush party, for they had found the ambush site where our ambush party had concealed themselves at night. Our former ambush site was strewn with our tin cans, cigarette butts and empty cigarette packages. Apparently the *mujahideen* thought that only 10-to-15 men were in the area.

I ordered one of my platoons to deploy near the company assembly area in ambush and prepare for battle. I ordered the two other platoons to move stealthily to the flanks of the *mujahideen* using the terrain folds to hide their movement. We waited for the enemy to move onto the large plain on the valley floor, so we could complete the encirclement. At the right moment, I called for a pair of helicopter gunships to come to our assistance and gave the order to open fire.

We killed 28 *mujahideen*, and captured 32 weapons, including three grenade launchers. We also captured valuable documents and Islamic official seals. My company had no casualties.

FRUNZE COMMENTARY: The ambush was successful for the following reasons: the thorough reconnaissance of the enemy forces and terrain; the precise planning of the group's actions; the skillful siting of the company in ambush using the terrain features; the uninterrupted and resolute control of the subunits during the fight; and the support of helicopter gunships.

EDITOR'S COMMENTARY: The Soviet Army seldom left a clean bivouac area or fighting position. They dug field latrines, but the troops were as likely to defecate and urinate around their area as to use the latrines. Trash was strewn everywhere. Apparently this sloppiness extended to their ambush sites and alerted the *mujahideen* to their presence. In this case, however, there apparently was not enough trash to reveal the true size of the ambush force and the company commander turned this to his advantage.

More disturbing than the trash is the fact that the ambush party was smoking in position. Even if the smokers were smoking under a poncho or tarp, cigarette smell carries-particularly in the damper, cooler night air. Russian cigarettes are strong and pungent. This demonstrates a basic lack of field sense or discipline.

Once again, the battalion commander or the battalion chief of staff were personally involved in training small groups. The lack of a professional NCO corps and the lack of trust in junior officers kept the battalion leadership doing jobs other armies would entrust to lieutenants and sergeants. As a result, other areas in the battalion suffered.

An airborne platoon conducts an ambush in Helmand Province
by Major A. A. Tolkachev[118]

Our airborne battalion's mission was to control part of the frontier located some 300 kilometers southwest of the city of Kandahar. Based on intelligence reports furnished by the Afghan KHAD, my battalion commander decided to employ ambushes to attack the enemy.

My ambush party was returning to our base camp by helicopter after conducting an ambush along the border. As we flew along the Helmand River, I discovered a road that skirted the green zone of the river. We dropped down to five-or-10 meters off the deck and I soon noticed fresh truck tracks. When we got back to our base camp to rest, I received information that a truck-mounted guerrilla force of about 50 men had arrived in our AO. I went to the battalion commander and suggested that I set up an ambush on the newly-discovered road.

My battalion commander told me to conduct an ambush in the area from 3 to 10 December 1984. My ambush party consisted of 25 men, two of which were officers. The force had three squads, each of which consisted of the squad leader and two three-man fire teams.

I picked out my ambush site independently as we flew to the area. The helicopters faked insertions at one false airhead with two phony LZs—one LZ some 10-to-20 kilometers away from our LZ and the other five to six kilometers away from it. We landed before darkness.

I had rations and water for 10 days. We took two days supply with us and buried and concealed the rest. Each man carried 35 to 40 kilograms of equipment. When night fell, we moved to our ambush site. When we came to the road, I personally selected the firing positions, organized sectors of fire, and specified how the positions were to be protected and concealed. Every soldier dug a prone firing position. They hauled the dirt away to a depression. Our two engineers laid in a mine field, using trip-wire and MON-100 com-

---

[118]A. A. Tolkachev served in the OKSVA from May 1983 through May 1985 as an airborne company commander. He was awarded the "Order of the Red Banner".

mand-detonated mines.[119] Two-thirds of the force were in battle
positions at night while one-third rested. During the day, I had three
look-outs, while the remainder rested. There was no sign of the
enemy during the first night. During the day, we defused the trip-
wire mines, so that wild animals would not set off the mines and disclose our ambush.

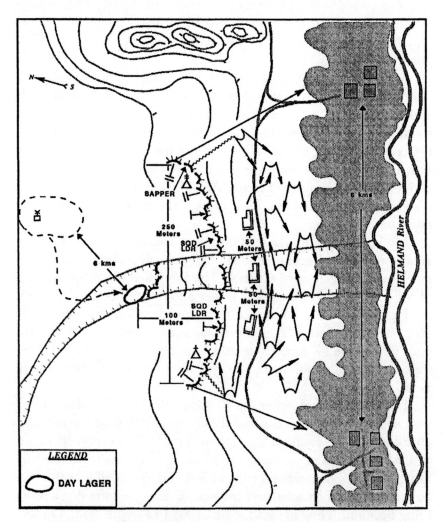

Map 43: Airborne platoon ambush in Helmand province.

[119]The MON *(minna oskolochnaya napravlenogo deistvie)* series of mines are
directional, anti-personnel mines similar to the U.S. claymore mine. They
can be set to detonate from a trip-wire or with a firing device (ed.).

Our ambush site was flat desert. I picked the site since it was higher than the green zone and allowed us to observe for a distance in any direction. During the day we could see for three-to-five kilometers, while at night, we could detect a truck with its headlights burning 20-to-25 kilometers out. We could hear a truck when it was three to five kilometers away.

On the next day, a shepherd drove a large herd of sheep through the area between the green zone and our minefield. Later, a nomad with three camels came through. Neither man discovered our ambush. I fed my force twice a day in the "day lager" located in the depression. They received a meal in the morning when they came off ambush and in the evening before they went back to their positions. I gave each soldier a liter of water every 24 hours. Nothing happened during the first two nights. The next morning, I sent the platoon leader with several soldiers to our rations and water cache to replenish our on-site supply.

On 5 and 6 December, we had a sand storm, but finally on the evening of the 6th, the wind calmed down. Suddenly on the night of 6 and 7 December, we heard the sounds of truck engines. I gave the command "To Battle". The men got their weapons ready and cocked their RPG-18s. After 30 minutes, three ZIL-130 heavy-duty trucks[120] and two light-trucks approached the site. Their lights were off. When all the trucks were in the kill zone, I detonated two mines, which was the signal to open fire. The platoon leader and I controlled the fire and used illumination flares and tracer rounds to adjust and shift the fire. All the trucks were hit by RPG-18 and small-arms fire within the first minute. One truck, which had tried to turn around and exit the ambush was destroyed by a mine. The enemy personnel were surrounded by burning, exploding ammunition. When they tried to get away from it, we cut them down. In this action, the enemy lost 44 KIA and three truck-loads of weapons, ammunition and gear. My group had no casualties.

FRUNZE COMMENTARY: The airborne subunit enjoyed success as a result of the correct, skillful organization of the ambush; the

---

[120]The ZIL-130 is a 150 horsepower, 4x2 Soviet truck that could haul 5.5 tons (ed.).

well-constructed and camouflaged firing positions; the skillful employment of mines; the use of close fire; and the control of night fire by an officer using illumination flares and tracer ammunition.

EDITOR'S COMMENTARY: The force went out for seven days with rations for 10. They stayed in the same spot with the same routine for four days before they had contact. Local inhabitants had been through the area, and although the commander was sure that they had not been detected, that possibility existed. Is it a good idea to remain in the same position for so long, or is this a good way to set up a force for counter-ambush?

A reinforced reconnaissance platoon conducts an ambush northwest of Surubi

by Major I. V. Solonin[121]

In December 1985, *mujahideen* activity increased in the provinces of Kabul, Kandahar and Takhar. Caravans moved increasing amounts of arms, ammunition and war supplies from Pakistan to the guerrilla forces. In order to stop this anti-government activity by the *mujahideen*, the high command decided to conduct ambushes in its areas of responsibility.

I was the commander of an airborne battalion. Together with my battalion chief of staff and my battalion chief of reconnaissance, I received our orders to conduct ambushes. We worked to prepare our subunits and to prepare an ambush plan in an organized manner.

A guerrilla force was active in the battalion AOR. Our AOR was centered on the village of Surubi, some 50 kilometers east of Kabul on the Kabul-Jalalabad highway. The guerrillas kept pressure on the local populace by forcibly kidnapping them and taking them to Pakistan, attacking government officials, blowing up electric power lines, attacking convoys, and shelling our base camps with launch bombs. KHAD intelligence, with whom we maintained close contact, reported the movement of weapons caravans from Pakistan to the Panjsher Valley. Their reports described how these caravans passed through the battalion AOR. Further KHAD reports described how the *mujahideen* routinely came from Dzhigdalay to Surubi to scout our garrison and commit acts of terror.

I decided to conduct ambushes on possible *mujahideen* routes located five kilometers northwest of Surubi. I selected the battalion reconnaissance platoon, an airborne platoon, and engineer squad and an AGS-17 crew for the ambush. This was a total ambush force of 23 personnel. We trained the force to react to all possible combat scenarios. We prepared the force in secret, under the guise of routine training. Self-propelled mortars would support the ambush.

At dusk one evening in the second half of December, the reinforced reconnaissance platoon, commanded by Captain V. P. Bobrov, moved to the ambush site. There was difficulty in getting

---

[121]I. V. Solonin served in the OKSVA from 1985 to 1987 as the commander of an airborne battalion.

there since the ambush party had to skirt an Afghan Army security position.[122]   We did not tell our Afghan neighbors about our ambush, since we wanted to safeguard the fact that we were conducting an ambush and prevent the leakage of information.

At 0030 hours, I received a radio message that the platoon had arrived on site and occupied their positions. The engineers mined

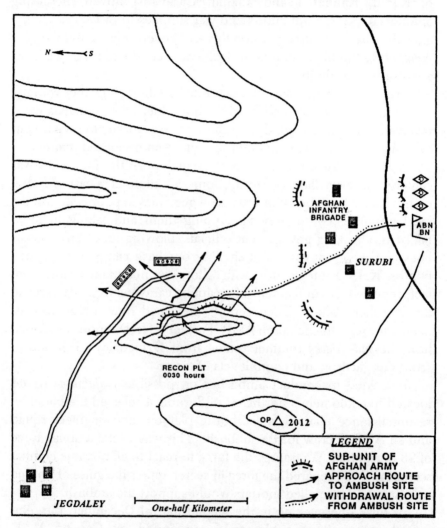

Map 44: Reconnaissance platoon ambush northwest of Surubi.

---

[122]The Afghan Army 14th Infantry Brigade and the Afghan 4th Sarandoy Brigade (ed.).

the possible *mujahideen* escape routes. They also emplaced a command-detonated mine. The ambush was positioned on the slope of a hill overlooking a path. The ambush force was positioned in two tiers. The snatch group occupied the first tier, while the support group was located 50 meters higher and occupied the second tier. The site was in constant radio communications with battalion. Nothing happened the first night. During the day, the personnel were concealed in a hide position and only lookouts stayed in the fighting positions. Additionally, the battalion OP on hill 2012 provided warning.

When night fell again, the ambush party reoccupied their positions. At 2345 hours, the ambush party saw a dark silhouette approach on the path from Jegdaley. They let him pass through, since they thought that he was a patrol. This was a variant that we had considered and trained against. The man returned and disappeared back down the path to Jegdaley. At 0300 hours, the ambush party saw 11 armed men approach. The platoon leader decided to capture the force. The force entered the kill zone, and after a short, intense fight, five *mujahideen* were killed and six were captured. The ambush party quickly started to withdrew by a different path. At that time, all the Afghan Army security posts were notified that the reconnaissance platoon was returning through their positions. At 0520 hours, the platoon returned to the battalion base camp. We had no casualties.

When the captured *mujahideen* were interrogated, they showed us a large weapons and ammunition cache in Surubi. Further, the prisoners gave us information which allowed us to prevent an attempt against the Surubi hydroelectric station.

FRUNZE COMMENTARY: This combat experience shows that conducting a successful ambush is very hard work. Up to 90% of our ambushes were without result. There were several reasons for this. First, our units did not always get to the ambush site undetected. Second, the high command issued regulations on ambushes which specified that no fewer than 25 men had to go on every ambush and that every ambush must contain heavy crew-served weapons. These precautions were not always justified. The composition of every ambush party depended on the actual situation. Third, regulations require an inordinate number of radio reports–departure for the ambush site, arrival at the ambush site, readiness of the ambush site for battle, hourly radio checks and the return of the subunit. As a result, the enemy discovered our intentions and did not move through these areas during the time our ambushes were out. Equipment for ambush was a particular problem. Practically all the officers and soldiers equipment and uniforms were unsatisfactory in that they were uncomfortable and inhibited movement. Army boots are totally unsuited for ambushes. They are uncomfortable and too heavy for mountain climbing and the *mujahideen* could readily determine our ambush sites from our boot tracks.

EDITOR'S COMMENTARY: The Soviets and Afghan government forces apparently did little to contest the *mujahideen* ownership of the night. Night patrols and ambushes were a singular planned event, not a routine mission. Battalions and companies moved into their bunkers at their base camps at night for protection from *mujahideen* mortar and rocket attacks. Consequently, *mujahideen* supply caravans routinely passed by base camps unmolested. Squad-sized ambushes were prohibited by 40th Army regulations, yet a platoon-sized ambush is frequently too cumbersome. The Soviets did not allow squad-sized ambushes in Afghanistan since their NCOs were not professional and perhaps not trusted. Yet, squad-sized ambushes, as well as platoon-sized ambushes, were part of the training program for Soviet forces not deployed in Afghanistan. In Afghanistan, two officers usually accompanied every ambush. This successful ambush still did not accomplish its mission—the interception of supply caravans from Pakistan.

Two Vietnam innovations, the mechanical ambush and the "claymores and grenades only" ambush are not mentioned. The mechanical ambush, which uses claymore mines rigged with trip wires, takes control from the ambush-site commander, but leaves the ambush party undetected. The "command-detonated claymores and grenades only" ambush gives the commander control and leaves the ambush party undetected until the ambush party resorts to small-arms fire. The Soviets apparently did not employ these ambushes.

The Soviet desire for positive control at all times did generate an unnecessary number of radio reports. Radio security was not always practiced and when traffic was encoded, it was often sloppily done. As a result, the *mujahideen* were sometimes able to determine Soviet activities or intentions from radio traffic.

Conducting ambushes on the basis of radio intercept data in the area of Khanabad

by LTC A. M. Tangaev[123]

At the beginning of March 1986, the enemy began to amass arms and ammunition in his bases near Ishkamesh, located some 60-kilometers southeast of Kunduz. These armaments were intended for use by *mujahideen* subunits in the green zones of Kunduz and Khanabad. We received intelligence reports that four caravans carrying weapons and ammunition arrived at these bases in the middle of March.

After the arrival of these caravans in the enemy staging area, our radio interceptors began monitoring a wide range of radio traffic on the short wave and ultra-short wave bands. The radio traffic was encrypted in four-letter code groups. Part of the encoded radio text was broken by a higher headquarters. From a deciphered message, we determined that the enemy would transport arms and ammunition to Kunduz at the end of March, start of April. Based on this information, the division commander decided to conduct ambushes utilizing our separate reconnaissance battalion.[124]

Preparations for the ambush began when the commander of the 1st Reconnaissance Company and the commander of the Radio and Electronics Reconnaissance Company received their orders. The reconnaissance company commander was given the area of the future action, the mission, the composition of the ambush force, the reinforcements and the sequence of events for preparing his force for the ambush. The commander of the radio and electronics reconnaissance company was ordered to increase his radio-intercept efforts in the direction of Khanabad and Ishkamesh and determine the enemy radio-traffic pattern during movement of caravans.

The reconnaissance company commander and his platoon leaders rode to an outpost which was located five kilometers from the

---

[123]A. M. Tangaev served in the OKSVA from 1985 to 1987 as the senior assistant to the chief of division reconnaissance. He was decorated with the "Order of the Red Star", the order "For Service to the Fatherland in the Armed Forces" Third Class, and the Republic of Afghanistan"s "Order of the Star" Second Class.

[124]The 201st MRD (ed.).

ambush site on the truck which normally delivered food to the outpost. They studied the terrain, the approach and withdrawal routes,
and the probable enemy approach route. The company commander
left one platoon leader behind to observe the area at night and
returned, with the other platoon leaders, to the company base camp.
During training for the ambush, the company conducted a systematic tactical exercise on terrain similar to that of the ambush site.[125]
The troops cleaned their weapons and drew ammunition and supplies for the ambush. On 2 April, the company stood a formal layout inspection to check the company's readiness for the ambush.

Radio-intercept and agent reconnaissance reported that the
enemy moved a caravan from Ishkamesh to Khanabad from 2000 to
2200 hours on 2 April. The division chief of reconnaissance set the
time to be ready to leave on ambush—1800 hours on 3 April.

The concept of the ambush was as follows: The 1st
Reconnaissance Company would move out secretly at nightfall on 3
April to some ruins. They would establish two OPs and conceal the
company. During the day, they would be in radio contact with the
battalion, the radio and electronics reconnaissance company and the
mortar battery. The company *bronegruppa* would move to a field
lager ready to advance rapidly to the ambush site and give it fire support. Then, on the evening of 4 April, the company would secretly
occupy its firing positions and prepare to ambush the enemy. They
would wait for a signal from the reconnaissance chief or the company commander of the radio and electronics reconnaissance company
that the enemy had started to move a convoy. They would allow the
enemy forward security patrol to pass through the ambush and then
destroy the main body. When the *bronegruppa* arrived, the ambush
party would withdraw from the ambush site, mount the carriers and
ride back to the base camp. There were 23 men in the ambush party.
They carried three PK general-purpose machine guns, three RPK
light machine guns, one 12.7 mm *utes* heavy machine gun (NSV), 16
AK-74 assault rifles, and five mines. The *bronegruppa* consisted of one
BRDM and three BMP-2s. A mortar battery supported the company.

---

[125]The systematic tactical exercise [*taktiko-stroevoe zanyatie*] was a field exercise by elements, in which the event was rehearsed step-by-step and progressed on as each step was mastered.

At 1900 hours on 3 April, the company set out for the ambush site on foot. They moved along a gully floor. Two patrols moved 50-to-60 meters in front of the main body and two patrols moved 40 meters behind it. By 0200 hours on 4 April, the company reached the ruins and established the OPs. The rest of the company moved to the day lager and concealed themselves.

At 0530 hours on the 4th of April, radio interceptors detected a radio transmitter in Ishkamesh talking to a radio transmitter in Khanabad. Traffic pattern analysis indicated the enemy was prepar-

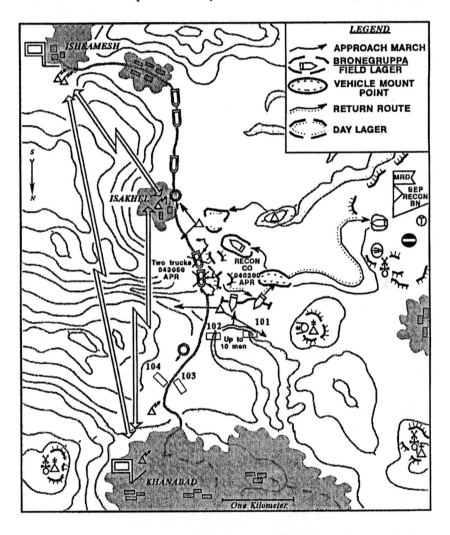

Map 45: Recon company ambush using radio-intercept data in the area of Khanabad.

ing to move a convoy. However, our observation posts saw nothing of the enemy during the day. By 1700 hours, our radio triangulation attempts had located several radio transmitters located along the Ishkamesh-Khanabad approach. As night fell, the company occupied the ambush. The ambush consisted of two OPs, a support group, a security group and a snatch group.

At 2005 hours, two men walked down the road. Twenty minutes later, a division OP reported that a truck had entered the canyon with its lights on. He let it pass. Twenty minutes later, two trucks roared into the ambush area at the maximum possible speed. As they entered the kill zone, the company commander detonated a mine which was the signal for the support group to open fire. They destroyed both trucks. At the commanders' signal, the snatch group then moved into the kill zone to inspect the trucks and pick up any weapons and ammunition. As the *bronegruppa* approached, the ambush party discovered a pocket of enemy who were moving toward the ambush. The ambush force cut down part of this group and the armored vehicle fire cut down the rest. The company then moved back to the mount-up site, loaded onto the carriers and rode back to our base camp.

Our ambush killed 12 *mujahideen*, and destroyed two trucks. We captured a lot of weapons and ammunition. The reconnaissance company had one soldier wounded.

FRUNZE COMMENTARY: The success of this ambush was due to the following factors: the use of intelligence generated by radio-intercept; the undetected deployment to the ambush site; the well-organized ambush on unfamiliar ground; the excellent employment of OPs, a support group, and a snatch group; the use of surprise; and the excellent combat training of the personnel. Further examination of the vignette, however, shows that the company commander could not adjust mortar fire effectively.

EDITOR'S COMMENTARY: This is the second example of the use of a *bronegruppa* in an ambush. In the first example (Vignette 38), the *bronegruppa* sneaks the ambush party closer to the ambush site. Then, the rest of the company mounts these vehicles. Later, when the Soviets spring the ambush, this mounted company drives to the ambush site to support by fire and cut off the enemy escape. In this vignette, the *bronegruppa* provides fire support from the same direction as the ambush party and provides a rapid, relatively safe exit for the ambush party.   Since ambush parties are frequently counter-ambushed on their way back to base camp, this appears to be a reasonable solution.

This is an interesting example since it shows that presumably strategic code-breaking assets were used to break tactical encoded radio traffic.   This emphasizes the importance that the Soviet high command placed on intercepting the *mujahideen* LOCs.

A reinforced motorized rifle company conducts an ambush to the northwest of Jalalabad
by Major V. P. Podvorniy[126]

In the second half of 1986, the general situation in Kunar Province began to turn in favor of the Soviet forces. The ambushes conducted by our separate motorized rifle battalion in our AOR in Kunar Province were successful.[127] The *mujahideen* had suffered appreciable losses which were causing him to improve his tactics for moving munitions and armaments by caravan.

Beginning in 1986, Soviet ambushes that had contact with the enemy noticed that the *mujahideen* had noticeably beefed up the forward security element on his caravans and their actions when ambushed had become more precise. When the *mujahideen* detected our ambush force, his counteraction took two forms. If the *mujahideen* had superiority in personnel and weaponry, he would try to flank the Soviet ambush force and destroy it from the flank or rear. If the *mujahideen* lacked superiority, then, as a rule, they would go around the ambush site using an alternate route leading to cover.

We learned that platoon-sized ambushes were pointless. A proper ambush required a motorized rifle company, reinforced with a sapper subunit and supported by artillery fire.

On the morning of 2 October, the 2nd MRC commander was directed to interdict the flow of *mujahideen* caravans along the road some 25 kilometers northwest of Jalalabad. The company had 96 men, 12 BTRs, and its TO&E weaponry. An artillery battery would support the company. The company would move to the ambush site in two stages. The dismounted company would hitchhike with a con-

---

[126]V. P. Podvorniy served in the OKSVA from March 1985 through March 1986 as the senior assistant to the chief of the operations section of a separate motorized rifle battalion. He was awarded the "Order of the Red Star". [An operations section at the battalion level is remarkable. This must have been a particular feature of this battalion (ed.)].

[127]This is probably the 2nd MRB of the 66th Separate Motorized Rifle Brigade. The 2nd MRB was
garrisoned in Asadabad, Kunar Province some 70 kilometers from the brigade headquarters in Jalalabad, Nangahar Province. The original text has the unit located in Kandahar Province. This must be a typographical error, since this would require a company road march of some 600 kilome-

voy from its base camp to the Soviet military outpost on the Jalalabad-Kabul highway. The convoy would go on to Kabul for cargo. The company BTRs would arrive later. The company would stay in the outpost and depart at night on foot more than 24 hours prior to the time they would be required to be at the ambush site. They would carry TO&E weapons, three combat loads of ammunition (one of these loads would stay on the BTRs), and three days of dry rations. They had to be ready to deploy by 0500 hours, 3 October.

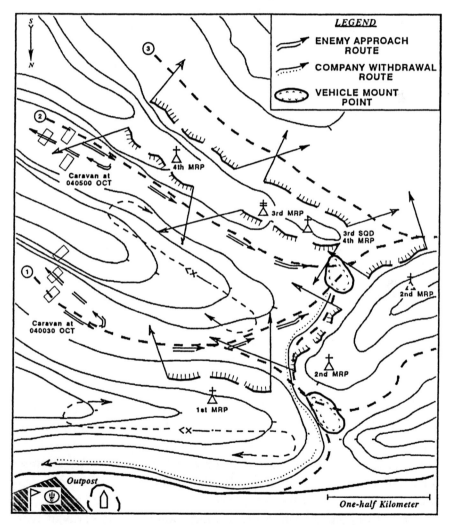

**Map 46: Ambush by a reinforced MRC supported
by an artillery battery**

The organization of combat activity in a separate motorized rifle battalion requires maintaining high combat readiness: one company was usually on combat duties, another company was on round-the-clock details and the third company was involved in combat and political training, but was kept ready for combat. The 2nd MRC was in combat training, so we had them prepare to conduct the ambush. The training included: the organization of combat; personnel training in weaponry and mission accomplishment; political-educational work; and practical work by the battalion commander, his deputies and the chief of the operations section.

The organization for combat included: the company commander's decision and his briefing it to the battalion commander; issuing orders to the platoon leaders; and working out coordination on a terrain model. Company preparations included: studying the assigned area of combat; training in the applications of tactical fire support and engineering relevant to mission accomplishment; conducting radio checks to insure that the radio sets were working; checking the night-vision devices; resting the personnel; and reporting to the battalion commander that the company was ready.

The battalion commander, his deputies and his chiefs of services approved the company commander's plan; assisted in coordination with the artillery battery and the supply and maintenance support to the company; issued the battalion order to the company for combat; and conducted a full lay-down inspection of the company to check its readiness for combat.

At 0600 hours on 3 October, the company moved out secretly with the convoy to the outpost. When night fell, the company moved out by dismounted platoons to the ambush site. By 2300 hours, they were in ambush positions with overlapping and interconnected fields of fire. Their flanks and gaps were covered by minefields.

At 0300 hours 4 October, the forward security patrol for a *mujahideen* caravan moved down route #1. They moved through the kill zone of the 1st Platoon and in an hour were in the kill zone of the 2nd Platoon. This particular caravan stretched out over 1.3 kilometers. The company commander decided that the bulk of the caravan was located in front of the two platoons and ordered the 1st and 2nd Platoons to open fire while the artillery pounded the caravan rear guard. The majority of the *mujahideen* and their pack animals were destroyed, but a part of the caravan was able to withdraw.

At 0500 hours, the caravan again began moving, but this time on route #2. The enemy thought that, as was the rule, Soviet ambush forces were small groups and were unable to cover several routes simultaneously. Further, they knew that usually these small groups rapidly abandoned their ambush sites after they sprang the ambush.

When the caravan was in the kill zones of the 3rd and 4th Platoons, the company commander gave the order to open fire. Part of the *mujahideen* moved to the tail of the caravan and began to withdraw hurriedly. The company commander radioed the artillery in the outpost and ordered them to open fire on the withdrawing enemy. But five-to-seven minutes passed from the fire command to the start of the firing and the enemy escaped.

At dawn, the company commander called in the *bronegruppa* and helicopter gunships. When they arrived, he arranged a search of the destroyed caravans and gathered weapons, ammunition and supplies. At 0700 hours, the company loaded onto their BTRs and, under the cover of the helicopter gunships, returned to their base camp.

FRUNZE COMMENTARY: It proved advantageous, in this situation, to have a motorized rifle company with four motorized rifle platoons.[128] The company was able to cover three possible caravan routes simultaneously. After they destroyed a caravan on one route, they did not abandon their positions, but continued to perform their mission. As a result, the company destroyed yet another caravan on another route that same night. It follows that one should note the skillful organization of troop control by the company commander. However, the combat revealed that the company commander could not quickly, correctly, precisely and clearly call in an artillery fire mission and adjust its fire.

---

[128]Usually an MRC has three MRPs. During the first half of the 1980s, an MRC had three MRPs and a machine gun/anti-tank platoon in BTR-mounted units or three MRPs and a machine gun/automatic grenade-launcher platoon in BMP-mounted units. This is not the case here. A separate motorized rifle battalion had four MRPs per MRC as well as other reinforcements (ed.).

EDITOR'S COMMENTARY: Poor artillery adjustment by company-grade officers is a constant theme in this book. Since the book is didactic and designed to illustrate key points, this is one point that the Soviets chose to emphasize. They solved this problem by putting Forward Observers (FOs) down to company and platoon level. This suggests a training deficiency for what should be a universal skill for professionals.

It is a commander's call whether to leave forces in place after an ambush to guard supplies and weaponry left in the kill zone or to exit the ambush site. Any enemy who revisits the ambush site following the ambush is either unaware of the previous ambush or in sufficient strength to wipe out the ambush party. The force had night-vision devices and could also have called for battlefield illumination by the artillery in order to police up the first caravan and then shift to another site. The 2nd MRP had an alternate site planned, but did not move to occupy it.

In this incident, the *bronegruppa* did not have a direct fire mission in support of the ambush. Rather, it remained passively near the outpost until dawn.

In this region, guerrilla forces apparently moved in large groups and, consequently, platoon-sized ambushes were insufficient. Company-size ambushes are much harder to place and control and were probably a unique tactic of this border region.

A recon platoon conducts an ambush in enemy-controlled territory
by Major V. A. Stolbinskiy[129]

Our separate motorized rifle brigade was located some 40-to-50 kilometers from the Afghanistan-Pakistan border.[130] In the middle of February 1987, we received orders to deny the delivery of weapons and ammunition from Pakistan to the guerrilla forces. Our brigade commander decided to use ambushes to stop caravans from transporting weapons, munitions, and military supplies to the central region of Afghanistan.

Our battalion controlled the northwest outskirts of Kandahar City. Intelligence reports made it clear that at the end of March, a large weapons caravan would travel along the road that connected the Rega Desert with Kandahar. This road ran through *mujahideen*-controlled territory. The battalion commander told me, an air assault company commander, to prepare and lead the reconnaissance platoon in ambush. In the event that the recon platoon found the caravan, it would have air support.

I went to the "Pipe" outpost with Senior Lieutenant A. N. Kholod, the platoon leader, Sergeant A. R. Babaev, and two scouts. From the outpost, we studied the *mujahideen*-controlled territory and plotted our approach route. The ambush party would have to cross three mountain ridges to get to the ambush site. According to intelligence, the *mujahideen* had several OPs which they manned around the clock, on the ridges closest to the outpost. The *mujahideen* used them to monitor Soviet movements. The "Pipe" outpost was held by

---

[129]V. A. Stolbinskiy served in the OKSVA from March 1985 through May 1987 as the commander of an air assault company. He was awarded the "Order of the Red Banner" twice.

[130]Probably the 70th Separate Motorized Rifle Brigade. There are some inconsistencies in this vignette. The city of Jegdaley, which appears on the map, is in the Kabul area, not the Kandahar area. However, the Rega desert, cited in the vignette, and the terrain of the vignette are closer to that of Kandahar, not Kabul. And there was not a separate motorized rifle brigade in Kabul. This vignette must have taken place near Kandahar (ed.).

the 12th MRC[131], with a 122mm howitzer battery and a MRLS platoon.

After three weeks of close observation, the lookouts at "Pipe" outpost had found a *mujahideen* OP. After two more weeks, they discovered a second one. The OPs were located on the dominant heights about 1.5 kilometers apart. I decided to move my force between these outposts on New Year's Eve night (by the Muslim calendar). My trip to the "Pipe" outpost helped me fine-tune my ambush plan and the approach route.

Usually, our battalion commander would report the time, coordinates and number of personnel in every ambush by radio to the higher staff. The majority of our ambushes were not successful. The enemy intercepted our radio messages, deciphered them and, in the best case, avoided our ambushes. In the worst case, the enemy would try to destroy our ambushing force. Since this ambush would be conducted deep in enemy territory, the battalion commander decided not to use the radio, but report the ambush details to the brigade commander in person.

The recon platoon trained for the ambush on a site similar to the actual one. Particular attention was given to training for crossing the mountains, coordination between groups and physical conditioning. Only the battalion commander, myself and the platoon leader knew the time and place of the ambush.

The recon platoon moved to "Pipe" outpost a week before the ambush. In order to deceive the enemy, soldiers of the 12th MRC mounted the three BTRs of the recon platoon and returned to our battalion base camp. They did this in full view of the enemy OPs. At the outpost, the recon platoon was hidden from sight in dugouts. I let them come out only at night.

At 2330 hours on 20 March, the 26-man recon platoon, reinforced with an AGS-17 squad, moved out from the outpost toward the ambush site. A three-man patrol moved 30 meters in front of the main body. The platoon traveled in a single column. Some five kilometers from the ambush site, I left a 16-man group commanded by the Deputy Platoon Leader, Senior Sergeant R. A. Usmanov. Their job was to cover the withdrawal of our look-outs, snatch group and covering group. They hid in a cave which they closed from the

---

[131]The 12th MRC, 3rd MRB, 70th Separate Motorized Rifle Brigade (ed.).

inside with stones.

My ten-man group continued on. At 0200 hours 21 March, we reached the ambush site. There was no cover close to the road. However, after awhile, we found a road culvert for a dry creek bed. I decided to post five men in the culvert. I sent the remaining five men, with the AGS-17 and a PK machine gun to the high ground some 800 meters from the road on the withdrawal route. They were commanded by my squad leader, Sergeant V. A. Sukhanov. The group's missions were to watch for the enemy, and if necessary, support the snatch group by fire. Communications were by radio. The

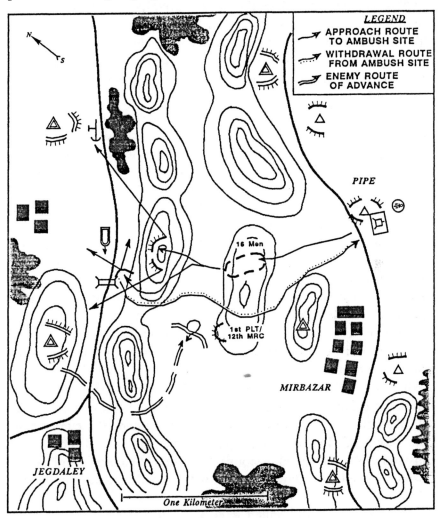

Map 47: Recon platoon conducts an ambush in enemy territory.

five men in the culvert were myself, Senior Lieutenant A. V. Kholod-the recon platoon leader, Private I. A. Dzhumaev-the translator, Sergeant A. N. Babaev, and a young machinegunner, Private A. N. Sivushkin.

When it became light, we could see that there were villages to the right and the left of the culvert. There was a field between the villages. At 0800 hours, armed people began to gather in the field. Sergeant Sukhanov reported that 140-150 people were there. The *mujahideen* began doing calesthentics. They finished these with running, crawling and other movements necessary in combat. All this took place 400 meters from the culvert. At 0900, Sergeant Sukhanov reported that the *mujahideen* had established guard posts on the road. The nearest posts were a kilometer left and right of the culvert where the snatch group sat. At 1000 hours, movement started on the road. In the culvert, we could hear the roar of the motors and the shouts of the people.

We stayed there for 48 hours without success. The caravan did not come. On the third day, I decided that we could not wait for the arrival of the caravan. I decided to capture one vehicle and return to the battalion. At noon, when it got really hot, the *mujahideen* usually quit training and went to the villages. I told Sergeant Sukhanov to tell me what was coming down the road. At noon, he reported that some armed bicyclists were coming down the road. I told Sergeant Sukhanov to keep reporting the distance of the bicyclists from the culvert. When they were at 20 meters, my group spilled out on the road and captured the *mujahideen.* They were not able to offer any resistance. We tied up our captives and pulled them and their bicycles into the culvert.

I then called Sergeant Sukhanov on the radio. He reported that a car was moving down the road at approximately 60 kilometers per hour. Eight motorcycles were about 1.5 kilometers behind the car. When Sergeant Sukhanov reported that the car was about 70 meters from the culvert, we again ran out onto the road and opened fire on it. We killed the driver instantly. The car coasted 40 meters further and stopped. Two *mujahideen* jumped out, but we cut them down instantly. We recovered weapons, four seals, documents and money from the dead. We blew up the car with grenades and began to withdraw.

The motorcyclists pulled over and began firing on my snatch group. Sergeant Sukhanov's group opened up on them. *Mujahideen* began running out of the villages. Some got on motorcycles and tractors and tried to cut off our escape. I called artillery fire in on the enemy. The 1st Platoon of the 12th MRC moved to previously-selected positions and supported the withdrawal of the recon platoon.

We killed five *mujahideen* in the ambush. Among them was Oka, the leader of a large guerrilla force, and his adviser, Turan, a former Afghan Army captain. We captured weapons, documents and money. Private A. N. Sivushin was wounded in the shoulder.

FRUNZE COMMENTARY: In this vignette, special attention should be given to how the commander got his platoon into the area from which to move out on his ambush. This area was constantly observed by the enemy, so he deceived the enemy by smuggling his platoon into the security outpost, while members of a different sub-unit rode back on his BTRs to his base camp. The platoon moved on foot to the ambush site under the cover of darkness. This is also a fine example of excellent coordination between lookouts, the snatch group and the fire support group. Finally, the brave, daring and decisive actions during the assault need to be noted.

EDITOR'S COMMENTARY: This is an interesting approach, but putting both officers in the snatch group is questionable. Granted that recon troops are better trained and motivated than the average, but these are conscript soldiers and NCOs. Who would take command and get the platoon out if the snatch group were destroyed? The support group was 800 meters from the snatch group. That is a long way to support and cover, particularly if done at night.

In Vietnam, American Army units put out ambushes every night on likely trails or where intelligence reports indicated likely activity would occur. In Afghanistan, the Soviets apparently conducted ambushes against specific intelligence and on an irregular basis.

There does not appear to be any standard distance between a patrol and the main body for night dismounted movement. In Vignette 43, the forward patrol is 50-60 meters out front, while the trail patrol is 40 meters behind. In Vignette 38, the patrol is 200 meters in front. In Vignette 37, the patrol is 20 minutes out front. In this vignette, the patrol is a mere 30 meters in front of the main body. This seems very close and seems to negate the advantage of having a forward patrol.

A reinforced recon company conducts an ambush west of Bagram

by Major V. N. Syemin[132]

The Republic of Afghanistan announced a period of national reconciliation for January and February 1987. It was officially announced that in the course of one or two years, the Limited Contingent of Soviet Forces would withdraw from Afghanistan. We did not conduct any combat during January and February. This allowed the guerrilla forces to stockpile a large quantity of weapons, ammunition and explosives. A large guerrilla force crossed the Pakistan border and transited the Panjsher valley unmolested. It selected the remote village of Dzhobal'-Ussarazgi in the Mirbachekot Massif as its base station. The village is located in the Bagram green zone. This force conducted missions against the Kabul-Salang stretch of highway. They would attempt to destroy our convoys, attack our security outposts and observation posts, and shell the Bagram military airfield.

During the time that we did not conduct combat, the enemy grew considerably stronger. The number of guerrilla forces and their stockpiles increased dramatically. Their arsenals swelled with weapons, ammunition, communications gear and heavy weapons.

Our separate reconnaissance battalion was stationed in Bagram. We were ordered to neutralize the enemy in our AO. Our battalion experienced good results from our planned ambushes during April 1987. We thoroughly prepared our companies for these ambushes. Officers began with sketches and maps of the area. We trained our personnel on ground that was similar to the actual ambush site. We paid a great deal of attention to preparing our weapons and equipment for the upcoming action.

Senior Lieutenant Yu. N. Petrov, the commander of a recon company, received the mission to destroy a caravan which was carrying arms and ammunition for a guerrilla force located in the mountain massif west of Bagram. The company was transported inside PX trucks to the "Closer" [blizh'nyaya] security outpost on the morning

---

[132]V. N. Syemin served in the OKSVA from 1986 to 1988 as the chief of staff of a separate reconnaissance battalion. He was awarded the "Order of the Red Star" twice and the medal "For Valor".

of 19 April. This outpost is located on the Kabul-Salang highway.
Two days prior, the company's *bronegruppa* had moved to the
"Southern" [Yuzhnaya] outpost as part of a reinforced road security
sweep. The battalion, which was securing the road from dominant
terrain, insured the ambush force's communications with the base
camp. The company commander precisely specified the approach
march and the order of movement to the ambush site to his group
leaders.

At 2240 hours, the company reached the ambush site and every
group occupied its position. The sapper group mined the probable

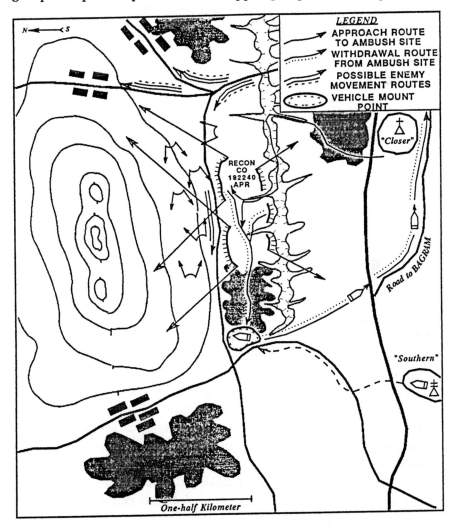

Map 48: Reinforced recon company ambush west of Bagram.

route of enemy withdrawal.

When the caravan appeared, the company commander let two groups, each with three or four pack animals, pass through the kill zone. When the main body of the caravan was in the kill zone, the company commander requested planned illumination fire from a supporting artillery battalion and gave the signal for his men to open fire. The mine field was in the right place, for the fleeing enemy ran right into it. All the emplaced mines exploded. Within minutes, we destroyed the caravan.

We killed 38 *mujahideen.* The search group captured a large amount of weapons, ammunition, and large-caliber rounds. The sappers blew up the weapons and equipment that we could not carry off. The company successfully withdrew to a mount site where they mounted their BTRs and moved back to the battalion base camp. Two of our soldiers were slightly wounded.

FRUNZE COMMENTARY: This vignette shows the use of artillery to provide battlefield illumination for an ambush. Uninterrupted communication and coordination with the artillery battalion insured the success of the subunits in the ambush. The company commander correctly determined the probable enemy route of withdrawal and selected this site to emplace his minefield.

EDITOR'S COMMENTARY: Again, reconnaissance forces are used for combat and not reconnaissance. Reconnaissance seems to be a secondary function. Yet, the lack of good tactical reconnaissance seems to have been a weakness of Soviet forces in Afghanistan. Once again, the Soviets use the *bronegruppa* for extrication of the force. The ambush party used a good covered approach through the woods and gully to the ambush site. The question is why the ambush site was located where it was, if the *mujahideen* had three possible routes in the area and the route junction was near at hand. Why didn't the commander put the ambush there, or at least put some observers at the junction and plan some RDM fires on the site? The Soviets established ambush positions on both sides of the woodline. This seems like a good idea. Were all positions fully manned or were they merely sited so that forces could shift between them?

Conducting an ambush on the
Yakpay Mountain Pass
by LTC V. I. Korotkikh[133]

During the spring and summer of 1987, guerrilla forces increased their attacks on government and Soviet forces. To support this combat, the *mujahideen* leaders increased their deliveries of weapons and ammunition from Pakistan. The deliveries would start at the Pakistan border with caravans of some 300 pack animals. Later, these would break into caravans of 15-20 animals which would cross the mountain passes to the guerrilla base camps.

By this time, the *mujahideen* knew Soviet reconnaissance and SPETSNAZ subunits' tactics well and used this knowledge to good advantage. Thus, if their caravan was traveling during the day and was approaching a likely ambush site, the *mujahideen* would block the pass before-hand and hold it for two or three hours until the caravan passed through. The *mujahideen* would post two or three armed lookouts every 200 or 300 meters on the pass. The caravan would then come through in groups of 15-20 pack animals, with an hour between groups, until they had all crossed this dangerous area.

If the caravan were to approach a pass at night, they would send out one or two unarmed patrols at twilight. These patrols were disguised as shepherds and often accompanied by children. The caravan would start to move when it became dark. Five to seven men, armed with rifles, would move forward as a reconnaissance patrol. The caravan moved behind this patrol. Drovers, armed with pistols or assault rifles, moved between every two pack animals. A rear security force of two to three men, armed with small arms, moved behind the caravan.

Based on this situation, the high command decided to increase our ambush activity. On 27 August 1987, I was ordered to select a group from my battalion to conduct ambushes in Yakpay Pass in Paktia Province.[134] My commander gave me the order to move out at night to the area of Yakpay Pass and to conduct ambushes there from 28 August to 2 September to destroy a caravan. The distance

---

[133]V. I. Korotkikh served in the OKSVA from 1986 to 1988 as a battalion commander.

[134]A battalion from the 56th Separate Air Assault Brigade (ed.).

from our base camp to the pass was 12 kilometers. I was the ambush commander. My 45-man party included 12 scouts from the recon platoon, 24 air-assault troopers from one of my companies, and up to two men each from my signal platoon, the sapper company and the chemical defense platoon. I also took the surgeon and the battalion's physician's assistant.

At 2030 hours on 28 August 1987, my group moved out for the ambush site. A three-man patrol with night binoculars moved out in front. The main body followed the patrol in a single column. By 0230 hours 29 August, my group finished its ascent and went into a

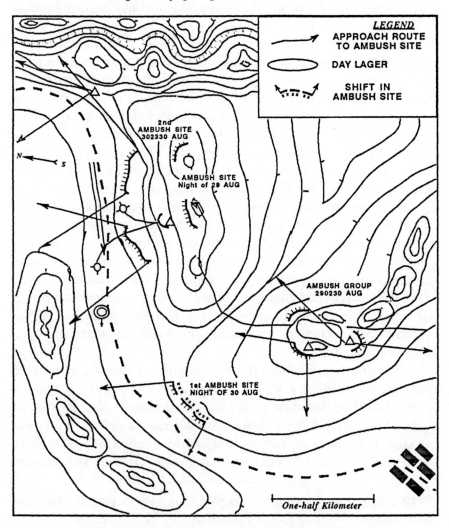

Map 49: Ambush on the Yakpay Mountain Pass.

day lager some 1.5 kilometers from the pass. I established two look-out posts. Toward evening, these posts spotted a caravan moving toward the guerrilla base camp.

The caravan settled into a village. At twilight, my ambush group moved rapidly into the pass, took up ambush positions and got ready for combat. However, after we waited until 0200 hours 30 August, I decided that the caravan would not come through the pass that night. I decided to take my force back to the day lager, pick up the material that we had cached there and move further down into the pass.

During the day of 30 August, we continued to observe the area. During the afternoon, we spotted 30 armed *mujahideen* moving toward the pass. After they climbed the mountain, they began to establish posts in the pass. It was clear that the stretch of pass I had chosen to ambush would not do. I conferred with the recon platoon leader and then decided to put the ambush in a different place. To do so, it was necessary to move five kilometers in an uninterrupted bound. I called my unit commander on the radio, reported my situation and advised him of my decision.

I ordered my force to move to the new site and we set out at 1800 hours. We reached the new site at 2330 hours. During the next 10-to-15 minutes, I fine-tuned the plan and coordinated the group's actions while the personnel got into firing positions. After a few minutes, a caravan started to move up from the valley. A six-man patrol moved in front of the caravan. We let it pass. When the caravan was in the kill zone, I gave the signal and my men opened fire. My illumination group fired off parachute flares to illuminate the kill zone. We destroyed the caravan within a few minutes. We killed 14 *mujahideen*, captured two others and seized 15 pack animals loaded with arms, ammunition and medicine. Our sappers blew up the captured ammunition.

I reported our ambush results by radio to my brigade commander. He ordered us to withdraw to an area where our BTRs would pick us up at 0800 hours. We took the prisoners, weapons and documents; linked up with our BTRs at the appointed time; and returned to our unit base camp.

FRUNZE COMMENTARY: In this example, the bravery and initiative displayed by the commander should be noted. He skillfully evaluated the situation, made the decision to change ambush sites, and in a short time organized it in another area. He constituted a special illumination group to provide light so that aimed fire could be placed on the enemy.

EDITOR'S COMMENTARY: The commander took both a surgeon and a medical assistant along on the ambush. The Soviets rediscovered that slight wounds at high altitude can rapidly turn fatal. Medical evacuation by helicopters in these areas was problematic and often wounded soldiers had to be carried to lower altitudes for MEDEVAC helicopters to pick them up. Wounded soldiers sometimes could not survive the hours needed to reach treatment centers.

CHAPTER 7:
AND IN CONCLUSION....

FRUNZE CONCLUSION: Combat experience in the Republic of Afghanistan confirms the correctness of the basic tenets of our directive documents. However, in addition, it confirms the need to reassess some of them which touch on forces and means in special circumstances.

Several combat principles lay at the heart of the *mujahideen's* tactics. First, they avoided direct contact with the superior might of regular forces which would have wiped them out. Second, the *mujahideen* practically never conducted positional warfare and, when threatened with encirclement, would abandon their positions. Third, in all forms of combat, the *mujahideen* always strove to achieve surprise. Fourth, the *mujahideen* used examples from the Basmachi movement[135] and employed terror and ideological conditioning on a peaceful populace as well as on local government representatives.

The *mujahideen* knew the terrain intimately, were natural scouts, and were capable of rapidly transmitting the necessary information about secret Soviet unit and subunit movements over great distances using rudimentary communications gear and signalling devices. Among the guerrilla forces' tactical strong suits were all types of night actions, the ability to rapidly and clandestinely move in the mountains, and the fielding of a very broad agent reconnaissance network.

The constant changes in the military-political situation in Afghanistan, the outfitting of the guerrilla forces with new weaponry, and the *mujahideen* use of various techniques and procedures of mili-

---

[135]The Basmachi were resistance fighters in Central Asia who resisted the imposition of Red rule from 1918 to 1933. The Bolsheviks attempt to extend their revolutionary order into Muslim Asia was resisted by hit-and-run raids and ambushes. A good English-language account of the Basmachi resistance is in Dr. Robert F. Bauman's *Russian-Soviet Unconventional Wars in the Caucasus, Central Asia, and Afghanistan,* Leavenworth Paper Number 20, Combat Studies Institute, Fort Leavenworth, Kansas, 1993 (ed.).

tary action worked to keep pressure on the tactics of Soviet forces. This demanded a constant, creative search for fundamentally new approaches for successful completion of the military mission. The TO&E structures of subunits and units were perfected. This was done in accordance with the techniques and procedures of combat which would be most effective in the given TVD. This placed increased demands on the production of improved uniforms, load-bearing equipment and gear for the soldiers.

Experience shows that the basic conditions for achieving success in battle are making a well-informed decision in accordance with the specific combat situation; thorough and complete preparation for mission accomplishment; securing tactical surprise and insuring tight coordination between subunits and units of various branches and aviation performing common missions; hard but flexible and uninterrupted control of subunits; and daring, brave and enterprising actions by the commander and his troops as well as comprehensive support for the combat actions.

Military cunning was given great importance. As a rule, when subunits went into battle, they were thoroughly prepared. Several hours or several days were set aside for this. Special attention needs to be paid to practical training of the soldier, sergeant, and officer. Training was frequently conducted on terrain similar to that on which they would fight. This allowed subunits to work out several scenarios for the conduct of battle.

It must be remembered, however, that the experience of Soviet forces in the Republic of Afghanistan is specific to that locality. The practical application of this experience will require creativity and will have to take into account the specific nature and types of enemy actions.

EDITOR'S CONCLUSION: The Soviet Army had extensive experience in subjugating and controlling unhappy populations and break-away Marxist-Leninist governments. During and after the Russian Civil War, well into the 1920s, the Bolshevik government employed political pressure, subversion, or outright military actions to incorporate into the Soviet Union numerous regions and nationalities which had asserted their independence during the confusion of revolution and civil war. In Ukraine, Central Asia, the Transcaucasus, and finally, the Far East, nascent republics were subjugated and reintegrated into the Bolshevik fold, often by force. In the early

1920's the Red Army put down political rebellion in city and countryside alike (Kronstadt and Tambov). In the mid-1920s, the fledgling Red Army campaigned for years against Basmachi tribesmen in Central Asia, leaving a legacy of military experiences which the Soviet Army attempted to draw upon sixty years later in Afghanistan.

Similarly, as the Red Army advanced through German-occupied territory in the Soviet Union in 1944 and 1945, it faced underground and open resistance from nationalist forces in the region. The Ukrainian UPA openly resisted the Red Army and Soviet political authorities, and in March 1944 claimed as one of its victims one of the best Soviet front commanders (Army General N. F. Vatutin of the 1st Ukrainian Front). So serious was the opposition that resistance to Soviet authorities continued in Ukraine and parts of Belorussia until the early 1950's, when Soviet military and security forces finally prevailed. In all of these post-Civil War and post-Second World War experiences, Soviet military power earned for itself a reputation as a seemingly invincible pillar of the state. Where Soviet military power tread, political domination would inexorably follow.

This reputation was born out during the Cold War years, when the Soviet Union wielded military power in support of its Socialist Empire. Their experiences in subjugating the Hungarian revolution of 1956 (where they suffered 669 KIA, 51 MIA and 1540 WIA) led to improved methods and techniques. In the 1968 invasion of Czechoslovakia, the Soviet Army lost a total of 96 killed.[136] The elements of their invasion plan included the establishment of an in-country Soviet military and KGB element to assist the invasion force and the production of a cover or deception operation to divert attention away from the future invasion. A General Staff group would tour the country in advance of the invasion, under some pretense, in order to assess and fine-tune invasion plans. When the invasion began, the in-country Soviet military and KGB element would disarm or disable the national military forces. Airborne and SPETSNAZ forces would spearhead the invasion and seize major airfields, transportation choke points, the capital city, key government build-

---

[136]G. F. Krivosheev (editor), *Grif sekretnosti snyat: Poteri Vooruzhennykh Sil SSSR b voynakh, boevykh deystviyakh i voennykh konfliktakh* [Removing the secret seal: Casualty figures of the Armed Forces in war, combat action and military conflicts], Moscow: Voyenizdat, 1993, p. 397-398.

ings, and communications facilities. They would seize or execute the key government leaders. Soviet ground forces would cross into the country, seize the major cities and road networks, suppress any local military resistance, and occupy the key population centers. A new government would then be installed, supported by the armed might of the Soviet Armed Forces.

This invasion plan was also used in Afghanistan. Soviet military and KGB advisers permeated the structure of the Afghanistan Armed Forces. In April 1979, General of the Army Aleksiy A. Yepishev, the head of the Main Political Directorate, led a delegation of several generals in a visit to Afghanistan to assess the situation. General Yepishev made a similar visit to Czechoslovakia prior to the 1968 invasion. In August 1979, General of the Army Ivan G. Pavlovski, CINC Soviet Ground Forces, led a group of some 60 officers on a several-weeks-long reconnaissance tour of Afghanistan. General Pavlovski commanded the invasion force in Czechoslovakia in 1968. The invasion of Afghanistan was launched on Christmas Eve, certainly not a Muslim holiday, but a time when the Western governments were not prepared to react. Soviet advisers disabled equipment, blocked arms rooms and prevented a coordinated Afghan military response. Soviet airborne and SPETSNAZ forces seized the Salang tunnel, key airfields, and key government and communications sites in Kabul. Soviet SPETSNAZ soldiers killed President Amin. The Soviet ground invasion force crossed into the country, fought battles with pockets of Afghan military resistance and occupied the main cities while the Soviet government installed their Afghan puppet regime.

The Soviets expected the resistance to end here. It did not. The rationalizing that pervades the West did not hold in the mountains of Afghanistan. The Afghans' values, faith and love of freedom enabled them to hold out against a superpower, although they suffered tremendous casualties in doing so.

How did the Soviets get it so wrong? The Russian Empire studied the area and maneuvered against the British over Afghanistan in "the great game" of the last century. The Soviet Union had diplomatic ties with Afghanistan since 1919 and extensive bilateral trade contacts since the 1930s. Soviet economic and military advisers had been a constant feature in Afghanistan since 1950. The Soviets built much of Afghanistan's road network (including the Salang tunnel) and airfields. The Soviet General Staff must have been quite knowledgeable about the geography, economy, sociology and military forces of Afghanistan.

The Afghan war was fought under four general secretaries-Brezhnev, Chernenko, Andropov and Gorbachev. Many senior military officers want to blame the debacle of Afghanistan solely on the Soviet political leadership, yet, there were evidently some high-ranking military accomplices who carried out Politburo directives without protest. And, although many in the West view Gorbachev as a liberal democrat and point out that he ordered the Soviet withdrawal from Afghanistan, the bloodiest years of fighting in Afghanistan (1985-1986) were under his leadership. Ideologically, the Soviet leadership was unable to come to grips with war in Afghanistan. Marxist-Leninist dogma did not allow for a "war of national liberation" where people would fight against a Marxist regime. So, initially the press carried pictures of happy Soviet soldiers building orphanages–and did not mention that they were also engaged in combat and filling those very orphanages. By the end of 1983, the Soviet press had only reported six dead and wounded soldiers, although by that time, the 40th Army had suffered 6,262 dead and 9,880 combat wounded. Soviet solutions for Afghanistan were postponed, as one general secretary after another weakened and died and the military waited for a healthy general secretary who could make a decision. It was only during the last three years of the war, under Gorbachev's *glasnost* policy, that the press began to report more accurately on the Afghanistan war.

The Soviet Army that marched into Afghanistan was trained to fight within the context of a theater war against a modern enemy who would obligingly occupy defensive positions stretching across the northern European plain. The Soviet Army planned to contend with this defensive belt by physically obliterating hectares of defensive positions through the weight of massed artillery fires and then driving through the subsequent gap to strike deep and pursue the shattered foe. Soviet tactics and equipment were designed solely to operate within the context of this massive strategic operation. Future war was seen as a lethal, high tempo event where forces and firepower were carefully choreographed. Consequently, Soviet tactics were simple. They were designed to be implemented rapidly by conscripts and reservists and to not get in the way of the unfolding operation. Spacing between vehicles and the ability to dismount a personnel carrier, form a squad line and provide suppressive small-arms fire were prized components of motorized rifle tactics. Tactical initiative was not encouraged as it tended to upset operational timing.

The *mujahideen* did not accommodate the Soviet Army by fighting a northern-European-plain war. They refused to dig in and wait for Soviet artillery. The Soviets found that massed artillery and simple battle drills had little effect on the elusive guerrillas. Tactics had to be reworked on site. The most tactical innovation was seen among the airborne, air assault and SPETSNAZ forces and the two separate motorized rifle brigades. These forces did the best in the counterinsurgency battle. Far less innovation was apparent among the motorized rifle regiments. Tanks were of limited value in this war, but helicopters were a tremendous asset. Engineers were always in demand.

The Afghanistan War forced the 40th Army to change tactics, equipment, training and force structure. However, despite these changes, the Soviet Army never had enough forces in Afghanistan to win. From the entire book, it is apparent that Soviet forces were spread very thin. Often, they could not assemble a single regiment for combat and had to cobble together forces from various units to create a make-shift unit. Base-camp, airfield, city and LOC security tied up most of the motorized rifle forces. KGB border troops were also stationed in Afghanistan in a security role.

This book shows that the Soviet Union failed to maintain adequate personnel strength in its line units. Regiments were often at single battalion strength, battalions at single company strength and companies at single platoon strength. First priority on personnel replacement always went to filling the driver, gunner and vehicle commander slots for the unit combat vehicles. This left few personnel to dismount and fight the resistance. There was also an evident dislike of close combat and a preference to use massive amounts of fire power instead. Disease cut into units' present-for-duty-strength in Afghanistan as poor field sanitation practices and poor diet contributed to the spread of disease. From 1/4 to 1/3 of a unit's strength was normally sick with hepatitis, typhus, malaria, amoebic dysentery, and meningitis. Units were filled twice a year from the spring and fall draft call-ups. Conscripts sent to the Turkestan Military District had six months to a year's training before going to Afghanistan for the rest of their service. Further, military districts and Groups of Forces were levied for troops twice annually. These levies were quite large. Yet, the unit field strengths remained appallingly low. The Soviets learned, like the Americans learned in Vietnam, that units need to be filled well in excess of 100% (in some regions of the world) if one hopes to field and maintain a reasonable fighting force. The 40th Army was chronically short of resources to carry out its mission and was an embarrassing reminder to its political masters of their political hubris and miscalculations which pushed this army into the inhospitable mountains of Afghanistan. Once the Soviet Armed Forces were in Afghanistan, it was very difficult to get out. The political-military climate and the subsequent decisions belong in another book. What remains is to examine tactical-level change in the Soviet Ground Forces in Afghanistan.

Tactics: The Soviet Ground Forces developed the *bronegruppa* concept to use the firepower of the personnel carriers in an independent reserve once the motorized rifle soldiers had dismounted. It was a bold step, for commanders of mechanized forces dislike separating their dismounted infantry from their carriers. However, terrain often dictated that the BMPs, BMDs and BTRs could not follow or support their squads. The *bronegruppa* concept gave the commander a potent, maneuverable reserve which could attack independently on the flanks, block expected enemy routes of withdrawal, serve as a mobile fire platform to reinforce elements in contact, serve as a battle taxi to pick-up forces (which had infiltrated or air-landed earlier and had finished their mission), perform patrols, serve in an economy-of-force role in both the offense and defense, and provide convoy escort and security functions.

The Soviet Ground Forces adopted bounding overwatch for their mounted ground forces. One combat vehicle, or a group of combat vehicles, would occupy dominant terrain to cover another vehicle or groups of vehicles as they would advance. The advancing group would then stop on subsequent dominant terrain to cover the forward deployment of their covering group. When dismounted, however, the Soviet motorized rifle units normally placed some crew-served weapons in overwatch positions, but did not usually bring them forward periodically to cover the advance. Reconnaissance forces, however, used bounding overwatch when dismounted.

Air assault tactics and helicopter gunship tactics changed and improved steadily throughout the war. However, the Soviet Army never brought in enough helicopters and air assault forces to perform all the necessary missions. Helicopter support should have been part of every convoy escort, but this was not always the case. Dominant terrain along convoy routes should have been routinely seized and held by air assault forces, yet this seldom occurred. Soviet airborne and air assault forces were often the most successful Soviet forces in closing with the resistance, yet airborne and air assault forces were usually understrength. Air assault forces were often quite effective when used in support of a mechanized ground attack. Heliborne detachments would land deep in the rear and flanks of *mujahideen* strongholds to isolate them, destroy bases, cut LOCs and block routes of withdrawal. The ground force would advance to link up with the heliborne forces. Usually, the heliborne force would not go deeper than supporting artillery range or would take its own artillery with it. However, as the book demonstrates, the Soviets would sometimes insert heliborne troops beyond the range of supporting artillery and harvested the consequences. And, although the combination of heliborne and mechanized forces worked well at the battalion and brigade level, the Soviet preference for large scale operations often got in the way of tactical efficiency. Ten, large, conventional offensives involving heliborne and mechanized forces swept the Pandshir Valley with no lasting result.

Enveloping detachments were used frequently in Afghanistan. Battalion or company-sized forces were split off from the main body and sent on a separate route to the flank or rear of the *mujahideen* to support the advance of the main body, perform a separate mission, prevent the withdrawal of *mujahideen* forces, or to conduct a simultaneous attack from one or more unexpected directions. If the enveloping detachment was dismounted, it was usually composed of airborne, air assault or reconnaissance forces. If the enveloping detachment was mounted, it was frequently just the unit's *bronegruppa*.

In general, ground reconnaissance personnel were better trained and better quality soldiers than the average motorized rifle soldier. But, they appear to be used for more active combat than reconnaissance duties. The Soviets relied primarily on aerial reconnaissance, radio intercept, and agent reconnaissance for their intelligence production. Quite often, these reconnaissance sources failed to produce usable tactical intelligence. However, since the ground forces were always critically short of combat elements, reconnaissance forces were used for active combat. Consequently, the Soviets often failed to find the *mujahideen* unless the *mujahideen* wanted them to.

Equipment: Many new systems were field tested and introduced during the Afghanistan war, but most of these had been designed and tested prior to the war. The most notable of these were the BMP-2, the BTR-80, the *vasilek* 82 mm automatic mortar, the self-propelled mortar, the AGS-17, the BM-22 MRLS, the Mi-8T helicopter, the Su-25 ground support aircraft and the ASU-74 assault rifle. Tanks were present, but were not too useful in mountain warfare. Consequently, the newest tank models did not fight in Afghanistan. Several models of the Mi-24 helicopter gunship were introduced during the war.

The concept of the motorized rifle force was a marriage of soldiers and armored personnel carriers. The soldier was never supposed to be more than 200 meters from his carrier. His load-bearing equipment, uniform, weaponry, and other field gear reflected this orientation. Yet, Afghanistan was a light-infantryman's war–and the Soviets did not have light infantry. In general, the Soviet ground soldier remained tied to his personnel carrier and to the equipment which was designed to be carried by that personnel carrier. Consequently, the standard flak jacket weighed 16 kilograms (35 pounds). This was okay when dismounting a carrier and assaulting for less than a kilometer. However, a dismounted advance of three kilometers in flak jackets would stall due to troop exhaustion. The reconnaissance flak jacket was lighter and better, but in short supply.

The Soviet field uniform was inappropriate for Afghanistan. It was restrictive and uncomfortable. The camouflage pattern was designed for northern Europe, not the high mountains. Soviet boots were noisy and unsuited for climbing in mountains. Commanders, who could scrounge them, put their soldiers in track shoes.

Most Soviet load-bearing equipment and rucksacks were not designed for continuous field use outside of an armored personnel carrier. The technology was from the 1950s. Some modern rucksacks, boots, ice axes, and load bearing equipment were issued to mountain rifle battalions and SPETSNAZ, but they were in short supply.

The Soviet sleeping bag was made of cotton and was not waterproof. When it rained, which it did in the mountains, the sleeping bag soaked up water and gained several pounds in weight. It was hard to stay warm in this bag. The premier trophy for a Soviet soldier was a *mujahideen* sleeping bag from the West. They were lightweight, waterproof and warm.

Dry rations (field rations) were also a problem. They were unpalatable and consisted of a series of shiny tin cans which reflected sunlight. Digging garbage pits in the mountains was difficult and the Soviet soldier usually just threw his empty cans around his fighting or ambush position. This aided *mujahideen* reconnaissance. The heat tabs for heating rations frequently crumbled or were not available.

The Soviet emphasis on massed firepower instead of accuracy meant that the dismounted soldier carried a lot more ammunition than his Western counterpart would. Further, heavy crew-served weapons always accompanied the dismounted force. The 12.7 mm heavy machine gun weighs 34 kg (75 pounds) without its tripod and ammunition. The AGS-17 automatic grenade launcher weighs 30.4 kg (66 pounds) and each loaded ammunition drum weighs 14.7 kg (32 pounds). Dismounted Soviet soldiers were less agile and could not catch up with the Afghan guerrillas.

Experimental systems were developed during the war. The AGS-17 was mounted on trucks and BTRs. Various ordnance racks were developed for helicopter gunships. New mine-clearing gear, mine plows and mine rollers were tried with varying success. Dogs were trained to detect mines and guerrillas. The Soviets developed a new helmet, which provided better protection.

Force structure: The Soviets experimented with several force structures during the Afghanistan war. They constituted self-sustaining separate motorized rifle brigades and separate motorized rifle battalions for independent actions. They formed mountain rifle battalions. They experimented with combined arms battalions and motorized rifle companies with four line platoons. All of this was done to come up with an optimum troop mix for counterinsurgency and independent actions. Materiel support brigades and battalions were formed to provide more effective support to the combat units. Airborne, air assault and SPETSNAZ forces were refitted with roomier BTRs and BMPs instead of their BMDs. Forces were up-gunned with extra machine guns, AGS-17 and mortars. The Soviets used these new formations as a test bed and the post-Afghanistan force structure for the Russian Army currently envisions a mix of corps and brigades for maneuver war and non-linear combat and divisions and regiments for conventional, ground-gaining combat.

Morale: During the war, draft-age Soviet youth increasingly tried to avoid the draft and Afghanistan duty. Large bribes were paid to exempt or safeguard the children of the privileged. A disproportionate number of youth from factories and collective farms served in Afghanistan. The conscript's morale was not great when he was drafted. At the training centers, they were told that they were going to fight Chinese and American mercenaries. When they got to Afghanistan, they soon discovered that they were unwelcome occupiers in a hostile land. Morale further plummeted at this realization. As in other armies, the field soldiers were too busy to get into much trouble, but those soldiers in the rear with routine supply, maintenance and security duties had too much time on their hands. Many conscripts developed a narcotics habit in Afghanistan. They financed their habit by selling equipment, ammunition and weapons. Many turned to violent crime. Soviet soldiers robbed merchants and passersby. At Soviet checkpoints, the soldiers would search Afghan civilians' luggage for weapons. Routinely, Afghans carrying large amounts of money were "sent to Kabul". That meant isolating the civilian and his luggage behind a wall and out of sight of the checkpoint. Once there the civilian was killed and his money taken.

Officer's morale also suffered. Although an officer got two years service credit toward his pension for every year served in Afghanistan, he saw that the officer corps had been given an impossible task and would be the scapegoats for its failure. There was constant tension within the officer corps at base camps as they vied for the affections of the female PX cashiers, nurses and secretaries. Afghanistan service saw the rebirth of the Soviet World War II tradition of the field wife. But, with a shortage of women, competition was fierce and sometimes violent among the officers. Vodka was the officers' drug of choice and some quarrels were settled with grenades and small arms.

In the field, villages were razed and the occupants murdered in retaliation for ambushes or suspected aid to the guerrillas. Some of these seem to have been officially sanctioned while others appear to have resulted from a break-down in discipline.

Hearts and minds: The Soviet policy seems to have been to terrorize the population, not to win them over to the government's side. Despite all the press photos showing Soviet soldiers with Afghan adults and children, genuine fraternization between Soviets and

Afghans was discouraged. During field operations, the Soviets called in artillery and airstrikes on villages without warning the inhabitants. Press gangs followed many sweeps and Afghan youth were conscripted into the Afghanistan Army on the spot. The most-infamous Soviet crimes against Afghans were prosecuted, but many more were ignored. Often, Soviet actions seemed deliberately designed to harden the resolve of the resistance.

And in the end, the soldier and officer returned to a changing Soviet Union. Many were unable to fit back into this staid, bland society. Many of the officers asked to go back to Afghanistan.

The war in Afghanistan lasted almost 10 years and inflicted heavy casualties on all sides. The effects of the war will last for decades. The tactical lessons that the Soviets learned are not uniquely Soviet, but equally apply to other nations' forces caught in the middle of a civil war on inhospitable terrain.

GLOSSARY

This is a list of common abbreviations and terms used in the book. Since the Soviet system is very different from the U.S. system, many of the translated terms are approximations. Where necessary, I have often included the transliterated Soviet term for the specialist.

AAslt   **Air Assault** [takticheskiy vozdushnyy desant]. Helicopter borne assault into an area.

AAsltB   **Air Assault Battalion** [Desanto-shturmoviy batal'on].

AAsltC   **Air Assault Company** [Desanto-shturmovaya rota].

AAG   **Army Artillery Group** [armeyskaya artilleriyskaya gruppa]. A temporary group of three to five artillery battalions under the control of the Army Chief of Rocket Troops and Artillery for a particular mission. During army operations, a gun AAG and a MRLS AAG are usually formed.

AO   **Area of Operations** [naznachennyy rayon]. The area in which a unit is authorized to conduct combat.

Airborne   **Parachute trained forces** [parashutno-desantiy] deployed by parachute or helicopter.

AOR   **Area of Responsibility** [zona otvetstvennosti]. The area that a unit is responsibile for securing and controlling.

BMP   **A tracked infantry fighting vehicle** [boevaya mashina pekhoty].

BrAG   **Brigade Artillery Group**. A temporary group of two-to-five artillery battalions under the control of the Brigade Chief of Rocket Troops and Artillery for a particular mission.

BRDM   **A four-wheeled armored reconnaissance vehicle.**

bronegruppa   **An armored group of 4-5 tanks, BMPs or BTR or any combination of such vehicles.** The BMPs and BTRs are employed without their normally assigned motorized rifle squad on board and fight away from their dismounted troops.

BTR   **An eight-wheeled armored personnel carrier** [bronetransporter].

CINC	**Commander in Chief.**
CP/OP	**Command Post/Observation Post** [komandno-nablyudatel'nyi punkt].
DAG	**Division Artillery Group** [divizionnaya artilleriyskaya gruppa]. A temporary group of three-to-five artillery battalions under the control of the Division Chief of Rocket Troops and Artillery for a particular mission.
FAC	**Forward Air Controller** [gruppa boevogo upravlenie]. An airman or soldier who requests, coordinates, and adjusts aviation strikes in support of the ground force. He can be on the ground or flying above the battlefield.
FDC	**Fire Direction Center** [punkt upravleniya ognyem].
FSC/FO	**Fire Support Coordinator or Forward Observor** [artilleyskiy korrektirovshchik]. A soldier who requests, coordinates, and adjusts artillery fire in support of the ground force.
FSE	**Forward Security Element** [golovnaya pokhodnaya zastava}. A reinforced company-sized element that normally moves in front of the battalion during a road march.
Full-field	**An exhaustive inspection** by a higher headquarters layout of forces field gear and personnel with everything laid out on tarps in front of the vehicles [smotr].
KHAD	**Secret police** of the Afghan government patterned after the Soviet KGB.
KIA	**Killed in Action**
Kyarizy	**An Afghanistan system of underground tunnels** used for the collection of ground water and for carrying water for surface irrigation. The *mujahideen* used them for shelter and ambush.
Launch bomb	**A 122mm rocket, used in the BM-21 MLRS system.** This rocket can be fired individually from a homemade tripod or two crossed sticks. It is inaccurate, but when it connects with a target, it is devastating.
LOC	**Lines of Communications** [put' soobshchenniya].
LZ	**Landing Zone** [ploshchadka prizemleniya].
MEDEVAC	**Medical Evacuation** [meditsinskaya evakuatsiya].
MIA	**Missing in Action.**
MRD	**Motorized Rifle Division** [motostrelkovaya diviziya]. The Soviet equivalent to a western mechanized division.
MRR	**Motorized Rifle Regiment** [motostrelkovyy polk].
MRB	**Motorized Rifle Battalion** [motostrelkovyy batal'on].
MRC	**Motorized Rifle Company** [motostrelkovaya rota]

MRP	**Motorized Rifle Platoon** [motostrelkovyy vzvod].
MRLS	**Multiple Rocket Launcher System** [reaktivnaya artilleriya]. A truck-mounted rocket artillery system capable of firing a salvo of rockets at a target.
MRS	**Motorized Rifle Squad** [motostrelkovoe otdelenie].
Mujahideen	**Afghan resistance** [holy warrior].
OKSVA	**Limited Contingent of Soviet Forces in Afghanistan** [ogranichennogo kontingenta sovetskikh voysk v Afganistane].
POL	**Petroleum, oil and lubricants** [goryuche-smazochnye materialy].
PX	**Post Exchange** [voyentorg]. A store for soldiers where they can buy non-issue items.
RAG	**Regimental Artillery Group** [polkovaya artilleriyskaya gruppa]. A temporary group of two-to-five artillery battalions under the control of the Regimental Chief of Rocket Troops and Artillery for a particular mission.
RDM	**Remotely Delivered Mines** [sredst distantsionnogo minirovaniya]. Mines which can be emplaced by aviation, artillery or MRLS fire. Similar to the US FASCAM (Family of Scatterable Mines).
Recon	**Reconnaissance** [razvedka].
RTO	**Radio-Telephone Operator** [svyazist].
Sarandoy	**Afghan Ministry of the Interior armed police** [Defenders of the Revolution].
Subunit	**Soviet term for a battalion, company, battery, platoon or squad** [podrazdelenie].
SOP	**Standard Operations Procedures** [poryadok deystviy].
SP	**Self-Propelled** [samokhodnaya], as in self-propelled artillery.
SPETSNAZ	**Troops of Special Designation.** For this book, Soviet forces trained for long-range reconnaissance, commando and special forces type combat.
TCP	**Traffic control point.**
TO&E	**Table of Organization and Equipment** [shtat]. An official document specifying the number of personnel by military specialty, the types of weapons and the type of equipment that an organization should have assigned.
unit	**A regiment or independent battalion with its own colors** [chast].
WIA	**Wounded in Action**
ZSU-23-4	**Self-propelled air defense weapon** which fires four 23mm machine guns simultaneously.

ABOUT THE AUTHORS

The Frunze Military Academy is a ground forces command and staff college located in Moscow on Proyezd Devich'yevo Polya near the Novodevichiy Monastery. It trains select captains and majors over a three year course of instruction. It has chairs of operational-tactical disciplines, history of war and military art, foreign languages and scientific research sections. It primarily trains ground forces officers in combined arms warfare, but has representatives from all branches and services. World-famous military historians are included in its faculty.

Lester W. Grau is a retired U.S. Army Lieutenant Colonel. He served as an infantry officer and a Soviet Foreign Area Officer (FAO) throughout his career. He fought in Vietnam. In 1981, he completed one year of Russian language training at the Defense Language Institute at Monterey, California and then graduated from the U.S. Army Russian Institute (USARI) in Garmisch-Partenkirchen, Germany in 1983. USARI was a two-year post-graduate school which dealt with all aspects of the then Soviet Union and all classes were taught in Russian. He has served in Moscow and traveled extensively in the former Warsaw Pact and former Soviet Union and continues that travel today. Since 1983, his work has exclusively been in the area of Russian and Soviet tactics and operations. As a combat infantryman, he finds it fascinating to compare and contrast how both the US and USSR fought and fight. Mr. Grau currently works at the Foreign Military Studies Office at Fort Leavenworth where he continues to work on operational and tactical issues.

MAP SYMBOLS

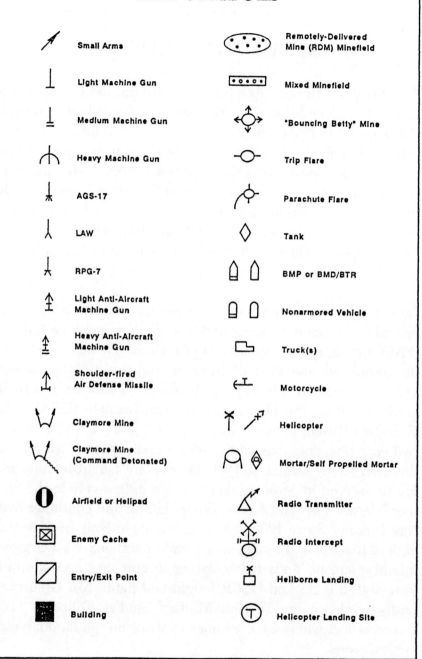

Small Arms		Remotely-Delivered Mine (RDM) Minefield
Light Machine Gun		Mixed Minefield
Medium Machine Gun		"Bouncing Betty" Mine
Heavy Machine Gun		Trip Flare
AGS-17		Parachute Flare
LAW		Tank
RPG-7		BMP or BMD/BTR
Light Anti-Aircraft Machine Gun		Nonarmored Vehicle
Heavy Anti-Aircraft Machine Gun		Truck(s)
Shoulder-fired Air Defense Missile		Motorcycle
Claymore Mine		Helicopter
Claymore Mine (Command Detonated)		Mortar/Self Propelled Mortar
Airfield or Helipad		Radio Transmitter
Enemy Cache		Radio Intercept
Entry/Exit Point		Heliborne Landing
Building		Helicopter Landing Site

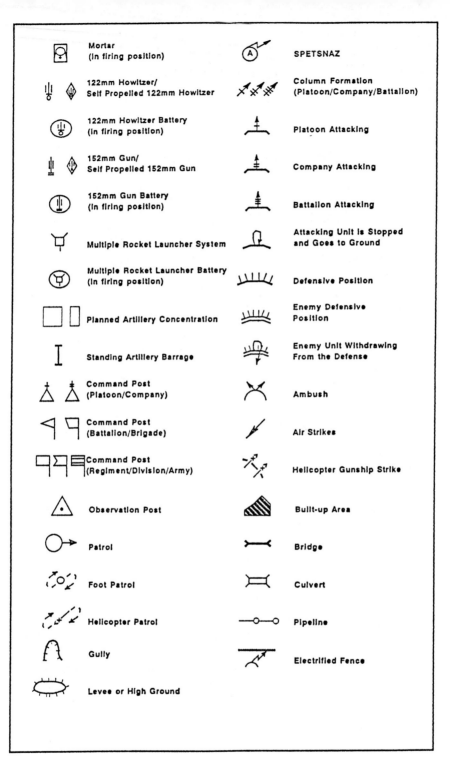

Mortar (in firing position)		SPETSNAZ	
122mm Howitzer/ Self Propelled 122mm Howitzer		Column Formation (Platoon/Company/Battalion)	
122mm Howitzer Battery (in firing position)		Platoon Attacking	
152mm Gun/ Self Propelled 152mm Gun		Company Attacking	
152mm Gun Battery (in firing position)		Battalion Attacking	
Multiple Rocket Launcher System		Attacking Unit is Stopped and Goes to Ground	
Multiple Rocket Launcher Battery (in firing position)		Defensive Position	
Planned Artillery Concentration		Enemy Defensive Position	
Standing Artillery Barrage		Enemy Unit Withdrawing From the Defense	
Command Post (Platoon/Company)		Ambush	
Command Post (Battalion/Brigade)		Air Strikes	
Command Post (Regiment/Division/Army)		Helicopter Gunship Strike	
Observation Post		Built-up Area	
Patrol		Bridge	
Foot Patrol		Culvert	
Helicopter Patrol		Pipeline	
Gully		Electrified Fence	
Levee or High Ground			

AFGHANISTAN
MAP 1

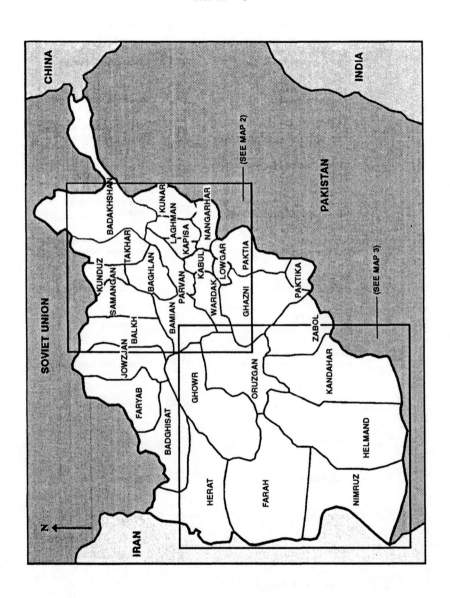

AFGHANISTAN
MAP 2

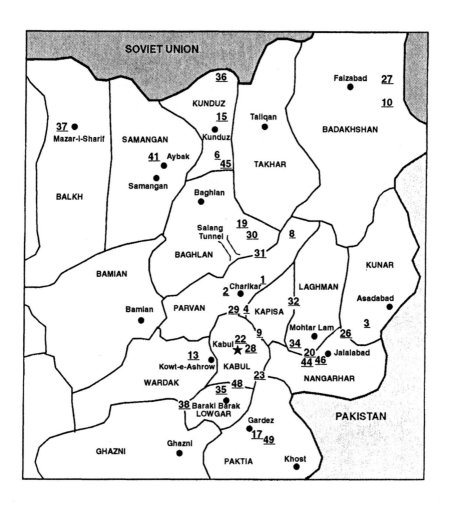

AFGHANISTAN
MAP 3

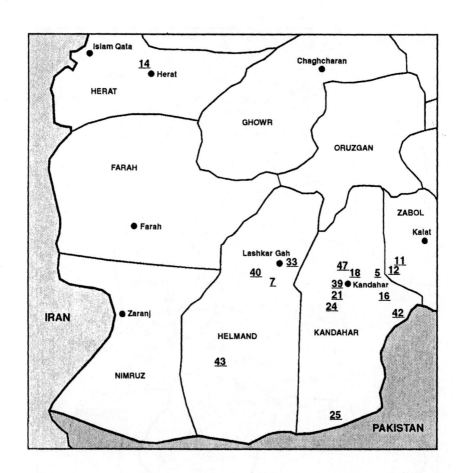

INDEX

SOVIET (RUSSIAN) MILITARY INSTITUTIONS

Series Editor: David M Glantz, Carlisle, Pennsylvania

This series examines the nature and evolution of Soviet (Russian) military institutions in peace and war and the human dimension of the Soviet (Russian) Army. Separate volumes address such subjects as the General Staff, key functional military or security organizations, specific force formations, as well as the role and experiences of Soviet military personnel of all ranks in peace and in war.

ISSN 1462-1835

Fallen Soviet Generals

Soviet General Officers Who Were Killed by Enemy Fire in the War Against Nazi Germany 1941–1945

A A Maslov
Translated and Edited by **David M. Glantz,** *Carlisle, Pennsylvania*

No war has caused greater human suffering than the Second World War on Germany's Eastern Front. Victory in the war cost the Red Army over 29 million casualties, whose collective fate is only now being properly documented. Among the many millions of soldiers who made up that gruesome toll were an unprecedented number of Red Army general officers. Many of these perished on the battlefield or in prison camps at the hands of their German tormentors. Others fell victim to equally terrifying Stalinist repression. Together these generals personify the faceless nature of the war of the Eastern Front – the legions of forgotten souls who perished in the war. This book reveals for the first time a hidden dimension of the human cost associated with the Soviet Army's victory over the German *Wehrmacht* in the Second World War.

304 pages   1998   0 7146 4790 X cloth   0 7146 4346 7 paper

FRANK CASS PUBLISHERS
Newbury House, 900 Eastern Avenue, Newbury Park, Ilford, Essex IG2 7HH
Tel: +44 (0)181 599 8866 Fax: +44 (0)181 599 0984 E-mail: info@frankcass.com
NORTH AMERICA
c/o ISBS, 5804 NE Hassalo Street, Portland, OR 97213 3644, USA
Tel: 1 800 944 6190 Fax: 503 280 8832 E-mail cass@isbs.com
Website: http://www.frankcass.com

SOVIET (RUSSIAN) MILITARY EXPERIENCE

Series Editor: David M Glantz, Carlisle, Pennsylvania

This series focuses on Soviet military experiences in specific campaigns or operations. Individual volumes investigate single operations or groups of operations and assess Soviet combat performance deriving from them what contemporary Soviet theorists deem relevant to future war.

ISSN 1462-0944

The Initial Period of War on the Eastern Front
22 June–August 1941

David M Glantz, *Carlisle, Pennsylvania*

'*Colonel Glantz has assembled a valuable collection of Soviet materials, many of them previously classified secret or top secret to which must be added his excellent introduction analysing the Red Army in 1941. This is a volume at first sight formidable in appearance but a treasure-trove in its own right and unique in its historical value.*'

The RUSI Journal

'*... amply illustrated ... their lavish display is invaluable to any student of war, especially in its operational and tactical context. If there is a lesson to be learned from Colonel Glantz's skilful re-creation of the campaign, it lies in his revealing the grossly inflated self-confidence of the members of the German High Command.*'

War in History

528 pages   1993; Repr.   1997   0 7146 3375 5 cloth   0 7146 4298 3 paper

FRANK CASS PUBLISHERS
Newbury House, 900 Eastern Avenue, Newbury Park, Ilford, Essex IG2 7HH
Tel: +44 (0)181 599 8866 Fax: +44 (0)181 599 0984 E-mail: info@frankcass.com
NORTH AMERICA
c/o ISBS, 5804 NE Hassalo Street, Portland, OR 97213 3644, USA
Tel: 1 800 944 6190 Fax: 503 280 8832 E-mail cass@isbs.com
Website: http://www.frankcass.com

From the Don to the Dnepr
Soviet Offensive Operations, December 1942–August 1943

David M Glantz, *Carlisle, Pennsylvania*

'What Glantz does is to produce a coherent narrative of the whole complex of Soviet offensive operations.'
The Journal of Military History

This book provides an in-depth study of the Soviet Army during the offensive operations that started with Battle of Stalingrad in December 1942 and went until Spring 1943. The lessons learned by the Soviet Army from these experiences helped design the military steamroller that decimated the German panzer divisions at Kursk in the Summer of 1943.

464 pages   1991   0 7146 3350 X cloth   0 7146 4064 6 paper

The Soviet Invasion of Finland 1939–40

Carl Van Dyke

This is the first-ever concerted effort to use Russian archival and previously classified secondary sources to document the experience of the Red Army in the conflict with Finland. Van Dyke examines the diplomatic, organisational and social aspects of Soviet's 'strategic culture' by first exploring the Leninist interpretation of violence in international relations, and how this legacy influenced Stalin in his use of diplomacy and threat of force to enhance the Soviet Union's 'forward defence' and to address the Baltic Problem in 1939.

288 pages illus.   1997   0 7146 4753 5 cloth   0 7146 4314 9 paper

FRANK CASS PUBLISHERS
Newbury House, 900 Eastern Avenue, Newbury Park, Ilford, Essex IG2 7HH
Tel: +44 (0)181 599 8866 Fax: +44 (0)181 599 0984 E-mail: info@frankcass.com
NORTH AMERICA
c/o ISBS, 5804 NE Hassalo Street, Portland, OR 97213 3644, USA
Tel: 1 800 944 6190 Fax: 503 280 8832 E-mail cass@isbs.com
Website: http://www.frankcass.com

Soviet Partisan Movements, 1941–44
Critical Analysis of Historiography

Leonid D Grenkevich

In history guerrilla warfare always played an important role whether it was of a large scale or of a limited character fighting. Grenkevich traces its impact on military history in the 18th and 19th century in Europe and North America. He carefully analyses the Russian partisan movement from the first bloody encounters in the 1870s, taking into account the social, economic and political configurations of Russia. The work details how the Communist Party studied the Red guerrillas' fighting experience at the end of 1918 and included in the Red Army's Field Manual a special chapter named 'Partisan Operations'. During the Second World War the most significant partisan war took place. The relationship between the Party, the Red Army and the Partisan Movements is covered in the main body of Grenkevich's historical research. This study is a response to the lack of a comprehensive bibliography and reliable books on the Partisan Movement. In preparing this research the author conducted interviews with surviving partisans; in addition, a significant amount of new Russian information on the activity of the Soviet partisans has become available in recent years.

264 pages 1998 0 7146 4874 4 cloth 0 7146 4428 5 paper

If War Comes Tomorrow
The Contours of Future Armed Conflict

M A Gareev
Edited by **Jacob W. Kipp** *Translated by* **Yakov Fomenko**

A forecast concerning the military, technical and political transformations that will re-shape military affairs into the second decade of the twenty-first century by a leading Russian General Staff Officer and military theorist. Over the last few years major changes affecting military affairs have occurred. But the world has not become more stable. It has even become more dangerous. Gareev is concerned with the basic question of military theory: is war still a continuation of politics by other means or has the political, ideological, and technical transformation heralded by *perestroika* broken that long-standing connection? Both information warfare and the revolution in military affairs are analysed.

216 pages 1998 0 7146 4801 9 cloth 0 7146 4368 8 paper

SOVIET (RUSSIAN) MILITARY THEORY AND PRACTICE

Series Editor: David M Glantz, Carlisle, Pennsylvania

This series examines in detail the evolution of Soviet military science studying the Soviet method of converting theory into military practice. Separate volumes focus on how successful the Soviets were in applying their theories in combat and on how they structured their forces to suit the requirements of changing times.

ISSN 1462-0936

A History of Soviet Airborne Forces

David M Glantz, *Carlisle, Pennsylvania*

For almost 70 years Soviet and Russian military theorists have been fascinated with the concept of airborne operations. Now Russian theorists tackle the problems posed to such operations by high-precision weaponry. This work, using newly released and formerly classified Soviet and East German archives, provides a detailed record of the performance of Soviet airborne forces during peace and war.

446 pages   1994   0 7146 3483 2 cloth   0 7146 4120 0 paper

The Military Strategy of the Soviet Union

A History

David M Glantz, *Carlisle, Pennsylvania*

This study of Soviet military strategy is based upon the relationship between the army and politicians as well as Soviet writings on the subject of military strategy. Thanks to the policy of glasnost, it incorporates Soviet materials hitherto unavailable in the West. It should not be considered simply as a retrospective account of what was; it forms at least part of the context for what will be in the future.

368 pages   1993   0 7146 3435 2 cloth

FRANK CASS PUBLISHERS
Newbury House, 900 Eastern Avenue, Newbury Park, Ilford, Essex IG2 7HH
Tel: +44 (0)181 599 8866 Fax: +44 (0)181 599 0984 E-mail: info@frankcass.com
NORTH AMERICA
c/o ISBS, 5804 NE Hassalo Street, Portland, OR 97213 3644, USA
Tel: 1 800 944 6190 Fax: 503 280 8832 E-mail cass@isbs.com
Website: http://www.frankcass.com

The Soviet Conduct of Tactical Maneuver

Spearhead of the Offensive

David M Glantz, *Carlisle, Pennsylvania*

'There can be no doubt that this represents an impressive contribution to the study of Soviet military doctrine: intelligent, learned, comprehensive and convincing.'

The Slavonic Review

264 pages   1991   0 7146 3373 9 cloth   0 7146 4079 4 paper

Soviet Military Intelligence in War

David M Glantz, *Carlisle, Pennsylvania*

422 pages   1990   0 7146 3374 7 cloth   0 7146 4076 X paper

Soviet Military Operational Art

In Pursuit of Deep Battle

David M Glantz, *Carlisle, Pennsylvania*

'There is immense value to be derived from Col. David M Glantz's masterly study ... This is a richly textured volume, the notes and references themselves being nothing short of encyclopaedic and deserving of a review essay in their own right.'

The Journal of Military History

295 pages   1991   0 7146 3362 3 cloth   0 7146 4077 8 paper

Soviet Military Deception in the Second World War

David M Glantz, *Carlisle, Pennsylvania*

'Once again, Glantz has provided the authoritative study ...'

The Journal of Military History

684 pages 200 maps   1989   0 7146 3347 X cloth

FRANK CASS PUBLISHERS
Newbury House, 900 Eastern Avenue, Newbury Park, Ilford, Essex IG2 7HH
Tel: +44 (0)181 599 8866 Fax: +44 (0)181 599 0984 E-mail: info@frankcass.com
NORTH AMERICA
c/o ISBS, 5804 NE Hassalo Street, Portland, OR 97213 3644, USA
Tel: 1 800 944 6190 Fax: 503 280 8832 E-mail cass@isbs.com
Website: http://www.frankcass.com

THE SOVIET (RUSSIAN) STUDY OF WAR

Series Editor: David M Glantz, Carlisle, Pennsylvania

This series examines the lessons Soviet military theorists and commanders have learned from the study of their own military operations. Separate volumes contain annotated translations of Soviet works analysing their own experiences, as well as the works of important Soviet military theorists and collections of Soviet articles concerning specific campaigns, operations and military techniques.

ISSN 1462-0960

Winter Warfare
Red Army Orders and Experiences

Richard N Armstrong *Colonel, US Army and* **Joseph G Welsh**

Based on German and Soviet military archival material, this book provides a rare insight into the tactics and planning for combat in a winter climate. It also studies the mechanisms for change in an army during the course of battle.

The first part of the book looks at the tactical pamphlet 'People's Commissar for Defence Order No. 109', as passed by Red Army units on 4 March 1941, which provided regulations for combat in Winter. The document came to the West through the German military intelligence files of the High Command of Forces, Foreign Armies East (Fremde Heere Ost) and represents a distillation of lessons learned from Red Army experiences during the Russo-Finnish War.

The second part of the book, using material from the Soviet military archives, reveals Red Army General Staff supplements to the winter regulation. Orders and directives alone are insufficient to ensure the passing of tacit knowledge in winter warfare. Within the Red Army, an institutional process existed for the collection of combat lessons which provided the tactical and operational examples for subordinate commands to emulate in training and battle.

208 pages   1997   0 7146 4699 7 cloth   0 7146 4237 1 paper

FRANK CASS PUBLISHERS
Newbury House, 900 Eastern Avenue, Newbury Park, Ilford, Essex IG2 7HH
Tel: +44 (0)181 599 8866 Fax: +44 (0)181 599 0984 E-mail: info@frankcass.com
NORTH AMERICA
c/o ISBS, 5804 NE Hassalo Street, Portland, OR 97213 3644, USA
Tel: 1 800 944 6190 Fax: 503 280 8832 E-mail cass@isbs.com
Website: http://www.frankcass.com

Soviet Documents on the Use of War Experience

Translated by **Harold S Orenstein**

Volume One: The Initial Period of War 1941
109 pages 1991 0 7146 3392 5 cloth
Volume Two: The Winter Campaign, 1941–1942
269 pages 1991 0 7146 3393 3 cloth
Volume Three: Military Operations 1941 and 1942
238 pages 1993 0 7146 3402 6 cloth

The Evolution of Soviet Operational Art, 1927–1991

The Documentary Basis

Translated by **Harold S Orenstein**, *Chief of the Central and East European Defence Studies Group at SHAPE, Belgium*
Foreword and Introduction by **David M Glantz**, *Carlisle, Pennsylvania*

'*What the historical development of operational art underlines is expertly conveyed in these volumes ... There is vivid and abundant illustration here, tables, figures and sketches of how an "acute understanding" of operational issues, in the context of strategy, can further provide deep and original insights into future war. The relevance of that cannot be overstated.*'
                    John Erickson, *University of Edinburgh,*
                    The Journal of Slavic Military Studies

This collection of texts has been taken from formerly classified material in the official Red Army General Staff journal 'Military Thought'. The results are two volumes of great scope based on archival evidence. They stand as a compulsory reference point for anyone with an interest in the operational endeavours of the Soviet Army from the 1920s onward.

Volume 1: Operational Art, 1927-1964
336 pages 1995 0 7146 4547 8 cloth 0 7146 4228 2 paper
Volume 2: Operational Art 1965-1991
368 pages 1995 0 7146 4548 6 cloth 0 7146 4229 0 paper

FRANK CASS PUBLISHERS
Newbury House, 900 Eastern Avenue, Newbury Park, Ilford, Essex IG2 7HH
Tel: +44 (0)181 599 8866 Fax: +44 (0)181 599 0984 E-mail: info@frankcass.com
NORTH AMERICA
c/o ISBS, 5804 NE Hassalo Street, Portland, OR 97213 3644, USA
Tel: 1 800 944 6190 Fax: 503 280 8832 E-mail cass@isbs.com
Website: http://www.frankcass.com

Red Armour Combat Orders
Combat Regulations for Tank and Mechanised Forces 1944

Richard N Armstrong, *Colonel, US Army*

Soviet military leadership is unable or unwilling to disassociate itself from past experiences. *Red Armour Combat Orders* illustrates through captured regulations that many of the Soviet Techniques in armoured warfare have remained unchanged over the last four decades. Study of the regulations provides a fundamental understanding of current Soviet armoured tactics and the ways in which they may develop.

168 pages   1991   0 7146 3401 8 cloth

The Nature of the Operations of Modern Armies

V K Triandafillov
Edited by **Jacob W Kipp** *and translated by* **William A Burhans**

V K Triandafillov was an outstanding young commander who shaped the military theory and doctrine of the Red Army as it came to grips with the problem of future war. A conscript soldier who rose through the ranks to become an officer in the Tsarist Army, he saw combat in both the First World War and the Russian Civil War. A student of some of the finest military specialists teaching the first generation of young Red commanders, he sought to link theory and practice by using past experience to comprehend future combat.

182 pages   1994   0 7146 4501 X cloth   0 7146 4118 9 paper

FRANK CASS PUBLISHERS
Newbury House, 900 Eastern Avenue, Newbury Park, Ilford, Essex IG2 7HH
Tel: +44 (0)181 599 8866 Fax: +44 (0)181 599 0984 E-mail: info@frankcass.com
NORTH AMERICA
c/o ISBS, 5804 NE Hassalo Street, Portland, OR 97213 3644, USA
Tel: 1 800 944 6190 Fax: 503 280 8832 E-mail cass@isbs.com
Website: http://www.frankcass.com